Teaching with Disney

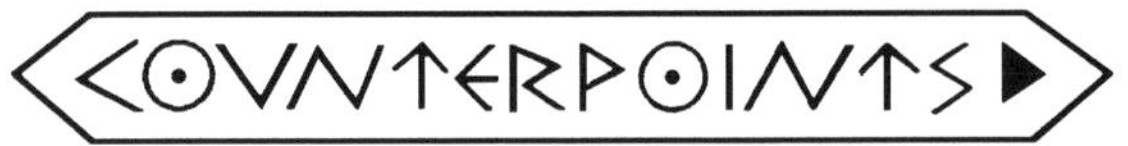

Studies in the Postmodern Theory of Education

Shirley R. Steinberg
General Editor

Vol. 477

The Counterpoints series is part of the Peter Lang Education list.
Every volume is peer reviewed and meets
the highest quality standards for content and production.

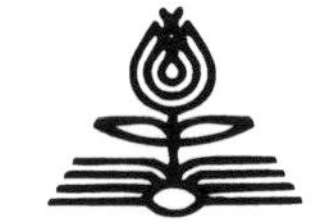

PETER LANG
New York • Bern • Frankfurt • Berlin
Brussels • Vienna • Oxford • Warsaw

Teaching with Disney

Edited by Julie C. Garlen and Jennifer A. Sandlin

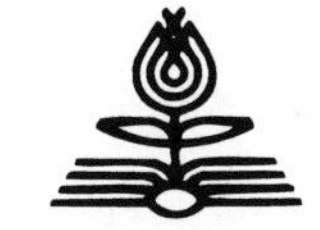

PETER LANG
New York • Bern • Frankfurt • Berlin
Brussels • Vienna • Oxford • Warsaw

Library of Congress Cataloging-in-Publication Data

Names: Garlen, Julie G., editor. | Sandlin, Jennifer A., editor.
Title: Teaching with Disney / edited by Julie G. Garlen, Jennifer A. Sandlin.
Description: New York: Peter Lang, 2016.
Series: Counterpoints: studies in the postmodern theory
of education; vol. 477 | ISSN 1058-1634
Includes bibliographical references and index.
Identifiers: LCCN 2015038043 | ISBN 978-1-4331-2882-0 (hardcover: alk. paper)
ISBN 978-1-4331-2881-3 (paperback: alk. paper) | ISBN 978-1-4539-1789-3 (e-book)
Subjects: LCSH: Walt Disney Company. | Motion pictures in education—United States.
Popular culture—Study and teaching—United States.
Classification: LCC PN1999.W27 T43 2016 | DDC 384/.80979494—dc23
LC record available at http://lccn.loc.gov/2015038043

Bibliographic information published by **Die Deutsche Nationalbibliothek.**
Die Deutsche Nationalbibliothek lists this publication in the "Deutsche
Nationalbibliografie"; detailed bibliographic data are available
on the Internet at http://dnb.d-nb.de/.

The paper in this book meets the guidelines for permanence and durability
of the Committee on Production Guidelines for Book Longevity
of the Council of Library Resources.

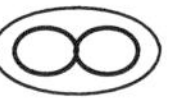

29 Broadway, 18th floor, New York, NY 10006
www.peterlang.com

Printed in the United States of America

Contents

Acknowledgments

We dedicate this book to our older sisters, Jennifer C. Garlen and Cindy Sandlin, who were our first pop culture pedagogues. It was Jennifer who first introduced Julie to the weird and wonderful worlds of *Monty Python*, *Doctor Who*, *Star Wars*, *The Muppet Show*, and of course, all things Disney. At the Magic Kingdom, Jennifer patiently endured Julie's early obsession with Dumbo and the People Mover as well as her lifelong fear of costumed characters, and eventually introduced a slightly older Julie to the thrill of Space Mountain. Jennifer also shared her love of musical theatre with Julie, who still knows almost every song from the *Cats* soundtrack. Jennifer, who is not only a Disney fan extraordinaire, but also a brilliant writer and literary scholar, taught Julie to question, challenge, and critique traditional norms and familiar narratives and inspired her toward an academic career. Cindy introduced Jenny to the wonders of popular culture, directing her in stupendous reenactments of *Grease* and *Saturday Night Fever*, which led to a lifelong love of show tunes, show choir, and karaoke. Jenny also has many fond childhood memories of reading and singing along with the "Disney Little Long Playing Records" played on a little plastic Fisher Price record player, as she and Cindy belted out songs from *Davy Crockett*, *The Hobbit*, the *Jungle Book*, and more, and waited patiently to turn the page only when Tinkerbell "waved her little wand like this." Cindy was also Jenny's companion on her first and only trip to Walt Disney World when they were in Junior High, where they endured getting stuck on the *It's a Small World* ride, and came home in love with Figment, the little dinosaur they encountered at EPCOT. Above all, Cindy has always and continues to gift Jenny with an appreciation for the pleasures and joys popular culture can bring, as she tempers her critique and at times curmudgeonly ways, reminding her that it's okay to critique and question, but it's also okay to have a little fun.

In addition to our sisters, there are many others to whom we are grateful for their contributions to this book. We want to say a special thank you to the editor of this series, Shirley Steinberg, for her enthusiastic and unflagging support of our work. We also want to thank all of the authors who are featured in this book—your dedication to this work as well as your careful attention to our (endless and probably annoying) editorial requests has produced what we believe is a valuable contribution to the Disney studies literature. We feel especially grateful to Misoo Filan, the brilliant artist who so graciously allowed us to feature her work on the cover of this book.

Julie would also like to thank the Department of Teaching and Learning and the College of Education at Georgia Southern University (GSU) for supporting this work. She is also appreciative of her GSU colleagues for the support and encouragement they have offered, especially her mentors, John Weaver and Bill Reynolds, who introduced her to cultural curriculum theory and encouraged her to pursue her interest in popular culture. Julie is also extremely grateful for the patient support and encouragement of her family, especially her children, Taylor, James, and John, and her parents, Bill and Virginia Garlen, who funded many childhood trips to Walt Disney World and provided important emotional support during the final phase of this project. Finally, there is a saying that I have come to cherish: If I am ready to learn, anyone can be my teacher. I came to this project with a desire to learn, and I encountered many teachers—contributors, colleagues, and friends—who informed, motivated, and challenged me along the way. May you always know how grateful I am for what you have inspired in me.

Jenny would like to thank the students in her recent Disney, Culture, and Society class at Arizona State University, who helped challenge her to create a meaningful and critical space within which to both critique and to find pleasure in Disney, and to explore the tensions between those two practices. I would also like to thank Mary Margaret Fonow, Daniel Schugurensky, and Bryan Brayboy from ASU's School of Social Transformation for allowing me to take a year sabbatical to work on this and other Disney projects—the time away was healing to my soul and allowed me to dive fully into this Disney scholarship. I also want to thank friends who have supported me in these last few years, both professionally and personally: Jake Burdick, Will Letts, Jory Brass, Sandro Barros, Deb Freedman, Jennie Stearns, Erik Malewski, Cole Reilly, George Bey, Melinda Hollis Thomas, Jeff Johnson, Torie Lynch, Lyndee Kelver, and Christian Payne—I love y'all truly and deeply. ☺ Special thanks also go to Julie Garlen for enduring countless hours of work with me on this and on so many other exciting popular culture projects—your friendship over the years has meant so much to me. Finally, I want to thank my parents, Richard and Patricia Sandlin, and my uncle, Marcel Bloch, for their unwavering support, and my son, Grant St. Clair, who always introduces me to new arenas of popular culture and is a constant source of laughter, love, and life.

CHAPTER ONE

Introduction

Popular Culture and Disney Pedagogies

JULIE C. GARLEN AND JENNIFER A. SANDLIN

In their groundbreaking work on the impact of Disney's global media domination on the lives of children, Giroux and Pollock (2010) argue that Disney is a "teaching machine" that "exerts influence over consumers but also wages an aggressive campaign to peddle its political and cultural influence" (p. xiv). The purpose of this volume is to further interrogate this notion of Disney as a pedagogical force and to explore what it means to teach, learn, and live in a world where many familiar discourses are dominated by the global media conglomerate. Giroux and Pollock encourage citizens to ask themselves, "How does the power of a corporation like Disney affect my life and shape my values as a citizen, consumer, parent, and individual?" (p. xv). In this volume, we ask, How do the powerful messages of Disney shape the ways we teach and learn? As a multinational entertainment conglomerate that is represented in almost every media platform, generating over $48 billion per year (Iger, 2014) through its various products, movies, and theme park experiences that are consumed by hundreds of millions of people, The Walt Disney Company is one of the most influential contributors to the global landscape of popular culture. Considering Giroux's (1999) assertion that "media culture has become a substantial, if not the primary, educational force in regulating the meanings, values, and tastes that set the norms that offer up and legitimate particular subject positions" (p. 2), the ubiquitous culture of Disney has profound potential to shape how we think, learn, and live. The Walt Disney Company is a major cultural force that shapes everyday life practices and identity formations through its representations of family values, gender, sexuality, race, class, ethnicity,

"Americanness," childhood, pleasure, entertainment, education, and community. Thus, Disney operates as pedagogy—both inside and outside of schools—that helps teach us into particular ways of understanding the world, our selves, and others.

Underlying our desire to better understand how Disney functions as pedagogy is a belief in the study of popular culture as an ethical imperative. As Miller (1999) explained, "it is increasingly important for educators to take seriously the processes by which media texts are produced and disseminated, and to understand the ways in which media images and constructions pervade all our lives" (p. 234). Echoing this sentiment, Steinberg (2007) argued that it is the responsibility of educators to "prepare our student/citizens to learn how to use it, consume it, and to have personal power over it" (p. xiv). The study of popular culture helps us understand and perhaps intervene in how we, through our interactions with popular culture, produce, reproduce, and re-imagine social life and everyday social practices and relations. As Hall (1992) asserted, studying popular culture can help build understandings about "the constitutive and political nature of representation itself, about its complexities, about the effects of language, about textuality as a site of life and death" (p. 285). We believe these understandings to be significant to the educative process, particularly in a media-saturated consumer society in which representation, language, and identity interact in complex ways.

The landscape of Disney as a site of popular culture is difficult to concisely map because the age of digital media has produced a wide range of cultural artifacts that include not only films, theme parks, and branded toys, clothing, and accessories, but also blogs, interactive websites, mobile applications, and on-demand entertainment. Within the vast cultural landscape of Disney, each of these varied and numerous artifacts are "texts" with which consumers engage and through which they produce new negotiated meanings. That is, these texts provide information we view, listen to, read, consume, interpret, negotiate, and produce. Of particular interest to us in this volume are the Disney texts in which children and adults actively and intentionally invest by devoting their time, money, and attention. However, Disney also operates as pedagogy—rather powerfully, we assert—through more passive interactions that occur through prolonged exposure to a Disney text. We do not need to have actively and intentionally "engaged" with a Disney text or be a fan of Disney to learn from it. The rapid (and we would argue, annoying) ubiquity of the recent Disney animated musical fantasy, *Frozen* (2013), propelled by viral videos of its theme song, "Let It Go," which, in 2014, won an Academy Award, provides an example of the way a text can become embedded in an individual's popular culture landscape even in the absence of an intentional or conscious engagement. Yet, where Disney is concerned, these opportunities for secondary exposure emerged long before the digital age. As Marsh and Millard

(2001) note, even in the era of the original *Snow White and the Seven Dwarfs* (1937), children who did not see the film might have received the accompanying picture book, “which required the famous red and green glasses to produce three-dimensional versions of key scenes” or “a packet of Snow White fruit pastilles, with a cut-out figure of the heroine inside” (p. 2). By the 1950s, a new generation of Snow White products appeared, including paper dolls, comic books, collectible cards in cereal boxes, and dress-up clothes (Marsh & Millard, 2001). Of course, the information age has multiplied exponentially the number of opportunities that Americans have to engage with Disney texts, whether actively or passively. By investigating these engagements, both our own and those of our students, we can better understand how The Walt Disney Company “represents the new face of neoliberal power, capable of not merely providing entertainment but also shaping the identities, desires, and subjectivities of millions of people across the globe” (Giroux & Pollock, 2010, p. xv).

In this book, we analyze those identities, desires, and subjectivities to explore the ways Disney teaches, in order to inform an understanding of how teachers, as well as learners, interact with Disney within the classroom and beyond. We believe that understanding how Disney works pedagogically is important for educators across all levels and disciplines, not only because of Disney’s cultural ubiquity, but also because of the long-standing relationship between The Walt Disney Company and education. During World War II, Disney was educating the American public through propaganda shorts and health education films, such as *The Winged Scourge* (1943), a film about malaria that featured the seven dwarfs (Robb, 2014), and *Cleanliness Brings Health* (1945), one of many educational films about “health and hygiene” that were distributed throughout rural Latin America as part of the U.S. government’s Center for Inter-American Alliance (Griffin, 2000, p. 35; see also Cartwright & Goldfarb, 1994). Walt told a national radio audience in 1943 that he anticipated “the use of our own medium in the curriculum of every schoolroom in the world” (quoted in Gabler, 2006). Indeed, Disney touts itself as the first studio to bring educational films into schools, as the company created the Educational and Industrial Film Division in 1944 (Mannheim, 2002), which, during 1945–1951, produced a series of educational films that were funded by corporate sponsors and then rented to American schools. These films included *The Story of Menstruation* (1946), which was shown to over 100 million American students in health classes through the 1960s (Griffin, 2000; Vostral, 2008). Walt Disney was recognized for his contributions to education in 1954, when he was awarded the American Education Award by the National Education Association (Watts, 1997). More than 70 years after it was founded, the special division, now called Disney Educational Productions, continues to produce educational videos, toys, furniture, and instructional supplies for the classroom. Today, the division website provides free lesson plan guides to accompany many of the products for sale and offers access to some free educational content, most recently a video series produced in cooperation with Disney's corporate ally, Siemens, called "Real Disney Theme Park Science," in which Disney Imagineers teach viewers about force and motion, electricity, and magnetism through an insider's look at the inner-workings of the theme parks. Featuring the logo, "Building thinkers every day," the website reminds visitors of the company's "legacy of education," noting that "Education has always been a core value of the Walt Disney Company" (Disney Educational Productions, 2014).

The particular brand of education advanced by The Walt Disney Company, grounded in Walt Disney's ideologies of white middle-class American heterosexual domesticity and child rearing (Griffin, 2000), emphasized "a model of learning based on practical work, fun, morality, and the wise counsel of parents and teachers" (Watts, 1997, p. 359). In an essay entitled, "Deeds Rather Than Words" (Disney, 1963), which appeared in an edited collection on the religious philosophies of great Americans, Walt Disney described the pedagogical potential of his productions in moral terms, explaining that his animated features and live action films reflected the virtues that make individuals desirable and were designed to keep children out of trouble, not by lecturing them, but by keeping them interested. Disney saw himself as the ultimate father figure, admonishing the parents of troubled children with public pronouncements against juvenile delinquency that emphasized the core American values of God, family, and country (Griffin, 2000; Watts, 1997).

In the decades since, The Walt Disney Company has explored a number of educational reform initiatives, most notably the establishment of a master teacher institute in the planned "New Urbanism" town of Celebration that was developed in the 1990s. The Celebration Teaching Academy, a joint project of the National Education Association and Stetson University, was housed within what was envisioned as a "school of the future" with experiential methods and state-of-the-art facilities (Giroux & Pollock, 2010, p. 67). The Celebration Teaching Academy and K–12 school, built in conjunction with the Osceola County School District, was designed to attract teachers, administrators, school board members, and parents from all over the world to learn about best practices in education and see them being implemented in real classrooms (Marcus, 1997; Natale, 1995). However, parents, who wanted a more traditionally structured curriculum, eventually rejected the school's progressive curriculum (Giroux & Pollock, 2010; Ross, 1999), and the teaching academy suffered costly delays due to disagreements between The Walt Disney Company and Stetson University. While both the plans for a more innovative school and the Celebration Teaching Academy failed to significantly influence public education reform writ large, they perhaps achieved the Disney Development Company's goal of increasing Disney's credibility in education (Natale, 1995). Since then, The Walt Disney Company has continued to develop that reputation by focusing on more lucrative educational products such as the Disney Imagicademy line of learning tools launched in 2014. Designed for children ages 3 to 8, Disney Imagicademy learning tools currently include 4 interactive games that teach math, science, and art skills, along with an additional mobile application that allows parents to track their children's progress and access daily tips for family-friendly learning activities, reflecting an ongoing commitment to the family values that drove Walt Disney's early educative ideals. The initial line of apps will gradually be expanded to include products designed for older children as well as other products such as books and interactive toys (Ortutay, 2014). Although there are over 100,000 educational applications to choose from in the interactive media market, it's not hard to imagine that parents and children alike will be drawn to apps that feature familiar characters and storylines (Ortutay, 2014).

DISNEY IN THE CLASSROOM

The Walt Disney Company's long-standing and ongoing interest in education, as illustrated above, positions Disney as a rich source for understanding the relationship between popular culture, teaching, and learning. Scholars writing and teaching across many different disciplines and locations and utilizing a wide range of practical and theoretical perspectives have explored this relationship in the academic literature. These texts, which are primarily articles appearing in academic journals, tend to approach Disney's pedagogical potential through one of three perspectives on popular culture: as a tool for instructional engagement, as a form of multicultural education, and as a source for teaching critical literacies. In the sections that follow, we describe among these perspectives some notable academic texts in order to position this volume within educational scholarship on Disney and to place it within the context of work that, like this volume, offers critical approaches to and insights on learning and teaching with Disney.

Disney as Instructional Engagement

Surprisingly, in spite of Disney's long-standing association with education, most of the scholarship that explores, critically or otherwise, the role of Disney within the classroom has emerged within the last few decades, particularly within the last five years. This timing may be attributed to the rise of what Budd (2005) calls "Contemporary Disney Studies" in the late 1980s, which helped legitimate Disney as a source of scholarly interest. In particular, the relative density of twenty-first-century Disney scholarship, by enthusiasts and critics alike, might be due to the polemical and highly influential work of Henry Giroux, whose book, *The Mouse that Roared: Disney and the End of Innocence*, harshly critiqued Disney's corporate ideologies and their destruction of American democracy and childhood. Whatever the reasons for the particular timing of the body of literature we describe here, all of these texts emerged at a time when it was widely accepted that the use of popular culture in educational settings motivates students of all ages to be more engaged in learning (Dyson, 1997; Marsh, 2000; Marsh & Millard, 2001). This belief was recently further validated by Dunn, Niens, and McMillan (2014), who, utilizing a children's rights approach, conducted a participatory study on children's views on the use of popular culture to motivate students and engage them in writing. They found that, when given a choice, children were more motivated to write about popular culture, particularly their favorite Disney characters. Educational psychology has long recognized the impact of interest on student motivation—as Hidi and Renninger (2006) note, "The level of a person's interest has repeatedly been found to be a powerful influence on learning" (p. 111). It is the powerful influence of interest that drives many educators to utilize Disney as a tool for instructional engagement.

Margaret K. King (1994), a nationally recognized expert on theme parks and consumer behavior, published one of the first academic articles that explored Disney as a way of engaging learners. King described how a theme park could be a medium for bringing popular culture into the classroom. She considered the Disney theme park a model curriculum and a sort of modern museum where children could learn about history, science, communications, technology, and design in a highly engaging setting. Applying King's recommendation to the college classroom, Bouzarth, Harris, and Hutson (2014) described Math and the Mouse: Explorations of Mathematics and Science in Walt Disney World, a course offered by Furman University in South Carolina as part of their May Experience program. Students enrolled in the course travel to Epcot to study the complex mathematical and scientific protocols in operation there. While King suggested that teachers bring the classroom to the theme park, other scholars focused on ways to bring the theme park experience into the classroom, such as adding Disney music to the educational environment and embedding theme park elements into the curriculum. Giles, Cogan, and Cox (1991), for example, tested the effectiveness of music from Walt Disney films in promoting the emotional health of elementary students and found that Disney music was more likely than classical music to positively alter a child's mood. Their findings suggest that playing Disney music in the classroom can promote emotional health by raising students' spirits. Presenting another use for theme park content, Hoge and Perry (2012) described a math activity program for students in kindergarten through the sixth grade that uses word problems about Disney theme parks to teach multiplication, addition, and subtraction concepts.

The literature on Disney as a source of instructional engagement focuses primarily on the use of Disney's films, particularly popular animated features, as a motivating context for teaching particular content; educators at all levels of schooling have found ways to do this. For instance, within the context of a medical school, Winter (2013) examined the use of video and song clips from *The Many Adventures of Winnie the Pooh* (1977) and *A Day for Eeyore* (1983) to teach resident physicians in a Family Medicine program habits of mindfulness to help decrease the burnout associated with the stresses of residency training. Similarly, Guerrero (2015) described a method for observing family structure at the beginning and the end of Disney films, as well as the developmental characteristics and growth of the film's protagonist in order to teach psychiatric students concepts of family and child development. Finding yet another use for Disney films in a high school context, Nikirk (2011) described how *Toy Story 3* (2010) was used to introduce interactive media to secondary students in a Computer Game Development and Animation program clause by teaching them about media development, production, and promotion.

Within Disney educational scholarship, it is often language and language arts educators who write about engaging with Disney content to capture student attention in both domestic and international contexts. Khoshniyat and Dowlatabadi (2014), for example, tested the effectiveness of a strategy for using Disney films to teach English idiomatic expressions, which they found to be highly successful with Iranian students learning English as a second language. Similarly, De Cunto and Garcia (2014) described a classroom project implemented in a bilingual elementary school in Buenos Aires, in which the Disney animated film, *Tangled* (2010), along with the Grimm Brothers version of "Rapunzel" was used to teach the characteristics of fairy tales as a literary genre. Interested in the ways students make meaning of such visual texts when they are used to teach reading and writing concepts, Ajayi (2011) analyzed drawings and explanations produced by third-grade students who had been taught reading comprehension skills through Disney's *Sleeping Beauty* (1959). In a study that explored English instruction at the undergraduate level, Matthew and Greenberg (2009) described how Disney films were used alongside traditional texts to introduce students to literary criticism and theory.

While literary criticism necessarily involves evaluation and interpretation, the focus of instruction in literary criticism and theory, and thus the primary purpose for the use of Disney texts, is the analysis of literature's methods and goals. Therefore, literary criticism cannot be equated with what we understand as critical literacy, which involves exploring how popular culture operates to both perpetuate social inequalities and to promote positive change by shaping the ways we think, learn, and live. In Steinberg's (2007) words, critically reading popular culture involves a "political economic critique which we can use to comprehend our surroundings"

(p. xiv). Wright and Sandlin (2009) also explain that while some instructors use popular culture in apolitical ways to reach students with relevant content and to make learning interesting or fun, critically reading popular culture in classrooms involves analyzing popular culture as a space that teaches hegemonic ways of being in the world, as it helps foster particular points of view on race, class, gender, and sexuality that serve the status quo. Such critical analysis also involves agency, as learners and teachers become co-creators of their own knowledge and identities.

Mulder (2013) described another case that falls short of this kind of critical analysis in spite of its seemingly critical content. Mulder discussed how instructors can use the Disney Pixar film *A Bug's Life* (1998), to identify Marxian concepts of revolution, exploitation, collective action, and solidarity. While these concepts are certainly helpful, if not essential, in understanding the hegemonic aspects of popular culture, the critical analysis of popular culture must do more than present challenging content. In fact, each of the pedagogical projects explored thus far, are consistent with the typical approaches to integrating popular culture texts identified by Johnson (2012), which include incorporating popular texts to make connections with students, using movies and popular music to teach literary concepts, and using Marxian concepts to analyze texts. As Johnson (2012) notes "these routine practices with pop culture texts rarely include examination of the power dynamics that circulate micro-level struggles for popular culture text meaning in school between students themselves or students and teachers" (p. 160).

Disney as Multicultural Education

The second approach to utilizing Disney in the classroom that emerges from the academic literature views popular culture as a form of multicultural education, which is a field of study seeking to "create equal educational opportunities for students from diverse racial, ethnic, social-class, and cultural groups" and provide students with the "knowledge, attitudes, and skills needed to function effectively in a pluralistic democratic society" (Banks & Banks, 1995, p. xi). When using Disney to promote the goals of multicultural education, educators utilize texts that showcase diverse racial, ethnic, and cultural groups to present cultural and linguistic diversity in a positive light. Fairy tales, as a form of folklore originating from oral traditions throughout the world, provide an ideal source for exploring differences across texts, cultures, and time periods. Disney films that reinterpret fairy tales are particularly useful for multicultural work because, as Zipes (1994) asserts, Walt Disney "was a radical filmmaker who changed our way of viewing fairy tales" and "capitalized on American innocence and utopianism to reinforce the social and political status quo" (pp. 73–74). As a result, as Hurley (2005) explains, "the visual representation of fairy tale characters has been dominated by the Disney version of these tales," to such an extent that "children tend to believe that Disney's version of the fairy tale is the real story" (p. 222). Therefore, exposing students to traditional fairy tales alongside Disney retellings provides an opportunity to broaden their understanding of textual and cultural diversity and is a popular approach among educators using Disney in the classroom.

Among that work, Westland (1993) presented an early study in which Cornish primary school students studied Disney Princess fairy tales alongside alternative "upside-down" fairy tales, while Barchers (1988) was one of the first to explicitly describe classroom instruction in which "students would read beyond Disney's versions of fairy tales, learn to identify the major elements of the tales, and internalize the structure adequately to write their own tales" (p. 136). Similarly, Kaminiski (2000) described using a large collection of folktales featuring Cinderella characters to challenge the Disney version by eliciting literature responses comparing the characters, settings, plots, and the motifs of magic in the multicultural tales. As she explained, "By introducing children to stories from many cultures, teachers can help them build a strong foundation for multicultural understanding by teaching them to use the cognitive strategies that enable them to comprehend and experience cultures different from their own" (p. 14). Alexander (2006) described another project in which elementary school students read and discussed variations on the Cinderella story to promote positive attitudes toward diversity while improving their reading skills. In another article on teaching with fairy tales, Yenika-Agbaw (2014) examined African, African American, and Caribbean Cinderella tales and concluded that although Disney's version of Cinderella continues to inform the understanding of most girls, "it is encouraging to know that there are competing versions that attempt to construct Cinderella in culturally situated ways that position Black cultures at the centre" (p. 245).

Among these studies on teaching with fairy tales, the approaches to diversity fall within the dimensions of multiculturalism that Banks (2004) has identified as content integration, knowledge construction process, and prejudice reduction, or within what May and Sleeter (2010) identify as "liberal multiculturalism." These approaches stop short of the more critical methods recently surveyed by May and Sleeter, including antiracist, critical race theory, critical pedagogy, and postcolonial approaches. May and Sleeter advocate especially for what they call "critical multiculturalism," which they define as an approach that "gives priority to structural analysis of unequal power relationships, analyzing the role of institutionalized inequities, including but *not necessarily limited to* racism" (italics in original, p. 10).

Disney as Critical Literacy

While most of the fairy tales studies thus do not move past liberal multicultural approaches, there is one example that exemplifies the third perspective that emerges from the literature: popular culture as a source for teaching critical literacies. Chou

(2007) used fairy tales to engage students in a form of cultural production, which Gaztambide-Fernández (2007) describes as a straightforward way of talking about how we "represent ourselves, our perceptions of others, and our ideas and experiences through symbols" (p. 35). Cultural production takes seriously the notion of popular culture as cultural pedagogy and emphasizes the fact that popular culture texts do not "exist for themselves in a vacuum, but rather, we encounter and engage with them in socially and historically situated ways that require active rather than passive engagement" (p. 35). Chou (2007) provides an example of one way to engage learners in cultural production by leading them in the study of the social codes embedded in fairy tales, and by helping them explore how rewriting familiar fairy tales might help learners reflect upon how Disney has influenced their ideas about race, gender, and other social norms. In this project she led students in critically analyzing the "cultural assumptions and unexamined messages in texts" (p. 58). Students compared various versions of fairy tales to see "culturally dominant scripts from new perspectives" (p. 58). Students also engaged in their own cultural production as they participated in the critical "rewriting of familiar, but destructive, cultural scripts" (p. 59), a process Zipes (2001) terms "contaminating" the tales. The pre-service teachers were asked to "reform the cultural values and identities in the fairy tale based on their experiences and beliefs about gender roles, race, and sexual orientation" (p. 61).

Chou is one of a number of scholars whose approaches to using Disney texts to teach critical literacies resonate with the critical perspectives of *Teaching with Disney*. According to Anderson and Irvine (1993), critical literacy "is learning to read and write as part of the process of becoming conscious of one's experience as historically constructed within specific power relations" (p. 82). In other words, critical literacy involves reading texts in ways that expose power relationships, that disrupt dominant narratives that perpetuate inequalities, and that produce transformative educational experiences. Traditionally, these texts have included media artifacts that utilize familiar codes and conventions to deliver messages, such as books, songs, films, posters, and websites. We assert, however, that any form through which information can be communicated and meaning produced can constitute a text, even in the absence of overt language. As Wohlwend (2009) asserts, "Identity messages circulate through merchandise that surrounds young consumers as they dress in, sleep on, bathe in, eat from, and play with commercial goods decorated with popular culture images, print, and logos, immersing children in products that invite identification" (p. 57). Critical media literacy and critical cultural literacy are thus inextricably intertwined, and Disney's branded consumer products, including the theme parks themselves, can be understood as texts that, like language practices and texts, "are always informed by ideological beliefs and perspectives whether conscious or otherwise" (Jones, 2006, p. 65). Disney products, services, and experiences, like all texts, are never neutral; they are produced, marketed, and consumed within particular social, historical, and political contexts. As Tavin and Anderson (2003) explain, "These texts play a significant role in the symbolic and material milieu of contemporary society by shaping, and often limiting, perceptions of reality and constructing a normative 'vision' of the world" (p. 21).

A number of scholars have explored critical approaches for teaching with Disney in a variety of educational settings, from elementary school to college. Tavin and Anderson (2003) described ways in which to deconstruct Disney in the elementary art classroom. In their study, fifth grade art students examined race and gender stereotyping, historical inaccuracies, and violence in clips from animated Disney films and analyzed specific Disney characters to produce multi-layered artworks based on their interpretations. Muller-Hartmann (2007) presented an approach to engaging secondary school students in critically reflecting on the ideological subtexts of animated Disney films. Sun and Scharrer (2004) discussed the implementation of a college media literacy program that involved extended critiques and analyses of *The Little Mermaid* (1989). Here, the authors analyzed students' reflective responses to better understand why they so persistently resisted transformative critique. Crank (2005), however, found that teaching with Disney did help foster media literacy among freshmen in an introductory English course and observed that these students learned "to ask questions about ideology and values, and more importantly, to feel comfortable with cognitive dissonance, understanding that they will and should be challenged by their education" (p. 104).

Other scholars have applied critical approaches to teaching with Disney to specific disciplines, including psychology, social work, and social studies. Bonds-Raacke (2008), for example, described the development of a course called The Psychology of Disney and Fairytale Movies, in which students critically examined the gender stereotypes and depictions of romantic love in Disney films. Similarly, Cappiccie et al. (2012) examined the use of animated Disney texts to teach concepts of human behavior and social environments to undergraduate students in a social work program. Using a critical race theory framework, the authors engaged the students in examining microaggressions—subtle, ambiguous, and potentially unintended expressions of discrimination—within Disney animations. Finally, Ciechanowski (2012) explored the use of Disney texts in the bilingual elementary social studies classroom and found that while students used everyday popular resources such as Disney films to understand classroom content, they took up dominant cultural perspectives even though they came from linguistically and culturally nondominant backgrounds, revealing the need for critical approaches to teaching language and social justice in the bilingual classroom.

In addition to studies that examine critical approaches to teaching with Disney in different educational contexts, a larger body of work engages in the critical analysis of Disney as cultural pedagogy by examining discourses of gender and race within and about Disney texts. Because Disney texts operate as cultural pedagogy by constructing and often confining normative discourses and ideals, an understanding of how we learn from Disney is an important component of critical literacy. While all of these studies are situated within classrooms, they do not document the implementation of critical approaches to teaching with or about Disney; rather, they perform the important work of analyzing texts, language, and classroom discourses around gender and race in order to inform those teaching practices, primarily in Western educational settings.

Yeoman (1999), for example, offers one early exploration of how Canadian elementary school children used their intertextual knowledge to produce disruptive stories that challenged limiting storylines about race, gender, and class. Based on her analysis, Yeoman suggests ways in which to enhance children's critical literacies. More recently, the work of Karen Wohlwend (2009, 2012a, 2012b) has been particularly notable. In "Damsels in Discourse: Girls Consuming and Producing Identity Texts through Disney Princess Play," she (2009) uses discourse analysis to discuss how a group of girls in a kindergarten classroom interacted with Disney Princess dolls and negotiated the gendered identities associated with the characters. Drawing from the same ethnographic data, Wohlwend (2012a) examined boys' Disney Princess play as a site of identity construction through which children learn gender expectations and found doll play to be a productive way for children to mediate gendered identity texts. Wohlwend (2012b) further analyzed boys' classroom play with Disney Princesses to examine how they negotiated transgender identity within commercially constructed storylines.

Other scholars have also focused on gender identity among young children, finding that children tend to reproduce gender stereotypes in their language and peer interaction. Anggard (2005) analyzed the work of pre-school children who created their own books by reusing narratives from popular culture. While the stories tended to reinforce gender stereotypes, some creative reinterpretations emerged in the roles and interactions of the characters. Offering further insight into the ways children make meaning of Disney texts, Baker-Sperry (2007) investigated elementary school students' interpretations of *Cinderella* (Disney et al., 1950) to examine how peer interaction influenced the production of meaning, and found that gender stereotypes were consistently reinforced in the peer groups. More recently, Garofalo (2013) conducted focus groups with girls ages 7 to 11 to gain insight into their understandings of the female characters in Disney films, including *The Little Mermaid* (Musker et al., 1989), *Cinderella* (Disney et al., 1950), and *The Princess and the Frog* (Del Vecho et al., 2009). Her analysis revealed that the girls found powerful women to be mean and ugly, placed importance on heterosexual relationships, and viewed beauty and politeness as essential princess characteristics. Similarly, Moule (2013) observed fantasy narratives of superheroes and princesses among a group of 3- and 4-year-olds, who exhibited embodied discourses of commodified, gendered identities. Drawing on the findings of such studies, Jule (2011) discussed the importance of primary teachers using alternative and diverse representations of gender roles when choosing books, stories, and activities for the classroom.

A much smaller set of studies focused primarily on critically analyzing classroom discourses of race and ethnicity. Notable among these is the work of Dorothy Hurley (2005) whose article, "Seeing White: Children of Color and the Disney Fairy Tale Princesses," presented a careful comparison of six classic fairy tales with their Disney Princess counterparts and found that the images therein held particular importance for children of color in the ways White privilege and binary color symbolism are reinforced. Based on her analysis, Hurley argues for the development of critical literacy skills by children as well as by teachers. Although not one of the Disney Princesses featured in Hurley's study, *Pocahontas* (1985) was the subject of two studies on Disney's racial discourses. Pewewardy (1996–1997), a Comanche-Kiowa, analyzed the misrepresentation of American Indians in mainstream media by examining the animated Disney film, *Pocahontas,* and called for educators to engage students in reflective exploration and in deconstruction of racist misrepresentations of indigenous peoples. A decade later, Golden (2006) described a project in which fourth graders in a New York public school compared the fictionalized accounts of Native American life portrayed by Disney with historical accounts from factual sources in order to reveal historical inaccuracies.

While the articles and theses described here reflect the bulk of the scholarly work on Disney and the classroom, there also exists a number of academic books that address the relationship between critical literacy and children's culture, of which Disney is an important component. Marsh and Millard's (2001) *Literacy and Popular Culture: Using Children's Culture in the Classroom* offers guidance on how to use children's popular culture interests to teach critical literacy. In *Kidworld: Childhood Studies, Global Perspectives, and Education*, Cannella and Kincheloe (2002) trouble normative notions of childhood and disrupt adult/child dualisms by examining, among other topics, the construction of childhood by corporations such as The Walt Disney Company. Expanding on these early works as well as on her aforementioned ethnographic study on Disney Princess play, Wohlwend (2011) wrote *Playing Their Way into Literacies: Reading, Writing, and Belonging in the Early Childhood Classroom.* Another recent volume aimed at teachers and teachers-educators is Rosa and Rosa's (2011) *Pedagogy in the Age of Media Control: Language Deception and Digital Democracy.* While Disney is not prominent in most of the book, the first chapter offers an exploration of the "historicity of Disney as an enterprise and the systematicity with which the ideological discourses embedded within the textual productions of Disney can be represented as 'curriculum' in itself" and as a viable medium through which educators can engage students in exploring issues of linguicism, classism, and racism (p. xxvi).

In addition to the work that we have described here, there is a much larger and more comprehensive body of academic literature on Disney, which began as early as the late 1930s (Budd, 2005). As Wasko (2001) notes, "since the first Mickey Mouse cartoons were released, Disney films have been analyzed in the popular press by film critics and analysts, who have mostly employed an assortment of aesthetic and art criticism and literary analysis" (p. 109). While our focus in this volume is on those works that specifically address the relationship between Disney and teaching, we acknowledge that critical Disney literacies can, and should be, informed by the extensive body of work that constitutes Disney Studies scholarship, which we describe in detail elsewhere (see Sandlin & Garlen, 2016). As we have discussed above, the work of Henry Giroux, in particular, has informed evolving work on the relationship between popular culture, schooling, and learning. Otherwise, however, among the many volumes focusing exclusively on Disney, only Van Riper's (2011) *Learning from Mickey, Donald and Walt: Essays on Disney's Edutainment Films,* makes an explicit connection between Disney and education, with each chapter exploring a different type of Disney "edutainment" film. While the volume is the first to offer a comprehensive exploration of Walt Disney's educative mission, it does not address pedagogy or the classroom context. What makes *Teaching with Disney* unique, then, is its explicit focus on teaching and learning with/in and against the ubiquity of The Walt Disney Company.

TEACHING WITH DISNEY

As Tavin and Anderson (2003) note, "The Walt Disney Company and other multi-billion dollar oligopolies are the teachers of the new millennium" (p. 34). Disney's vast array of visual representations, objects, and experiences constitutes a cultural pedagogy from which, and through which, we, educators and students alike, are learning. That cultural pedagogy is part of what we see as a "Disney milieu," a cultural context in which corporate ideologies drive consumer identifications with childhood, family values, patriotism, and uncomplicated leisure. The powerfully seductive narratives of fantasy, hope, love, and escape that are constructed within Disney texts make possible a cultural ubiquity that is unparalleled in popular culture and yet largely unproblematized within the classroom. Yet as parents, educators, or simply fans, we are teaching ourselves and others through our own critical and not-so-critical engagements with Disney goods and services. In this sense, teaching "with" Disney is meant to acknowledge acts of teaching that take place alongside, within, and in opposition to the "big" curriculum (Schubert, 2006; see also Cremin, 1976 and Schubert, 1981) of Disney. Teaching "with" Disney also refers to bringing Disney into the classroom to engage students in critical, productive analyses of race, class, gender, and sexuality that are essential in exposing power dynamics and disrupting normative discourses. As Johnson (2012) explains, "Leaving micro-level negotiations of race, class, and gender (i.e., performative politics) out of classrooms, pop culture text work ignores radical possibilities these negotiations have to counter and confound reductive subjectivities in and beyond school" (p. 161). Thus, the chapters in this volume investigate both micro- and macro-level negotiations of race, class, gender, and sexuality, while exploring discourses that inform our collective identities as learners, teachers, parents, and consumers. While some contributors in this volume teach "with" Disney by engaging students in analyzing and reflecting on Disney texts to advance critical understandings, others examine the pedagogical potential of specific texts in regard to perspectives on particular aspects of identity that inform our roles as teachers and learners. The book is divided into four thematic sections, described below, each of which expands upon the body of scholarly work on Disney as cultural pedagogy we have described above by offering new insights into the ways we teach and are taught into the discourses of gender, race, class, sexuality, consumption, and subjectivity.

Teaching Gender

Of all of the lucrative franchises owned by The Walt Disney Company, Disney Princess undoubtedly ranks among the most widely recognized. As Mussman (2014) recently observed, "somehow, images of slender femininity with flowing hair and royal pedigrees strike a chord within the souls of small, female children across the globe" (¶ 2). Following and building upon the scholarship reviewed above that focuses on how teachers and learners negotiate gender and sexuality in and through Disney discourses that circulate in both Disney films and in classrooms where students engage with/in those discourses, the chapters in this section explore the promises and problems inherent in Disney's familiar Princess narratives in order to complicate understandings of gender and sexuality and to reveal agentic possibilities for teachers and students.

Alejandra Martinez opens the section with her chapter on analyzing and performing gender. Martinez describes an exercise in which she engages her undergraduate students in analyzing Disney films and in creating new stories and characters to disrupt the stereotypes discovered in the critical analysis. To conclude the exercise, Martinez and her students co-construct a performative text meant to interrupt Disney's gendered discourses. Next, offering a different perspective on teaching gender, Joyce Olewski Inman and Kelli M. Sellers describe a project in which they examined student writing produced for a composition course they collaboratively designed titled, The Disney Princess Dilemma, in which students analyzed and reflected upon Disney Princess narratives. In order to better understand why most of the students in their classes resisted critique and clung to normative gender discourses, Inman and Sellers analyze student essays to investigate moments of confrontation and change in their personal narratives. Finally, Cole Reilly suggests that Disney's gendered discourses might be changing for the better in his analysis of what he calls the "encouraging" evolution of Disney Princesses. Utilizing a critical feminist approach, Reilly offers a balanced analysis that examines the problematic aspects of Disney Princesses while simultaneously exploring signs of progress.

Teaching Race

Cultural critics and the general public have critiqued Disney's representations of African Americans in its animated films almost as long as the company has been "caricaturing such groups" (Budd, 2005, p. 20). Academic work took up critical analyses of race and ethnicity in Disney films in earnest starting in the 1980s and 1990s, exploring problematic and racist representations of Thai people in *Lady and the Tramp* (1955), African Americans in *Dumbo* (1941) and *Song of the South* (1946), Native Americans in *Peter Pan* (1953), *Davy Crockett King of the Wild Frontier* (1955), and *Pocahontas* (1995), and Arab characters and depictions of Islam in *Aladdin* (1992), among other examples (Budd & Kirsch, 2005; Cheu, 2012; Jhappan & Stasiulis, 2005; Sperb, 2012; Wasko, 2001). *The Lion King* (1994) has also been the subject of much scholarship, with the portrayal of the hyenas as "definitely recognizable … Black and Hispanic characters lurking about in a jungle version of a ghetto" (Wasko, 2001, p. 141). Following this and the more classroom-focused research on race and ethnicity that was just reviewed above, this section analyzes the ways in which race and ethnicity are constructed through the familiar narratives of Disney films and television shows. Here, authors explore how images and language inform our understanding of race and ethnicity and investigate how to engage students in the critical analysis of racialized images and colonizing discourses.

The section begins with Jessica Baker Kee and Alphonso Walter Grant's analysis of the ways in which the visual images in Disney films reinforce negative stereotypes about people of color. Taking up Disney films as coded texts, they examine how the images in the films reinforce dominant narratives and marginalize more positive alternative narratives, ultimately implicating themselves in the critique in order to explore the long-term impact of Disney's racially "naturalizing" curriculum. Next, Christina Berchini explores what happens when a new teacher is faced with teaching about issues of race and social justice to a predominantly White, rural student population. Drawing on critical research methodologies, Critical Whiteness Studies, and discourse analysis, Berchini describes the case of Mr. Kurt, who brings Disney into his classroom in order to challenge his students' normative assumptions about race. Finally, Manisha Sharma describes how she engaged her college students with Disney's portrayals of ethnicity and discusses their analytical and emotional responses based on the semiotic analyses those students performed on Disney texts. Drawing from the themes that emerged from the students' analyses, Sharma describes how their ideas of ethnic identity were deeply entwined with ideas of nationality, immigration, and racial identity, illustrating an understanding of American identity that is constructed by defining "ethnic" as "other."

Teaching Consumers

As Steinberg and Kincheloe (2004) note, corporations like Disney have used fantasy and desire to develop a worldview that "melds with business ideologies and free-market values" (p. 16). They recommend a form of critical media literacy that works to expose the social and political effects of the corporate curriculum. The chapters in this section largely take up that call by exploring the ways in which Disney operates to shape how we enact our identities as consumers of products, images, and experiences. Authors here examine how the experience of childhood is appropriated for corporate profit and investigate formal and informal sites of youth and childhood cultural consumption.

In his chapter on teaching Disney critically in what he calls the "Age of Perpetual Consumption," William M. Reynolds describes his experiences of teaching Disney critically to undergraduate education students, arguing that engaging students in critical media literacy requires an understanding of the ways in which they are emotionally and nostalgically invested in consumption. Reynolds positions Disney within the context of a culture of consumption to explain current attitudes of youth toward Disney as well the relationships between Disney loyalty and neoliberal educational policies that are driven by free market ideologies. As Laura Rychly and Stacie Pettit illustrate in their chapter, the American culture of consumption is being exported to China via Disney English. Rychly and Pettit use critical discourse analysis to examine how Disney English is teaching "Americanness" through English language instruction and commodifying language through a vocabulary of consumption. Next, Dennis Attick explores the intersections between consumer culture and teacher identity by examining the ways in which teachers are portrayed in Disney Channel sitcoms. Attick situates the portrayals of teachers around the theme of teachers as apathetic adults and explores how such portrayals trivialize both teachers and students as they perpetuate a notion of education as spectacle. Finally, Marna Hauk explores the domination narratives that emerge from a consumer culture, exploring alternative understandings of regenerative creativities that might heal our colonized imaginations. Focusing on the actual, physical space of Disneyland, she applies a Gaian lens to consider what could be possible if the imagination of the Earth liberated the Disney culture of consumption toward a notion of education that is creative, collaborative, and connective.

Teaching Ourselves

Without an understanding of how we, as educators, are also invested in, and shaped by and through our engagements with popular culture, it is difficult to fully engage learners in the kinds of critical analyses of popular culture described both here in the literature review and in the various chapters throughout this book. Understanding how we learn from popular culture and how our investments in various cultural commodities teach us into certain ways of knowing, being, and doing provides a foundation for designing instruction that allows learners to engage in critical analyses of their own investments with/in popular culture. The essays in this final section of the book take up Miller's (1999) call for educator self-reflexivity with regard to our own engagements with popular culture. Miller (2000) further advocates for interrogating our reactions to popular culture to understand our own personal experiences and to investigate our own "subjectivities and identities" (p. 267). Using the metaphor of media production, Miller (2000) proposes a self-journaling approach to analyze the effects of popular culture on our own learning and development. Miller asserts that educators can investigate their own learning through autobiographical narratives that reveal the intertextuality of life experiences and one's engagement with popular culture.

The chapters in this section engage in these kinds of personal critical narratives as they examine how our individual subjectivities are constituted through engagements with Disney goods, services, and experiences. As Tavin and Anderson (2003) note, "Disney appeals to many of us through a complex affective process where we negotiate our beliefs, values, desires, and expectations in the realm of pleasure and meaning" (p. 22), and the authors in this section explore how these processes work within their own engagements with Disney. Each of these authors thus examine different ways we are taught into various ways of interpreting and experiencing discourses of identity, which shape the ways we think about ourselves and how we relate to others. Embodied responses to and engagements with Disney are explored by several authors as they engage with recent theorizing around the importance of implicating "bodies in pedagogy" (Ellsworth, 2005, p. 6) in ways that are typically ignored within the field of education. This work focuses not only on how bodies are represented in Disney discourses, but also on the non-cognitive and embodied aspects of the learning that occurs as we engage with popular culture, and embraces notions of selfhood that are tentative and "becoming" rather than fixed or unitary (Sandlin, Wright, & Clark, 2013).

First, Shannon Puechner draws on collective memory work, literary analysis, and discourse analysis to analyze the experience of constructing herself through fairy tales she wrote as an adult woman whose "happily ever after" ended in divorce. Puechner explores the anxieties she experienced and the ways in which those anxieties limited how she could situate herself in the world. In the next chapter, Laura

Trafi-Prats and Gina Polencheck Ruchalski examine how pre-service teachers negotiate their subjectivities through the development of an embodied arts research curriculum centered on bodies and relationships between bodies in Disney fairy tale movies. They connect their embodied arts curriculum with disability theory in order to think differently about normalcy as it is expressed through Disney fairy tales. Their unique approach focused on moving students from what is familiar into what is new by engaging them in connecting their own experiences with new ideas, which is illustrated through the students' own artifacts. Offering another perspective on Disney's body pedagogies, Sara Leo discusses how Disney fans and consumers use social media to resist and disrupt Disney's problematic body pedagogies. She explores issues of body representation and policing within the context of a participatory Internet culture by describing specific examples of social media resistance to body shaming and policing in Disney texts, including Merida's Disney Princess makeover, the introduction of Disney Villains Designer Collection Dolls, and the failed Habit Heroes attraction at Epcot. Finally, Jessica L. Kirker offers an autoethnographic account of some of the challenges and moments of success she has experienced in learning to navigate the discourses of Disney in a variety of formal and informal educational settings. She highlights two vignettes that exemplify these crises in both her personal and professional life. Through these stories, she reflects on her experiences as a way of exploring "possibilities for critical theorists and critical pedagogues who have to make decisions about when to advance or suppress their own feminist/critical race/social justice agendas."

TEACHING WITH *TEACHING WITH DISNEY*

As has been noted by many educators who report "special difficulties in getting students to develop critical approaches in the face of the distinctive Disney mystique" (Budd, 2005, p. 3), Disney is in some ways "beyond criticism." In fact, Wasko, Phillips, and Meehan (2001), who surveyed 1,250 respondents in 18 countries for their "Global Disney Audiences Project," found that the vast majority have very favorable attitudes towards Disney and consider critiquing Disney to be taboo. When students do engage in meaningful critique of Disney, they are often left overwhelmed by its power and pervasive influence, and educators and pre-service teachers find themselves doubting whether they are equipped to teach Disney critically in their own classrooms. *Teaching with Disney* seeks to address this dissonance by focusing on the agentic possibilities that emerge from critical analysis and by seeking a balanced perspective that acknowledges the viewer/consumer as an active participant in the meaning-making process who can derive pleasure from *and* engage critically with the popular culture texts that shape public and personal pedagogies. Thus, this volume is not, as Tavin and Anderson

(2003) explain in their work on deconstructing Disney, "a call to censorship," nor a "plea for teachers to become psychic terrorists, destroying the real pleasure students receive from popular culture" (p. 34). We ourselves, two cultural curriculum scholars who write extensively on the ways that Disney's pedagogies perpetuate social inequalities, have been entertained and even, if we must admit, moved to tears by the "magic" of Disney. And yet, we are also scholars and educators dedicated to thinking and teaching more critically about how we learn from popular culture, which is what we hope this volume will enable us and others to do.

This book is not a textbook, per se, but we are envisioning that it could be used in undergraduate and graduate level education and cultural studies courses. Because it focuses on Disney, which engages with so many aspects of culture and society and which is thus relevant to many realms of education, and because it highlights scholars drawn from a wide range of educational contexts, including educational foundations, art education, higher education, K-12 contexts, adult education, media literacy, critical pedagogy, and curriculum studies and curriculum theory, this book will be relevant to a global audience of educational researchers, students, and practitioners. We envision the book being used by upper-level undergraduate and graduate courses in educational foundations, curriculum and instruction, curriculum theory, critical media education, art education, sociology of education, and related fields. Discussion questions are provided for each chapter to help facilitate individual reflection as well as class discussions and assignments.

REFERENCES

Ajayi, L. (2011). A multiliteracies pedagogy: Exploring semiotic possibilities of a Disney video in a third grade diverse classroom. *The Urban Review, 43*(3), 396–413.

Alexander, L. (2006). Multicultural Cinderella: "This is fun work!" *Kappa Delta Pi Record, 42*(4), 183–185.

Anderson, G. L., & Irvine, P. (1993). Informing critical literacy with ethnography. In C. Lankshear & P. L. McLaren (Eds.), *Critical literacy: Politics, praxis, and the postmodern* (pp. 81–104). Albany: SUNY Press.

Anggard, E. (2005). Barbie princesses and dinosaur dragons: Narration as a way of doing gender. *Gender and Education, 17*(5), 539–553.

Baker-Sperry, L. (2007). The production of meaning through peer interaction: Children and Walt Disney's *Cinderella. Sex Roles: A Journal of Research, 56*, 717–727.

Banks, J. A. (2004). Multicultural education: Historical development, dimensions, and practices. In J. A. Banks & C. A. McGee Banks (Eds.), *Handbook of research on multicultural education.* 2nd ed. (pp. 3–29). San Francisco: Jossey-Bass.

Banks, J. A., & Banks, C. A. M. (1995). *Handbook of research on multicultural education.* New York: Macmillan.

Barchers, S. (1988). Beyond Disney: Reading and writing traditional and alternative fairy tales. *The Lion and the Unicorn, 12*(2), 135–150.

Bonds-Raacke, J. (2008). *Cinderella* and *Sleeping Beauty*: Developing a course on Disney and fairytale movies. *Journal of Instructional Psychology, 35*(3), 232–234.

Bouzarth, L., Harris, J., & Hutson, K. (2014, November). Math and the mouse. *Math Horizons, 22*(2), 12–14.

Budd, M. (2005). Introduction: Private Disney, public Disney. In M. Budd & M. H. Kirsch (Eds.), *Rethinking Disney: Private control, public dimensions* (pp. 1–33). Middletown, CT: Wesleyan University Press.

Budd, M., & Kirsch, M. H. (Eds.). (2005). *Rethinking Disney: Private control, public dimensions.* Middletown, CT: Wesleyan University Press.

Cannella, G. S., & Kincheloe, J. L. (2002). *Kidworld: Childhood studies, global perspectives, and education.* New York: Peter Lang.

Cappiccie, A., Chadha, J., Lin, M. B., & Snyder, F. (2012). Using critical race theory to analyze how Disney constructs diversity: A construct for the Baccalaureate Human Behavior in the Social Environment Curriculum. *Journal of Teaching in Social Work, 32*(1), 46–61.

Cartwright, L., & Goldfarb, B. (1994). Cultural contagion: On Disney's health education films for Latin America. In E. Smoodin (Ed.), *Disney discourse: Producing the Magic Kingdom* (pp. 169–180). New York: Routledge.

Cheu, J. (2012). *Diversity in Disney films: Critical essays on race, ethnicity, gender, sexuality, and disability.* Jefferson, NC: McFarland.

Chou, W. H. (2007). Contamination of childhood fairy tale: Pre-service teachers explore gender and race constructions. *The Journal of Social Theory in Art Education, 27*, 55–73.

Ciechanowski, K. (2009). "A squirrel came and pushed Earth": Popular cultural and scientific ways of thinking for ELLs. *The Reading Teacher, 62*(7), 558–568.

Ciechanowski, K. (2012). Conflicting discourses: Functional linguistic and discourse analyses of Pocahontas texts in bilingual third-grade social studies. *Journal of Literacy Research, 44*(3), 300–388.

Crank, V. (2005). 'Doing Disney' fosters media literacy in freshmen. *Academic Exchange Quarterly*, 3, 100–104.

Cremin, L. A. (1976). *Public education.* New York: Basic Books.

De Cunto, M., & Garcia, M. L. (2014). From *Rapunzel* to *Tangled* and beyond: Multimedia practices in the language and literature classroom. *Argentinian Journal of Applied Linguistics, 2*(1), 14–25.

Del Vecho, P., Lasseter, J. (Producers), Clements, R., & Musker, J. (Directors). (2009). *The princess and the frog* [Motion picture]. United States: Walt Disney Pictures.

Disney Educational Productions. (2014). About Disney Educational Productions, 2014. httpp://dep.disney.go.com/aboutus.html

Disney, W. (1963). Deeds rather than words. In R. Gammon (Ed.), *Faith is a star* (p. 7). New York: E. P. Dutton.

Disney, W. (Producer); Geronomi, C., Jackson, W., & Luske, H. (Directors). (1950). *Cinderella.* [Motion picture] United States: Walt Disney Pictures.

Dunn, J., Niens, U., & McMillan, D. (2014). "Cos he's my favourite character!" A children's rights approach to the use of popular culture in teaching literacy. *Literacy, 48*, 23–31.

Dyson, A. H. (1997). *Writing superheroes: Contemporary childhood, popular culture, and classroom literacy.* New York: Teachers College Press.

Ellsworth, E. (2005). *Places of learning: Media, architecture, pedagogy.* New York: Routledge.

Gabler, N. (2006). *Walt Disney.* New York: Alfred A. Knopf.

Garofalo, M. (2013). *The good, the bad, and the ugly: Critical media literacy and Disney female characters.* MA Thesis, Brock University.

Gaztambide-Fernández, R. (2007). Inner, outer, and in-between: Why popular culture and the arts matter for urban youth. *Orbit 36*(3), 35–37.

Giles, M. M., Cogan, D., & Cox, C. (1991). A music and art program to promote emotional health in elementary school children. *Journal of Music Therapy, 28*(3), 135–148.

Giroux, H. (1999). *The mouse that roared: Disney and the end of innocence.* Lanham, MD: Rowman & Littlefield.

Giroux, H., & Pollock, G. (2010). *The mouse that roared: Disney and the end of innocence.* 2nd ed. Lanham, MD: Rowman and Littlefield.

Golden, M. (2006). Pocahontas: Comparing the Disney image with historical evidence. *Social Studies and the Young Learner, 18*(4), 19–23.

Griffin, S. (2000). *Tinker belles and evil queens.* New York: NYU Press.

Guerrero, A. (2015). An approach to finding teaching moments on families and child development in Disney films. *Academic Psychiatry, 39*(2), 225–230.

Hall, S. (1992). Cultural studies and its theoretical legacies. In L. Grossberg, C. Nelson, & P. Treichler (Eds.), *Cultural studies* (pp. 277–285). New York and London: Routledge.

Hidi, S., & Renninger, K. A. (2006). The four-phase model of interest development. *Educational Psychologist, 41*, 111–127.

Hoge, S. E., & Perry, K. E. (2012). Disney in December. *Teaching Children Mathematics, 19*(5), 290–291.

Hurley, D. (2005). Seeing white: Children of color and the Disney fairy tale princess. *The Journal of Negro Education, 74*(3), 221–232.

Iger, R. (2014). The Walt Disney Company fiscal year 2014 annual financial report and shareholder letter. Anaheim, CA: The Walt Disney Company. Retrieved from: http://thewaltdisneycompany.com/sites/default/files/reports/10k-wrap-2014_1.pdf

Jhappan, R., & Stasiulis, D. (2005). Anglophilia and the discreet charm of the English voice in Disney's *Pocahontas* films. In M. Budd & M. H. Kirsch (Eds.), *Rethinking Disney: Private control, public dimensions* (pp. 151–180). Middletown, CT: Wesleyan University Press.

Johnson, E (2012). Performative politics and radical possibilities: Re-framing pop culture text work in schools. *Journal of Curriculum Theorizing, 28*(1), 158–174.

Jones, S. (2006). *Girls, social class, and literacy: What teachers can do to make a difference.* Portsmouth, NH: Heinemann.

Jule, A. (2011). Princesses in the classroom: Young children learning to be human in a gendered world. *Canadian Children, 36*(2), 33–35.

Kaminiski, R. (2000). Using multicultural Cinderella books to engage students in comprehension strategies: Classroom connections. *Council Connections, 6*(1), 14–17.

Khoshniyat, A. S., & Dowlatabadi, H. R. (2014). Using conceptual metaphors manifested in Disney movies to teach English idiomatic expressions to young Iranian EFL learners. *Procedia-Social and Behavioral Sciences, 98*(6), 999–1008.

King, M. J. (1994). Instruction and delight: Theme parks and education. In R. B. Browne & M. T. Marsden (Eds.), The cultures of celebration (pp. 105–123). Bowling Green, OH: Bowling Green State University Press.

Mannheim, S. (2002). *Walt Disney and the quest for community.* Burlington, VT: Ashgate Publishing Company.

Marcus, J. (1997). Disney to open own teaching institute. *Times Educational Supplement* (4208), 16.

Marsh, J. (2000). Teletubby tales: Popular culture in the early years literacy classroom. *Contemporary Issues in Early Childhood, 1*(2), 119–133.

Marsh, J., & Millard, E. (2001). *Literacy and popular culture: Using children's culture in the classroom.* London: Sage.

Matthew, P. A., & Greenberg, J. (2009). The ideology of the mermaid: Children's literature in the Intro to Theory Course. *Pedagogy: Critical Approaches to Teaching Literature, Language, Composition, and Culture, 9*(2), 217–233.

May, S., & Sleeter, C. E. (2010). Introduction: Critical multiculturalism: Theory and praxis. In S. May & C. E. Sleeter (Eds.), *Critical multiculturalism: Theory and praxis* (pp. 1–18). New York: Routledge.

Miller, N. (1999). *Applying insights from cultural studies to adult education: What Seinfeld says about the AERC.* Proceedings of the 40th Annual Adult Education Research Conference (pp. 229–234), DeKalb, IL.

Miller, N. (2000). *Lifelong learning goes to the movies: Autobiographical narratives as media production.* Proceedings of the 41st Annual Adult Education Research Conference (pp. 267–272), University of British Columbia, Vancouver, Canada.

Moule, J. (2013). The masked masquerade: Superhero and princess narratives and gendered masquerade in an early childhood setting. MA Thesis, University of British Columbia. Available at: elk.library.ubc.ca.

Mulder, C. P. (2013). It's the time of your life: Marxism in animated films. *Rethinking Marxism, 25*(2), 284–292.

Muller-Hartmann, A. (2007). Is Disney safe for kids?—Subtexts in Walt Disney's animated films. *American Studies, 52*(3), 399–415.

Musker, J. (Producer & Director), Ashman, H. (Producer), & Clements, R. (Director). (1989). *The little mermaid* [Motion picture]. United States: Walt Disney Pictures.

Mussman, A. (2014, April 25). How Disney princesses lead young women to dystopic fiction. *The Federalist.* Retrieved from: http://thefederalist.com/2014/04/25/how-disney-princesses-lead-young-women-to-dystopic-fiction/

Natale, J. A. (1995). Education goes Mickey Mouse. *Education Digest, 61,* 29–32.

Nikirk, M. (2011, March). Introducing interactive technology—"Toy Story 3." www.acteonline.org. Retrieved from: http://files.eric.ed.gov/fulltext/EJ926075.pdf

Ortutay, B. (2014, December 4). Disney jumps in to educational apps market. *The Toronto Star.* Retrieved from: http://www.thestar.com/business/2014/12/04/disney_jumps_in_to_educational_apps_market.html

Pewewardy, C. (1996–1997). The Pocahontas paradox: A cautionary tale for educators. *Journal of Navajo Education, 14*(1 2), 20–25. Retrieved from: http://www.hanksville.org/storytellers/pewe/writing/Pocahontas.html.

Robb, B. (2014). A brief history of Walt Disney. London, UK: Little, Brown Book Group.

Rosa, J. J., & Rosa, R. D. (2011). *Pedagogy in the age of media control: Language deception and digital democracy.* New York: Peter Lang.

Ross, A. (1999). *The Celebration chronicles: Life, liberty, and the pursuit of property value in Disney's new town.* New York: Ballantine Books.

Sandlin, J. A., & Garlen, J. C. (Eds.). (2016). *Disney, culture, and curriculum.* New York: Routledge.

Sandlin, J. A., Wright, R. R., & Clark, M. C. (2013). Public pedagogy, adult learning, and adult development in the post-modern era: Re-examining theories of adult learning and development in the age of media. *Adult Education Quarterly, 63*(1), 3–23.

Schubert, W. H. (1981). Knowledge about out-of-school curriculum. *Educational Forum, 45,* 185–199.

Schubert, W. H. (2006). Focus on the big curriculum. *Journal of Curriculum and Pedagogy, 3*(1), 100–103.

Sperb, J. (2012). *Disney's most notorious film: Race, convergence, and the hidden histories of* Song of the South. Austin: University of Texas Press.

Steinberg, S. R. (2007). Preface: Reading media critically. In D. Macedo & S. Steinberg (Eds.), *Media literacy: A reader* (pp. xiii–xv). New York: Peter Lang.

Steinberg, S. R., & Kincheloe, J. L. (Eds.). (2004). *Kinderculture: The corporate construction of childhood.* 2nd ed. Boulder, CO: Westview Press.

Sun, C. F., & Scharrer, E. (2004). Staying true to Disney: College students' resistance to criticism of *The little mermaid. The Communication Review,* 7(1), 35–55.

Tavin, K., & Anderson, D. (2003). Teaching (popular) visual culture: Deconstructing Disney in the elementary art classroom. *Art Education, 56*(3), 21–35.

Van Riper, A. B. (2011). *Learning from Mickey, Donald and Walt: Essays on Disney's edutainment films.* Jefferson, NC: McFarland & Co.

Vostral, S. L. (2008). *Under wraps: A history of menstrual hygiene technology*. Plymouth, UK: Lexington Books.

Wasko, J. (2001). *Understanding Disney*. Malden, MA: Polity.

Wasko, J., Phillips, M., & Meehan E. (Eds.). (2001). *Dazzled by Disney? The global Disney audiences project*. Leicester, UK: University of Leicester Press.

Watts, S. (1997). *The Magic Kingdom: Walt Disney and the American way of life.* Columbia: University of Missouri Press.

Westland, E. (1993). Cinderella in the classroom. Children's responses to gender roles in fairy tales. *Gender and Education, 5*(3), 237–249.

Winter, R. O. (2013). The mindful physician and Pooh. *Journal for Learning Through the Arts, 9*(1). Retrieved from: http://files.eric.ed.gov/fulltext/EJ1018318.pdf

Wohlwend, K. E. (2009). Damsels in discourse: Girls consuming and producing identity texts through Disney Princess play. *Reading Research Quarterly, 44*(1), 57–83.

Wohlwend, K. E. (2011). *Playing their way into literacies: Reading, writing, and belonging in the early childhood classroom.* New York: Teachers College Press.

Wohlwend, K. E. (2012a). 'Are you guys *girls*?': Boys, identity texts, and Disney Princess play. *Journal of Early Childhood Literacy, 12*(1), 3–23.

Wohlwend, K. E. (2012b). The boys who would be princesses: Playing with gender identity intertexts in Disney Princess transmedia." *Gender and Education, 24*(6), 593–610.

Wright, R. R., & Sandlin, J. A. (2009). Cult TV, hip hop, shape-shifters, and vampire slayers: A review of the literature at the intersection of adult education and popular culture. *Adult Education Quarterly, 59*(2), 118–141.

Yenika-Agbaw, V. (2014). Black Cinderella: Multicultural literature and school curriculum. *Pedagogy, Culture & Society, 22*(2), 233–250.

Yeoman, E. (1999). 'How does it get into my imagination?': Elementary school children's intertextual knowledge and gendered storylines. *Gender and Education, 11*(4), 427–440.

Zipes, J. (1994). *Fairy tale as myth: Myth as fairy tale.* Lexington: The University Press of Kentucky.

Zipes, J. (2001). *Stick and stones: The troublesome success of children's literature from Slovenly Peter to Harry Potter.* New York: Routledge.

PART ONE

Teaching Gender

CHAPTER TWO

Awakening Rebellion in the Classroom

Analyzing and Performing Disney

ALEJANDRA MARTINEZ

March 26, 2015. It is the first class of the semester. I enter the classroom and I am already excited: I have a new cohort of senior students majoring in graphic design and advertising, with whom to share evenings of intense discussions about media content. I am especially cheerful today: Disney has just released a trailer for the film, Inside Out. *I cherish new Disney pieces because every movie is a land of discovery to me. In this trailer, a "typical" family interacts during a traditional dinner, in an average house. Inside their heads, tiny characters representing emotions guide their actions. For example, the mother is guided by little people in her mind to support her daughter after a bad day at school. These tiny characters guide the woman to involve the father in the conversation but, inside his head, little male characters are watching a sporting event, completely disconnected from the family. Tiny gender-biased people make contradictory decisions, and it all goes wrong: the daughter (and her own tiny characters, both female and male) is grounded and sent to her room.*

As the clip finishes, my students still cannot guess what I am trying to do. I love working that way.

"Well?" I ask. Nobody knows what they are supposed to say. Silence, nervous laughs. "It's fun," says a girl in the front row. She is the first student who dares to speak up. "It is, indeed," I say. But I'm looking for more. "Anyone else?" A girl with purple hair waves her hand almost indifferently: "I think it's something about stereotypes. ..." ("Yes," I say to myself; "you're getting it"). "Um. ... something about roles within the family?" It is time to double the bet. I grab the felt pen and draft a lesson on traditional gender norms.

Drawing on a long tradition of theorists, I explain that gender regulations are socio-cultural constructions that indicate to people what to do, think, and expect, according to their biological sex. I argue that those regulations are incorporated from the first days of life and are constructed from dichotomous relational assumptions: The female has been associated for a long time with the inside, with taking care of the home and the family, children, and the elderly and the ill, with dependence on others, passivity, private space, and emotion; while men have historically been linked to the productive role, providing for their wives and children, and also associated with the use of force, rationality, activity, and independence, among other things.

I play the video again, and when it finishes, most hands are up. I live for that moment.

We discuss the video for an hour. Excitement is contagious and the feeling of learning something new and interesting captures the students' attention. "Why does Disney repeat the same old stereotypes?" they ask. "Do they really believe all men are aggressive, sport fans, insensitive people, disconnected from their wives and children? And that women are all family laden, emotional, and helplessly romantic?" Time passes too quickly and we all leave the room reluctantly. I'm already looking forward to meeting with them again.

INTRODUCTION

I teach a subject that I love, Sociology of Media, at Siglo 21 University, in the city of Córdoba, Argentina. I also work as a researcher at the National Council for Scientific and Technical Research in Argentina, where I have analyzed children's films from a gender perspective for eleven years. My students will be the advertisers and graphic designers of years to come, and the future of mass communication lies in their hands. It is my responsibility to offer them tools so that they can be critical of media content. Otherwise, they will tend to reproduce the same stereotypes we have consumed in the past and still do today, so I feel it is my responsibility as a professor to awaken criticism within them. I do that using a two-stage exercise in which I ask them to analyze Disney films and to then create new stories and characters inspired by their critical analyses. I describe that exercise in this chapter, which I have organized into two parts. First, I describe research procedures and some of the results produced by our joint effort to analyze movies from a gender perspective. It represents the first stage of my work in the classroom, which involves sharing my research experience with the students. I replicate what I do as a researcher, encouraging them to develop their own interpretation of the material we analyze. I call this stage, "The Awakening." Second, students and I appropriate these analyses and, by creating new versions of Disney stories, break with the stereotypes we have observed while analyzing films. In this stage, students and I co-construct a performative text in an effort to demystify the aura that surrounds Disney products. I call this stage, "The Rebellion."

My interest in the study of Disney products is based on the certainty that media content aimed at children has enormous potential to instill its audiences with social regulations, as it has a privileged position in children's culture (Li-Vollmer & LaPointe, 2003). The rising consumption of media content increases the power of such messages. Boys and girls are now exposed to content more frequently and more intensely than in the past (Lacroix, 2004). Moreover, marketing strategies have become significantly more aggressive than at the beginning of Disney's existence. The company combines the consumption of objects and movies, multiplying the effect of its educational structure (Giroux & Pollock, 2010). Consistent with Giroux and Pollock (2010), Denzin (2002), and Sandlin and Maudlin (2012), I believe that entertainment is always an educational force, and that "popular culture is a primary arena of education and learning" (Sandlin & Maudlin, 2012, p. 177). With this "edutainment," as Giroux calls it, children's films operate as innovative teaching machines and have even more cultural authority and legitimacy to instill roles, values, and ideals than traditional teaching spaces do (King, Lugo-Lugo, & Bloodsworth-Lugo, 2010). Disney's narratives reproduce the idea that in order to access certain social "trophies" people need to fit a scheme that was introduced with *Snow White and the Seven Dwarfs* (Disney et al., 1937) and never updated (Booker, 2010).

The limitations and possibilities of characters are linked to objective conditions of existence[1] that determine what is thinkable or unthinkable for them. That is why many of these characters must break with such conditions to access the rewards they seek to obtain. A simple example of the relation established in films between condition and possibility is the repeated idea that beautiful princesses marry charming princes. Being beautiful is an objective condition of existence that introduces a certain range of options for a character (Bazzini, Curtin, & Joslin, 2010). Some of these seem to be unquestionable, such as finding true love and achieving what Disney defines as a "good" marriage (understood as catching a wealthy, powerful, and good-looking man). The objective conditions of existence and the possibilities they offer are embodied in social representations and are reproduced by the media. These have the potential to be apprehended by recipients as socially accepted and naturalized expectations. If being beautiful (in films) is an objective condition that allows access to love, a "good" marriage, and eternal happiness, beauty will be the natural aspiration for little girls who consume these films, and who aspire to live happily ever after. The idea of what is possible or impossible to people, according to their objective conditions of existence, is repeated incessantly in children's films, leaving a tangible mark in the subjectivity of the receivers (Martinez & Merlino, 2012).

"THE AWAKENING": ANALYZING DISNEY WITH MY STUDENTS

The methodology I use working with undergraduate students unites qualitative research and discourse analysis. We use discourse analysis to identify the ways in which animated characters are named, described, and placed (temporally and spatially) according to practices and regulations that define possibilities according to their biological sex. We draw on Philippe Hamon (1977), who focuses on the descriptive moments of a story, to analyze the semiotic surface structures in which the construction of the character is key. Hamon uses the term *referential character* to describe a meaning that has become fixed within culture, representing certain roles, narrative programs, and stereotypes. Referential characters are historical, mythological, allegorical, social, and easily recognizable because they are widespread in culture. To be identifiable to audiences, characters are built according to cultural patterns and to the use of shared meanings. The referential character is constructed from a *must be* that corresponds to certain qualities, spaces, and tasks, and consequently also a *must not be* that corresponds to the space of that which is unthinkable for such a character.

To analyze the narrative structure of Disney films in class, we also use discourse analysis based on the semiotic approach developed by Algirdas Greimas (1977, 1983, 1987; Greimas & Courtés, 1982). Drawing on his work, we approach narrative as a representation of actions. Referential characters mentioned by Hamon (1977) act at the surface level of the story supported by *narrative*. Narrative programs are abstract formulas that represent action in the narration. This action includes (always, as a part of the structure of the narration) the initial and the final relation of the subject with his or her object of value. For example: A *subject* (S) (the heroine) is in a disjunctive relationship (u) with her *object of value* (O) (love). By the end of the story (S) is expected to be in the opposite state (n) (conjunction) with that object. Greimas represents that situation with the following formula:[2]

$$(S\ u\ O) \rightarrow (S\ n\ O)$$

Conjunction is possible thanks to one or more *helpers* (usually characters who help the subject to obtain the object of value), and a *Sender*, a character who commands the subject to do something (initiating a program which includes obtaining the object of value) and provides him or her with the necessary skills to get that object. At the same time there are *opponents* who try to avoid the Subject in order to obtain the object of value (i.e., evil stepmother). The basis of the narrative lies with the movement of the *actants*. Actants are roles in the narration and can be fulfilled by different characters (or objects). According to Greimas, there are three pairs of actants:

Subject ----- Object (of value)
Helper ------ Opponent
Sender ------ Receiver

Actants represent cultural patterns (tradition, chauvinism, etc.) that must be analyzed in order to understand their nature and their consequences on the audience.

In what follows, I illustrate the ways in which these cultural patterns are expressed in Disney films.

Analyzing Traditional Gender Norms

Representations of gender norms in Disney films have remained relatively constant since 1937, when *Snow White and the Seven Dwarfs* was born (Disney et al., 1937). The stories repeat patterns that reinforce the idea of female as opposite and complementary to male (Martinez & Merlino, 2012; Martinez & Papalini, 2012), and there is a strong naturalization of marriage as an indisputable goal that organizes the stories (Byrne & McQuillan, 1999; Gillam & Wooden, 2008; Tanner et al., 2003). While several recent animated films, including *Tangled* (Conli et al., 2011) and *Frozen* (Del Vecho, Buck, & Lee, 2013), contain female characters who are resolute, courageous, and even rebellious, my students and I have found that these films continue to develop a narrative scheme that reproduces similar dénouements: The end comes when the girl gets a prince and he wins a trophy-woman, which is the means to obtain a more valuable object than love or marriage, including a crown, wealth, or inheritance. Thus, while the surface of films might have changed, the structure has remained the same: instead of appropriating their new skills (and possibilities), Disney animated heroines still need to be rescued by men who are stronger than they are. For those women who dare to be tougher than men, the only possible Disney destiny is to remain unmarried—for example, Merida in *Brave* (Sarafian, Andrews, & Chapman, 2012) and Elsa in *Frozen* (Del Vecho, Buck, & Lee, 2013).

In stories produced by Disney since 1989, heroines pursue objects of value that are not necessarily limited to getting married, but that are directly associated with marriage and romantic love. Examples include Ariel in *The Little Mermaid* (Musker, Ashman, & Clements, 1989); Belle in *Beauty and the Beast* (Hahn, Trousdale, & Wise, 1991); Jasmine in *Aladdin* (Clements & Musker, 1992); Megara in *Hercules* (Clements & Musker, 1997); *Mulan* (Coats, Bancroft & Cook, 1998); Rapunzel in *Tangled* (Conli et al., 2012); and Anna in *Frozen* (Del Vecho, Buck, & Lee, 2013). The eternal quest of women for love/marriage is consistent with representations that associate them with reproduction, the inside, passivity, dependence, and emotionality. Their associations with male characters allow heroines access to a fulfilling life, which they cannot achieve being single.

While widowhood is acceptable in Disney films, as it is a situation caused by an inevitable event, voluntary singleness appears rarely. When it does, it is due to at least two specific situations[3]—either (1) the heroine does not have *valid* options from which to choose a husband (available men are unacceptable), or (2) the heroine has a very impressive degree of power that makes her inaccessible (untouchable) and unacceptable as a wife. Merida from *Brave* (Sarafian, Andrews,

& Chapman, 2012) is a great example of the first scenario. She is not offered realistic fiancés to choose from, and she is also too strong, too independent, and too rebellious to be considered a marriageable Disney princess.[4] An example of the second scenario, is Elsa from *Frozen* (Del Vecho, Buck, & Lee, 2013), who exerts overwhelming powers and becomes a queen, but a lonely one. In these representations of singlehood, Disney seems to be whispering to little girls: "Don't be too strong or you'll die single." If love and marriage are shown as the only path to eternal happiness, Disney's message to girls is strong. My students and I affirm: the rebellion is still on hold.

"THE REBELLION": PERFORMING DISNEY WITH MY STUDENTS

While analyzing films in class has always been engaging for both students and me, I recently began to see that something else was needed for my students to go beyond "awakening" and change reified representations. I did not know what it was until May 2013, when I began developing performance exercises in the classroom after Dr. Norman K. Denzin (during a visit I recently made to the University of Illinois at Urbana-Champaign) encouraged me to ask myself two key questions about my work analyzing children's films: What are *my* feelings and sensations when I analyze children's films? What happens *to me* when I work with those cultural pieces? Dr. Denzin (2003a) had just introduced me to performance ethnography:

> This way of doing ethnography imagines and explores multiple ways in which we can understand performance, including understanding it as imitation, or *mimesis*; as construction, or *poiesis*; and as motion or movement, or *kinesis*. The interactionist moves from a view of performance as imitation, or dramaturgical staging, to an emphasis on performance as liminality and construction, to a view of performance as struggle, as an intervention, as breaking and remaking, as kinesis, as a sociopolitical act. (p. 187). I quickly realized that I could apply performance ethnography to my research and use it in class to encourage rebellion among my students by having them break (and remake) crystallized representation within children's films.

I was still visiting the University of Illinois at Urbana-Champaign when I contacted my former students through their Facebook accounts and asked them to write down what they had felt when we analyzed animated films in class. Seventeen students responded to my invitation. Some said they were excited to explore the idea of biased models in the movies, and others wrote about their disillusion about the idea of childhood characters not being transparent. From my former students' expressions I wrote the first sketch of a script that I shared with them while it was still a rough draft. Together, we wrote a text that illustrates the impact the films had on them and on me.

With this exercise, I sought to provoke "conflict, curiosity, criticism, and reflection" (Freire, quoted in Denzin, 2003c, p. 226) as well as to "create a space for dialogue and questions, giving a voice to positions previously silenced, or ignored" (Denzin, 2003b, p. 247). Following Giroux (2010), I believe there is a need to produce a critical language in order to begin dismantling the discourses of innocence proposed by companies like Disney. I like to think of this exercise as a co-performative critical representation (Hamera, 2013), as well as a personal/political praxis and an aesthetic/epistemic performance (Spry, 2011). Performance ethnography criticizes and challenges naturalized senses, inviting participants into an ethical dialogue, while reflexively clarifying a moral position, engendering resistance while offering utopian thoughts about how things can be different (Denzin, 2014). It shows instead of telling; it commits politically, functionally, and collectively (Denzin, 2014). When doing performance ethnography, it is assumed that it is not possible to guarantee absolute methodological certainty in the social sciences, that all research reflects the point of view of the investigator, that all observation is theory laden, and that there is no possibility of constructing a free knowledge exchange (Denzin, 2014). That is why these exercises include emotion, action, introspection, self-awareness, and the body, and they demand the use of narrative and literary styles of communication.

My former students and I re-created the contents of the animated films, and wrote the first act of our play, *Waking Up Snow White: The Story of a Betrayal.* The synopsis of this first act is as follows:

> *Princesses Snow White and Merida meet in the forest. Snow White is longing to be rescued by a prince and to marry him. Merida tries to make her understand how ridiculous her expectations are. When Prince Charming arrives, instead of being gallant and courageous, he looks scruffy and decayed. Feminism, he says, has complicated his situation. Snow White decides to ignore him, as his looks and attitude differ from her own image of what a prince should be. Merida offers to help him improve his appearance, in exchange for a percentage of the profits from selling Disney merchandise.*

In August 2013, I returned to Argentina, excited to meet a new cohort of students and begin working with them on the second act of *Waking Up Snow White.* During the first class, we critically analyzed a corpus of popular animated films. In this initial approach to the films, students' reactions were typical (Martinez, 2015)—they were surprised, angry, and disappointed, but they were also enthusiastic to identify elements of sexism in seemingly innocent films. The students had begun to understand, with a certain amount of discomfort, that many of their expectations are the product of a set of cultural influences. How could they not be discontented at the notion of not owning their dreams? That same week I received many comments and questions through Facebook and through e-mails. Students sent me newspaper articles and YouTube videos about related issues and told me a dozen anecdotes of their experiences as movies consumers, and many of them asked what else they could read about this topic. I was ecstatic.

Then I gave them the first act of the play, *Waking Up Snow White,* which my former students and I had written three months before, and I invited them to develop the second act however they wished. They had carte blanche to change the characters, the course of the story, and even the format of the presentation. The continuation of the story could be produced in whatever format they wanted. The most important part of the task was for students to tap into their feelings and sensations in the performance. We agreed that from their performances I would write a draft of the second act of *Waking Up Snow White.* I would then share it with them to complete the piece together. This exercise would be a collaborative process between my students and me, a co-performance (Denzin, 2003a).

Reviewing my students' proposals, I understood that performance texts are "situated in complex systems of discourse, where traditional, everyday, and avant-garde meanings of theater, film, video, ethnography, cinema, performance, text, and audience all circulate and inform one another" (Denzin, 2003c, p. x). The students wrote not only about Disney films, but also about their own lives. They brought their anxieties, fears, and frustrations to texts that put into dialogue theories, media contents, and their own voices. The systematic observation of content, as well as the performative stimulus, awakened a kind of rebellion in them. Such feelings were expressed in creative pieces in which the harshest aspects of reality came into play; as shared emotional experiences were created, critical cultural awareness was awakened (Denzin, 2003c).

Most of my students had opted for collages of images, words, and sounds. They had produced two radio segments, a set of postcards, a sort of "antique Facebook" (shaped as an old book), a magazine, a comic strip, a poster, a game, a weblog, a website, three theatrical scripts, and three short films—one with human actors, another with puppets, and a third using the technique of stop-motion. The situations and characters they had proposed were so varied that it was almost impossible to make them coexist in the same story. Performances featured gay princes coming out of the closet, characters sent to prison, suicidal drug-addicted princesses, corrupt politicians, and cold-blooded murderers. There were no happy endings, no easy ways out. Anger, disappointment, sadness, and rebellion abounded. Their ideas came from their own contexts, contrasting sharply with the pink promises of children's films. The distress of this awakening became evident in witnessing the violent content in their performances, including the murder of Walt Disney. To students, he was no longer beloved "Uncle Walt," but a kind of evil traitor who deserved punishment.

Like Denzin (2003a), I believe that performances "interrogate and evaluate specific social, educational, economic, and political processes" and "become the vehicle for moving persons, subjects, performers, and audience members into new, critical, political spaces" (p. 198). By encouraging my students to critically analyze Disney films and afterwards to write critical performances about them, following their own feelings and sensations, I seek to help them identify and combat the hegemonic gender norms and sexual discrimination that are forwarded in popular culture (Aronowitz, 1998). The first step in achieving this goal is to awaken in my students a more critical perception of popular cultural products and encourage them to break and remake the narratives and ideologies they perpetuate. This exercise allows them to criticize Disney narratives and, hopefully, to stop reproducing them in their own work as professional advertisers and as graphic designers.

In conclusion, I would like to illustrate the exercise we developed with an example.[5] The postcard below (see fig. 1) was one of a set of twelve, in which students were determined to break Disney myths. Their final reflection was the following:

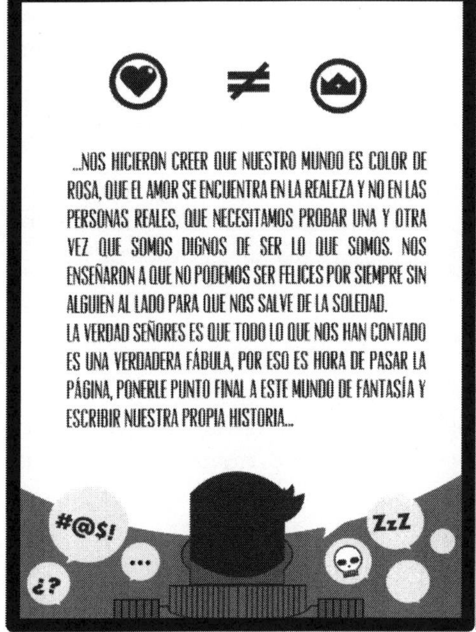

Text: "...They made us believe that our world is pink, that love lies in royalty and not in real people, that we need to prove again and again that we deserve to be what we are. We were taught that we cannot be happy forever without someone to save us from loneliness. The truth is that everything we have been told is a fable, so it's time to turn the page, put an end to this fantasy world, and write our own story."

(Courtesy of Carlos Llanos, Marcos Dalmasso, Martin Vinograd, and Stefano Brizzio)

Fig. 1. A New Ending.

FINAL WORDS

The reproduction of social representations clinging to traditional norms and stereotypes delays the symbolic and material advancement of women. Children's films contribute to stalling a feminist revolution and leave women with much left to achieve. As professors, we have the privilege to educate future professionals who will shape the world to come. With such privilege comes responsibility: within the classroom our words are performative and thus political (Denzin, 2003a). We must denounce what we learn through our own critical research and share new ideas with our students, so that they avoid doing what think tanks of our times have been doing for years. Professors know it will not be easy for students because *following* is easier than *resisting*, but we must motivate them towards change. As educators, we must seek to leave a mark on our students, to set them free from reified ideas that make them suffer, to help them see, and to try to change what they see, encouraging them to be conscious of making personal and professional decisions.

My last words are words of thanks to the editors of this book for their invitation to write a chapter. I doubly appreciate their effort of writing about Disney and asking colleagues around the world to do so, since it is not trouble free to expose sexism, consumerism, and racism in movies where the "good guys" win and endings are always happy. Questioning Disney involves breaking the mystique that sustains its products as well as shattering the purity that surrounds them (Budd & Kirsch, 2005). Disney has a sacred space in culture and it is widely protected from popular criticism (Byrne & McQuillan, 1999), and that is why traditional gender stereotypes and biases find fertile ground there (Martinez, 2013). I firmly believe that teaching with Disney is much more than spreading awareness among students: it is an effort to make their lives better and to contribute to a future in which cultural products are more than unquestioned reproductions of hegemonic meanings.

DISCUSSION QUESTIONS

1. Discuss the importance of questioning media content aimed at children.
2. Identify an animated film that proposes alternative representations of gender norms. Discuss differences between that film and the movies cited in this chapter.
3. Identify your favorite Disney movie and:
   (a) Reflect on what makes it special for you. What do you feel when you watch it?
   (b) Re-write the story. Re-create the characters and the narrative. Propose new ones that break the traditional path and destiny for Disney's heroes and heroines.
   (c) Insert yourself in the new story. What kind of character would you be? Why?
   (d) Experiment with creative ways to (re)present your story (writing poetry, painting, acting, etc.)

NOTES

1. I refer to objective conditions of existence as social determinants that are unlikely to be subject to modification: gender, social class, family origin, ethnicity, and nationality, among others (Martinez & Merlino, 2012).
2. I am presenting a very simplified version of the model in order to guide the readers toward the forthcoming analysis. Please see Greimas (1977, 1983, 1987; Greimas & Courtés, 1982).
3. Most readers may remember the controversy around Merida's makeover to be commercialized as a feminized princess (Fox 2 Now, St. Louis, 2013).
4. I should also mention Pocahontas, who is single by the end of the original movie, but interracial marriage as an obstacle deserves a whole paper to be discussed (see Cokely, 2004).
5. First published in Martinez (2015).

REFERENCES

Aronowitz, S. (1998). Introduction. In P. Freire, *Pedagogy of freedom: Ethics, democracy, and civic courage* (pp. 1–19). Boulder, CO: Rowman & Littlefield.

Bazzini, D., Curtin, L., & Joslin, S. (2010). Do animated Disney characters portray and promote the beauty-goodness stereotype? *Journal of Applied Social Psychology, 40*(10), 2687–2709.

Booker, K. (2010). *Disney, Pixar, and the hidden messages of children's films*. Santa Barbara, CA: Praeger.

Budd, M., & Kirsch, M. (Eds.). (2005). *Rethinking Disney: Private control, public dimensions*. Middletown, CT: Wesleyan University Press.

Byrne, E., & McQuillan, M. (1999). *Deconstructing Disney*. Sterling, VA: Pluto Press.

Clements, R., & Musker, J. (Producer & Director). (1992). *Aladdin* [Motion Picture]. United States: Walt Disney Pictures.

Clements, R., & Musker, J. (Producer & Director). (1997). *Hercules* [Motion Picture]. United States: Walt Disney Pictures.

Coats, P. (Producer), Bancroft, T., & Cook, B. (Directors). (1998). *Mulan* [Motion Picture]. United States: Walt Disney Pictures.

Cokely, C. (2004). Someday my prince will come. In C. Ingraham (Ed.), *Thinking straight: The power, promise and paradox of heterosexuality* (pp. 167–182). New York: Routledge.

Conli, R., Lasseter, J., & Keane, G. (Producers), Greno, N., & Howard, B. (Directors). (2011). *Tangled* [Motion Picture]. United States: Walt Disney Pictures.

Del Vecho, P. (Producer), Buck, C., & Lee, J. (Directors). (2013). *Frozen* [Motion Picture]. United States: Walt Disney Pictures.

Denzin, N. K. (2002). *Reading race*. London: Sage.

Denzin, N. K. (2003a). The call to performance. *Symbolic Interaction, 26*(1), 187–207.

Denzin, N. K. (2003b). Reading and writing performance. *Qualitative Research, 3*(2), 243–268.

Denzin, N. K. (2003c). *Performance ethnography: Critical pedagogy and the politics of culture.* Thousand Oaks, CA: Sage.

Denzin, N. (2014). *Interpretive autoethnography*, Thousand Oaks, CA: Sage.

Disney, W. (Producer), Hand, D., Cottrell, W., Jackson, W., Morey, L., Pearce, P., & Sharpsteen, B. (Directors). (1937). *Snow White and the Seven Dwarfs* [Motion Picture]. United States: Walt Disney Pictures.

Fox 2 Now, St. Louis. (2013). Disney Princess Merida re-design stirs up controversy. Retrieved from: http://fox2now.com/2013/05/20/disney-princess-merida-re-design-stirs-up-controversy/

Giroux, H. (2010). Stealing of childhood innocence—Disney and the politics of casino capitalism: A tribute to Joe Kincheloe. *Cultural Studies/Critical Methodologies, 10*(5), 413–416.

Giroux, H. A., & Pollock, G. (2010). *The mouse that roared: Disney and the end of innocence.* Lanham, MD: Rowman & Littlefield.

Gillam, K., & Wooden, S. R. (2008). Post-princess models of gender: The new man in Disney/Pixar. *Journal of Popular Film and Television, 36*(1), 2–8.

Greimas, A. (1977). Elements of a narrative grammar, *Diacritics* 7, 23–40.

Greimas, A. (1983). *Structural semantics: An attempt at a method.* Lincoln: University of Nebraska Press.

Greimas, A. (1987). *On meaning: Selected writings in semiotic theory.* Minnesota: University of Minnesota Press.

Greimas, A., & Courtés, J. (1982). *Semiotics and language: An analytical dictionary.* Bloomington: Indiana University Press.

Hahn, D. (Producer), Trousdale, G., & Wise, K. (Directors). (1991). *Beauty and the Beast* [Motion Picture]. United States: Walt Disney Pictures

Hamera, J. (2013). Performance ethnography. In N. Denzin & Y. S. Lincoln (Eds.). *The Sage Handbook of Qualitative Research* (pp. 317–331). Thousand Oaks, CA: Sage.

Hamon, P. (1977). Para un estatuto semiológico del personaje. In R. Barthes et al. (Eds.). *Poétique du récit.* París: Seuil.

King, R. C., Lugo-Lugo, C. R., & Bloodsworth-Lugo, M. K. (2010). *Animating difference: Race, gender and sexuality in contemporary films for children.* Plymouth, UK: Rowman & Littlefield.

Lacroix, C. (2004). Images of animated others: The orientalization of Disney's cartoon heroines from *The little mermaid* to *The hunchback of Notre Dame. Popular Communication. 2*(4), 213–229.

Li-Vollmer, M., & LaPointe, M. (2003). Gender transgression and villainy in animated film. *Popular Communication 1*(2), 89–109.

Martinez, A. (2013). Cruella de Vil and the fairy godmother: Watching Disney with my students. *Cultural Studies/Critical Methodologies 15*(1), 3–8.

Martinez, A. (2015). The story of a betrayal: Performing Disney with my students. *Cultural Studies/Critical Methodologies, 15*(2), 87–93.

Martinez, A., & Merlino A. (2012). Normas de género en el discurso cinematográfico: El eterno retorno del "final feliz." *Cuestiones de género: De la igualdad y la diferencia, 7,* 79–99.

Martinez, A., & Papalini, V. (2012). Valiente o la rebeldía amordazada. *Question 1*(36), 58–68.

Musker J. (Producer & Director), Ashman, H. (Producer), Clements, R. (Director). (1989). *The little mermaid* [Motion Picture]. United States: Walt Disney Pictures.

Pentecost, J. (Producer), Gabriel, M., & Goldberg, E. (Directors). (1995). *Pocahontas* [Motion Picture]. United States: Walt Disney Pictures.

Sandlin, J. A., & Maudlin, J. G. (2012). Consuming pedagogies: Controlling images of women as consumers in popular culture. *Journal of Consumer Culture 12*(2), 175–194.

Sarafian, K. (Producer), Andrews, M., & Chapman, B. (Directors). (2012). *Brave* [Motion Picture]. United States: Walt Disney Pictures and Pixar Animation Studios.

Spry, T. (2011). Performative autoethnography: Critical embodiments and possibilities. In N. K. Denzin & Y. S. Lincoln (Eds.), *The Sage handbook of qualitative research.* 4th ed. (pp. 487–512). Thousand Oaks, CA: Sage.

Tanner, L. R., Haddock, S. A., Zimmerman, T. S., & Lund, L. K. (2003). Images of couples and families in Disney feature-length animated films. *The American Journal of Family Therapy, 31*(5), 355–373.

CHAPTER THREE

The Disney Princess Dilemma

Constructing, Composing, and Combatting Gendered Narratives

JOYCE OLEWSKI INMAN AND KELLI M. SELLERS

Disney is in the business of educating, of making memories, and, ultimately, of telling stories. As Henry A. Giroux and Grace Pollock (2010) point out in their often-cited text, *The Mouse That Roared: Disney and the End of Innocence*, the multimedia conglomerate effectively reconstructs identities by creating entertaining and educational narratives: stories that shape our ideals, behaviors, and memories. What is remarkable is that Disney not only creates stories but also edits children's own life experiences, their personal narratives. A corporate, mouse-eared lens shapes the ways children understand the significant moments of their lives and make sense of the world around them. Giroux and Pollock argue that the "struggle over public schooling should be addressed as part of a struggle over the educational force of a culture that has come to play an increasingly powerful and influential role in shaping the minds, desires, and identities of the young and old alike" (p. 58). Since self-discovery is a hallmark of composition pedagogy, the writing course is an ideal space in which to explore how Disney has shaped the stories that form our individual and group subjectivities.

In the fall of 2012, we collaboratively designed an active-learning, first-year honors composition course titled, "The Disney Dilemma," and Giroux and Pollock's text served as our jumping-off point. Like these authors, we asked students to consider the ways in which Disney has shaped their ideas about gender, race, education, the family, community, education, place, and globalization. Ultimately, we wanted to counter students' internalization of the concept that Disney is a place where memories are made and push them to think about critiques of Disney as "the epitome of placelessness constructed" (Cresswell, 2004, p. 45) and as a company skilled "at making places" (Salamone & Salamone, 1999, p. 85) and at shaping identities. It was, perhaps, not surprising that the stories students most resisted and produced, involved gendered narratives. In this chapter, we will discuss our students' first essays of the semester, personal narratives in which they were asked to reflect on a learning experience with Disney. Namely, we seek to investigate what we believe to be moments of confrontation and change as students make sense of their own stories and of how Disney has affected their understandings of gender. Although we did not have discussions of Disney's constructions of gender until later in the semester, from the beginning of the semester students' own stories often adhered to Disney metanarratives. After analyzing these metanarratives, we more fully examine the work of one student, Anna, who challenged Disney's construction of gender. What we learn from Anna's essay in particular is that students must move away from their nostalgic, childhood memories of Disney in order to resist the gendered master narratives forwarded by Disney and to create their own.

DISNEY PRINCESS CULTURE AS A MASTER NARRATIVE

Our considerations of these stories about gender roles—those advanced by Disney and those told by our students—are influenced by Jean-Francois Lyotard's (1984) notions of the ways knowledge is justified via narratives. One of our hopes in designing this class was to help students begin to analyze the ways in which Disney princess culture serves as a master narrative that shapes our culture's understandings of gender roles and expectations of girlhood. Lyotard's view of master narratives as overarching stories that society clings to in an effort to rationalize our cultural experiences is not an uncommon lens through which scholars view Disney's shaping of stories about gender in our society (see Boje, 1995; Bryman, 1995; Herzogenrath, 2001). Indeed, the master narrative, according to Lyotard, is both appealing and limiting due to its perceived legitimacy and canonization in cultural story telling, and Disney's princess culture is based on a long history of fairytales in which women are granted little agency. The Disney versions of these fairytales, however, have an unprecedented reach in the lives of American children, who, via an onslaught of dedicated stories and merchandising, learn that a princess is a beautiful, demure, heterosexual, young woman who is coming of age with a wish to be rescued and domesticated. Such master narratives have also been given significant attention in the field of composition studies given the prevalence of narrative genres in first-year composition sequences (see Brodkey, 1989; Daniell, 1999; Alexander, 2011; Williams, 2003). For us, encouraging students to explore Disney as a master narrative capable of shaping identity and requiring them to write narrative essays about their experiences with Disney provided an opportunity to explore how our students accept, reconcile, and/or reject the master narrative formula.

As we describe here, each of our classes attempted to identify—with the assistance of our readings—the gendered master narratives that Disney perpetuates via its animated films. Our students easily understood that the vast majority of scholars who write about Disney claim that Disney promotes an idealized princess character defined by moral virtue and physical beauty and whose success and happiness are linked to securing a husband and finding contentment in the heteronormative domestic realm. They were willing to admit that this was indeed a simplistic and inaccurate trope that was obvious in most Disney films featuring a woman as the primary character. They were not, however, convinced that this narrative was powerful enough to "act invisibly to structure and define our lives" (Alexander, 2011, p. 610). Initially, they did not accept our assertion that Disney's representations of gender roles were a master narrative capable of shaping their expectations and desires about what it means to be a woman or a man. We were repeatedly told that we were simply reading too much into these innocent stories and that Disney films and the materials marketed alongside them were harmless and fun entertainment. We hoped that by exposing students to critical readings about gender and Disney as they began to write their narrative essays for our class, they would be more apt to see the relevance of this master narrative to their own experiences.[1]

While there are many scholarly works on the role of Disney in American culture, we chose as a primary text for our class Giroux and Pollock's (2010) influential book on the politics of innocence implicit to Disney's business and cultural model. The authors examine "the commonsense narratives often encoded by Disney as an important step in the process of interrogating the historical, institutional, and political conditions that shape, limit, and condition the way people decode such narratives" (p. 11). Because we designed our courses with these types of discussions in mind, we developed assignments that asked students to "interrogate," analyze, and evaluate Disney's narratives and their roles in shaping students' own stories. The scaffolded assignments required students first to navigate their own life stories and the ways Disney has affected their learning, then to analyze the life story of a popular Disney character in order to investigate the character's legacy, and finally to research an element of Disney and to explore the ways in which this particular element shapes our culture. At the end of the semester, students compiled final portfolios, which required them to revisit their first and last projects in the course. Each assignment required reflection, analysis, and evaluation by moving students' gazes from inward to outward, exploring how Disney "shape(s), limit(s), and condition(s)" cultural identity both individually and globally.

For the purposes of this chapter, we will focus on the first major writing assignment for the course, a narrative essay we titled, "Learning Disney," and students' revisions of this project for their final portfolios. The project asked students to explore a particular moment, experience, or memory pertaining to Disney and to analyze that moment in an effort to make their experiences relevant to an outside audience. Students responded with a variety of interesting essay topics pertaining to their Disney experiences, most of which included specific memories made while visiting Disney parks on vacation with their families, watching specific Disney movies, or identifying with specific Disney characters. In the section that follows, we will consider the stories our students composed that were related specifically to gender and how their retellings of those stories changed (or did not).[2]

DISNEY'S GENDERED METANARRATIVES

In *Narratology,* Mieke Bal (1998) explains that narrative events are defined in terms of transitions or processes of change; therefore, our analysis of student narratives is driven by the events that students encountered in the classes. Namely, we seek to investigate what we believe to be those moments of adherence to Disney's master narrative of princess culture or those moments of confrontation that result from students making sense of their own stories and how Disney has affected their understandings of gender. In order to consider the processes of change evidenced in our students' writings, we begin by examining tropes consistent with Disney's master narrative of princess culture in our students' original narrative essays. Our corpus of essays includes twenty-three first-year student narratives, five of which explicitly explore the writers' relationships to Disney princess films or characters; these five essays were each authored by female students in the class. In these essays, we identify three gendered metanarratives that reinforce students' unintentional internalization of Disney's master narrative for young women: youthful impertinence, physical beauty, and heteronormative domesticity. Each of the essays we explore here explicitly addresses at least two of these narrative threads, and none of the metanarratives was more or less common than another.

The first metanarrative, youthful impertinence, centers on the characterization of the princess as a rebellious teenager. Our students understandably identify with this concept, given their age and gender, but their willingness to embrace this stereotype is also interesting. Though our students often resisted the idea that Disney has influenced their ideas and behaviors, their writings demonstrate the significance of Disney's stories in their understandings of their own identities and power. In her narrative essay, Carie writes, "To be honest, I was spoiled growing up. Being daddy's 'little princess,' most of the time I could just turn to him and get anything I wanted." Carie goes on to explain that her house was "the house" in her neighborhood because it held a vast number of toys and entertainment opportunities, and she notes that "it was like being the princess with the biggest castle in all the land."

Laura Sells (2008) addresses the phenomenon of youthful impertinence in her analysis of the Disney film, *The Little Mermaid* (1989), as she describes the film as both insidious and liberatory in its representations of the main character of Ariel as a rebellious teenager who defies her father for her chance at true love. Giroux and Pollock (2010) also note that three of the most popular Disney heroines, Ariel, Belle, and Jasmine, are presented as teenagers whose strength is only evident in childish willful acts—acts that are liberating only until the young women find their true loves. Princess behavior, according to these popular texts, involves token and sometimes strategic rebellious acts and selfish behaviors that allow women to show a semblance of independence without becoming fully reliant on themselves as change agents. It was not surprising then that a different student writes about her memories of running to her room, throwing herself on the bed and crying, and then compares her actions to those of Ariel in *The Little Mermaid.* Indeed, our students, as illustrated in their personal narratives, embraced the rebellious spirit of these princesses while initially resisting the idea of self-reliance, using their youthful impertinence to get what they want.

The second common metanarrative evident in these essays involves the significance of physical beauty in the lives of women influenced by the Disney culture. Our students' essays both acknowledge and embrace a culturally accepted standard of beauty as a marker of the successful princess/woman. Jill, in fact, tells her story of coming to believe that she was beautiful when she realized while watching the parade at Disney World that her pale skin was similar to Snow White's skin. Another student writes about dressing up as a princess as a child and her desire to be as beautiful as a princess for her senior dance. Our students seemed to find little reason to critique Disney's animated representations of women, pointing out that these characters were diverse enough that most girls could relate to at least one of the princesses. Only Anna, whose essay we return to in the final portion of the chapter, talks about this standard of beauty as a negative aspect of princess culture. Yet, even her essay does not critique our culture's complicities with Disney's standards of beauty but rather attempts to grapple with the fact that she was not "pretty enough." Illustrating Disney's limited constructions of beauty regarding race and ethnicity, Bell (2008) notes that early "animated heroines were individuated in fair-skinned, fair-eyed, Anglo-Saxon features of Eurocentric loveliness, both conforming to and perfecting Hollywood's beauty boundaries" and goes on to explain how class and status are marked on these characters through the ways their movements are animated (p. 111). Though our students claimed in class discussions that Disney's princess culture had not influenced their own perceptions of beauty, the essays indicate that the physical characteristics Bell defines do affect students' attitudes of self-acceptance and self-esteem.

The third metanarrative, heteronormative domesticity, reinforces the master narrative of princess culture by insisting on marriage and happily-ever-after love as a formula for success and contentment. As Giroux and Pollock (2010) point out, "all of the female characters in [Disney's] films are ultimately subordinate to males and define their sense of power and desire almost exclusively in terms of dominant male narratives" (p. 104). While Disney has presented a number of new princess models over the past decade, the classic princess tales of Cinderella, Snow White, and Sleeping Beauty all reinforce domesticated, stereotypical gender roles for women, and these classic princess tales will always represent what a colleague of ours terms, "A-level princesses."[3] The impressions these characters made on our students are quite obvious in their Disney essays. Stephanie, for example, writes that, "After watching *Cinderella* (1950), I gained a love for romantic, fairy-tale endings that has remained with me to this day." Indeed, three students ultimately explore their desire to find a traditional fairytale romance that ends in marital bliss. Some students, however, began to see the ways in which this metanarrative negatively influences young girls. In her final essay of the semester, Carie admits, "Disney's idea of love has a universal influence no matter how hard we try to stray from it." Nonetheless, she refuses to entirely dismiss the appeal of the Disney princess and the positive role models she finds in princess films: "Even though a little girl may realize that Disney's love story is not something that happens to everyone, she can still dream. … That is the beauty of Disney, no matter how false his portrayal of love may be." For Carie and for others in the class, this kind of love may be misleading, but it is still something for which to strive.

As we have shown through these brief glimpses of our students' stories, most of our students initially resisted a critique of Disney's princess culture and the ways in which it affects girls' understanding of their positions in society. This resistance can be understood in two ways. First, their unwillingness to consider the negative influences of Disney reinforces what other scholars have shown about the far-reaching power of the corporation. In fact, students' resistance also reinforced our own goals for the class: the importance of investigating Disney's stories, recognizing their influence and then attempting to combat the narratives. Second, we believe that students found it difficult to challenge Disney narratives because they struggled with separating the corporation from their own childhood memories. In other words, we were not simply asking students to challenge a powerful part of American culture; we were asking them to critique their nostalgic memories of childhood. In her initial blog post, Stephanie explains, "I couldn't even tell you my first experience with Disney because it is so ingrained in my memory that I don't even know when it first began. My mom had my brother and I watching the old, classic Disney movies pretty much from the time we were born." Although it is true that most students adhered to Disney's narrative because of their early experiences, others made moves that challenged the stories Disney tells. The narrative that follows indicates Anna's struggle with the three metanarratives we previously identified, but more significantly, Anna's story shows that in order for students to combat Disney narratives by rewriting their own narratives, they must be willing to confront their constructed childhood stories and to move past them.

ANNA'S NARRATIVE OF CHANGE

When Anna first entered the classroom, she attempted to fade into the background. She offered little to class discussions and often stared at the table rather than make eye contact with her peers. Anna's response to the introductory blog assignment, which asked students to introduce themselves to the class and to discuss their general experiences with Disney, was, therefore, surprising. Like most students in the class, Anna describes watching Disney films and the paraphernalia she owned as a child (including "baby boots that were white with blue trim and had Tigger and Pooh Bear on them"). However, Anna did something in her blog that no other student even attempted; she positioned herself for change, eagerly writing,

> I cannot wait to dig into Disney with a critical eye rather than a child's eye. I am anticipating a change in my perspective of Disney by the end of the semester, whether it is for good or bad. I know I will always love Disney and the movies, but perhaps the way I view the movies and the corporation will shift.

Most notable about Anna's post is that she recognizes the difference between a child's perspective and a critical one. As she enters her first year of college, she is moving over the threshold between childhood and adulthood and is ready to see the world around her with a "critical eye rather than a child's eye." Perhaps because Anna "anticipated" a change, her work and subsequent class narrative is one of the few that not only confronted the Disney master narrative but also attempted to counter the narrative by creating a new life story and identity.

Although Anna's story is the exception rather than the rule, she also had to face the difficult task of confronting the stories Disney tells, especially in terms of gender. When working on the narrative assignment, Anna struggled to make sense of her experience with her favorite Disney film, *Beauty and the Beast* (1991). Her draft, titled, "Thou Shalt Never Judge a Book by Its Cover," focused on the theme of beauty versus goodness, and it did not go beyond her own initial observations that Disney had taught her never to judge a book by its cover. Part of the problem, Kelli later discovered, was that Anna was holding back. In a discussion about her essay, Anna told Kelli that she felt she could not formulate her ideas because she was not sure if she wanted to write about her sexuality. She made a choice, however, to take a risk with the narrative. The resulting essay developed into a sort of coming-out narrative that indicated her willingness to, as she puts it, "shift her perspective" about

Disney and about her own sexual identity. In the essay, she attempts to explain how the prologue of Disney's *Beauty and the Beast* had "changed [her] life completely" and had even "ruined some of [her] high school experiences." Though Anna attempts to understand Disney's negative influences by exploring themes of beauty versus goodness, the result is not a straightforward analysis. Rather, the essay is replete with mixed and confused messages about identity. Anna never mentions the princess in this Disney film; instead, she focuses on the Beast by first comparing the cursed character to the people she distrusts. At the same time, Anna's language and the stories she tells reveal that she identifies with the Beast in this princess tale.

Throughout the essay, Anna is preoccupied with notions of ideal standards of beauty, but she does not engage the ways in which Disney constructs these standards. As she tells the story of a high school dance, Anna recounts that none of the boys wanted to dance with her. Crushed, Anna wonders, "Was I not pretty enough?" She finally attempts to connect the lessons she learned from Disney to those experiences at the dance: "I have my faults, but I am strong. When I look in the mirror I do not see some beautiful girl staring back at me, not by looks. I see a girl who is strong enough to face each day alone if she has to. The question is: do other people see me that way?" By attempting to reconcile what she sees in the mirror to the person she feels she is on the inside, Anna aligns herself with the Beast in her favorite film and concludes her essay with the vow never to "have a true relationship with anyone until they earn [her] trust completely."

Each of Anna's projects shows the evolution in her understanding of Disney's problematic standards of beauty and messages of heteronormative domesticity. In fact, there is a unifying theme to Anna's work throughout the semester. She continued to be concerned about topics of beauty and grotesqueness and their connections to gender, especially in terms of Disney princesses and villains. For her next essay, which asked students to explore the legacy of a Disney character, Anna made an interesting move by returning to her favorite film. In this essay, however, she is no longer concerned with the Beast or beauty. Rather, she seeks to understand definitions of goodness or morality as they are marked by socially accepted gender portrayals. In her essay, Anna analyzes the villain of the film, the hyper-masculine Gaston, and argues that he is not the villain he appears to be. Instead, she understands him to be a misunderstood figure who, by striving to conform to society's definitions of the "ideal man," turned to a life of wickedness. If he is wicked, she claims, it is because society has reinforced masculine ideals.

Anna's first two essays indicate that Disney's gender portrayals certainly can leave lasting, negative impressions, especially when children see them at such an early age. In their essay, "Gender Role Portrayal and the Disney Princesses," England, Descartes, and Collier-Meek (2011) observe the following:

> Consistently portrayed gender role images may be interpreted as "normal" by children and become connected with their concepts of socially acceptable behavior and morality. For

> example, when children see villainy in a character illustrated via gender transgression (e.g., a male villain appearing effeminate), they may develop lasting negative associations with non-stereotypical gendered behavior. (p. 557)

As the only openly gay student in our classes, Anna did not identify with Disney princesses. Instead, she continued to identify with the villains, first with the Beast and then with Gaston. Her understanding of her own identity, as marked by Disney at least, was conflicted between her realization of her own goodness (if not beauty) and her attempts to understand the perceived wickedness of the villainous characters. But, her first two projects also illustrate Anna's process of change and her ability to combat Disney's gendered narratives. Anna becomes a change agent as she begins to understand society's complicity in Disney's portrayals of socially acceptable gender roles. In doing so, she begins to understand that it is not she who is the villain, but the world around her.

By the end of the semester, Anna seemed to make a choice of self-acceptance, to confront Disney's master narrative, and to begin creating her own story. Her process of change is most evident in her research essay and in her revised narrative essay. Though Anna had never read the England, Descartes, & Collier-Meek (2011) essay we reference above, she wondered why so many Disney villains appeared effeminate and what that meant about Disney's influence. And in her research essay, she argues:

> Out of principle, wickedness would lie within the body of the effeminate, lanky, and scrawny man, and greatness would come from the burly, masculine man. Clearly, through their films, the Disney Corporation suggests that gender roles are black and white—men should be masculine and women should be feminine; therefore, Disney portrays male villains as effeminate to further emphasize their deplorable, grotesque characteristics and to reinforce predominate heterosexual values.

Anna clearly identifies the problems with Disney's gendered master narrative and views it with a critical eye, not that of a child. More importantly, she recognizes the influence of that narrative in her own life. In her narrative rewrite, Anna admits that because of Disney and her religion she had "felt obligated to enter into a heterosexual relationship despite [her] distaste" for it. However, unlike in her original narrative, Anna feels more confident to rewrite her own story. As she points out in the conclusion of her new narrative, "even the strongest of influences can be overcome sometimes."

PEDAGOGICAL RESPONSES TO THE PRINCESS NARRATIVE

Anna's ability to reflect on the ways young women are unconsciously shaped by Disney's master narrative was certainly not the typical student response. However, we are confident that each of our students came to new understandings of Disney's influence in defining acceptable roles for women, even if, like Carie, they still believe that this influence is not entirely negative. We, too, came to a new understanding of Disney's master and gendered narratives that our students both resisted and produced. When looking back at our students' narratives and how they adhere to and attempt to escape the gendered princess narrative, we realized that any exploration of our students' work must consider three things: (1) that students were affected by the assignment requirements they were asked to fulfill; (2) that students' understandings of princess culture and their own gender identities are nascent and evolving; and (3) that life stories are merely "partial, selective commentary on lived experience" (Goodson & Sikes, 2001, p. 16). In other words, the material that we analyzed is a glimpse into one moment of students' lives, and, therefore, we recognize that these processes did not end with the conclusion of the class. However, we have begun to learn more about the ways in which the course provided a catalyst for students' confrontations with Disney and gender identity, allowing them to begin revising their life stories. Although we cannot show how our classes affected students long term, we can gain insight into their "present" retellings included in their final portfolios and hopefully demonstrate the pedagogical importance of asking first-year writing students to confront the master narratives embedded in Disney's princess culture.

In hindsight, we realize that while we struggled with students' resistance to critiquing Disney and thought we were not making an impact, in reassessing our experiences, we discovered that the arc of students' writing tells its own story. Moving from the narrative essay to a research project and final portfolio, students wrestled with the inherent contradictions that Disney offers and ultimately began questioning competing notions of their new, academic, adult lives and Disney-constructed childhood memories. In the narrative essay, most of the students constructed stories that fondly looked back on their childhood experiences with Disney. But, as students completed their final projects for the course, they began to recognize the social influence of Disney and attempted to critique and combat Disney's stories with those of their own. The most notable changes that occurred (especially for the women in the class) were in students' perceptions of gender and in their recognition of their own agency when reconstructing gendered identities, their own power to recognize the role Disney plays in shaping a master narrative, and their abilities to rewrite and rethink childhood stories about who they are becoming and why. In asking students to reach for and reflect on childhood memories, we must not forget the significance that Disney plays in shaping those memories. By doing so, we are confident that "it is possible for everyone to utilize encounters with the cultural images and narratives that constitute the Disney curriculum in order to learn about themselves and others" (Giroux & Pollock, 2010, p. xvi).

DISCUSSION QUESTIONS

1. Consider the ways Disney influences today's students by taking some time to write about your own experiences with Disney. Pinpoint a specific experience with Disney (e.g., the first time you watched a favorite Disney film, an experience during a trip to Disney World, or your thoughts about a Disney hero). How might your own memories and experiences lead to fruitful class discussions about Disney's influence?
2. Part of students' resistance to critical ideas about Disney is that their experiences are rooted in nostalgic childhood memories. Critiquing Disney, therefore, places that nostalgia at risk. What kinds of discussions about home, school, ideas, and Disney can help students to navigate this danger zone in order to openly and freely critique the values, especially gendered values, embedded in Disney as a cultural icon?

NOTES

1. The class readings were divided into five primary units, focusing on gender, race, place, education, and globalization.
2. This study was approved by our institution's IRB. All student names are pseudonyms.
3. Charles Yow (2014), "The cost of happily ever after: Marxism and the Disney princess films and franchises."

REFERENCES

Alexander, K. P. (2011). Successes, victims, and prodigies: 'Master' and 'little' cultural narratives in the literacy narrative genre. *CCC, 62*(4): 608–633.

Bal, M. (1998). *Narratology*. Toronto: University of Toronto Press.

Bell, E. (2008). Somatexts at the Disney shop: Constructing the pentimentos of women's animated bodies. In E. Bell, L. Hass, & L. Sells (Eds.), *From mouse to mermaid: The politics of film, gender, and culture* (pp. 107–124). Bloomington: Indiana University Press.

Boje, D. M. (1995). Stories of the storytelling organization: A postmodern analysis of Disney as "tamara-land." *Academy of Management Journal, 38*(4), 997–1035.

Brodkey, L. (1989). On the subjects of class and gender in 'The literacy letters.' *College English, 51*(2), 125–141.

Bryman, A. (1995). *Disney and his worlds*. London: Routledge.

Cresswell, T. (2004). *Place: A short introduction*. Malden, MA: Blackwell Publishers.

Daniell, B. (1999). Narratives of literacy: Connecting composition to culture. *CCC, 50*(3), 393–410.

England, D. E., Descartes, L., & Collier-Meek, M. A. (2011). Gender role portrayal and the Disney princesses. *Sex Roles, 64*(7–8), 555–567.

Giroux, H. A., & Pollock, G. (2010). *The mouse that roared: Disney and the end of innocence*. Lanham, MD: Rowman & Littlefield.

Goodson, I., & Sikes, P. J. (2001). *Life history research in educational settings: Learning from lives.* Buckingham: Open University Press.

Herzogenrath, B. (2001). *From virgin land to Disney World: Nature and its discontents in the USA of yesterday and today.* Amsterdam: Rodopi.

Lyotard, J. F. (1984). *The postmodern condition: A report on knowledge.* Minneapolis: University of Minnesota Press.

Salamone, V., & Salamone, F. (1999). Images of Main Street: Disney World and the American adventure. *Journal of American Culture, 22*(1): 85–92.

Sells, L. (2008). 'Where do the mermaids stand?': Voice and body in *The little mermaid.* In E. Bell, L. Haas, & L. Sells (Eds.), *From mouse to mermaid: The politics of film, gender, and culture* (pp. 175–192). Bloomington: Indiana University Press.

Williams, B. (2003). Heroes, rebels, and victims: Student identities in literacy narratives. *Journal of Adolescent and Adult Literacy, 47*(4): 342–345.

Yow, C. (2014, October). The cost of happily ever after: Marxism and the Disney princess films and franchises. Paper presented at PCAS/ACAS, New Orleans, LA.

CHAPTER FOUR

An Encouraging Evolution Among the Disney Princesses?

A Critical Feminist Analysis

COLE REILLY

As a feminist researcher, theorist, pedagogue, and uncle, I am ever-curious about the messages taken up by children as well as by adults in response to consuming/being consumed by texts (Paul, 1998) designed primarily for children. It seems important to consider more than books alone—particularly when popular culture's multimedia presence unavoidably colors our notions of identity and even possibility. For years now, any visit with my nieces and nephews or with the children of my friends reveals just how iconic Disney's catalog of characters is in the minds of so many, particularly the young and those who teach/raise them. Perhaps no figures lend themselves more readily to such feminist work than the massively popular Disney Princess franchise. Marketed as they are to children—movies made for one and all, but the dolls, clothing, and accessories geared to growing girls, in particular—I both problematize the Disney Princess phenomenon regarding matters of gender, race, class, and age, and also shine a spotlight on signs of meaningful progress (albeit belated) in the Disney Princess narrative. I also illustrate an encouraging evolution of increasingly empowered femininities made available by the Disney Princess franchise in recent years.

I have chosen to focus specifically on the dozen full-length, animated feature films released in cinemas and later recognized by the Disney Princess line of marketing: *Snow White and the Seven Dwarfs* (Disney & Hand, 1937), *Cinderella* (Disney et al., 1950), *Sleeping Beauty* (Disney et al., 1959), *The Little Mermaid* (Musker, Ashman, & Clements, 1989), *Beauty and the Beast* (Hahn, Trousdale, & Wise, 1991), *Aladdin* (Clements & Musker, 1992), *Pocahontas* (Pentecoste, Gabriel, & Goldberg, 1995), *Mulan* (Coats, Bancroft, & Cook, 1998), *The Princess and the Frog* (Del Vecho et al., 2009), *Tangled* (Conli et al., 2010), *Brave* (Sarafian, Andrews, & Chapman,

2012), and *Frozen* (Del Vecho et al., 2013). I focus on how each of the thirteen princesses among the dynasty of Disney debutantes is introduced to the audience via her feature film debut. My aim is neither to defend Disney nor to credit Disney with ushering forth the next wave of feminism. I do, in fact, find much of the Disney Princess curricula irresponsible and at times repressive (Bell, Hass, & Sells, 1995; Davis, 2006; Giroux & Pollock, 2010; O'Brien, 1996) and acknowledge that other problematic representations could emerge as new material evolves. However, I maintain that there has been a noteworthy evolution among the Disney princess films in terms of offering progressively more substantive story arcs and characters with agency. Granted, it has taken more than 75 years to move from damsel in distress, Snow White, to Anna and Elsa, a pair of leading ladies who offer independent, empowered narratives in *Frozen* (2013). Many would argue that such delayed progress is too little too late, but if we wish to realize momentous change, we need to keep our eyes and ears open to it by recognizing small shifts and acknowledging that even slight progress *is* progress nonetheless. In this chapter, I *document* what I see as meaningful measures of movement from a boulder that has historically proven difficult to budge at all.

AN ENCOURAGING EVOLUTION

Through my personal and pedantic consumption of Disney and my ongoing efforts to refine my theoretical lens of queer feminism (Wilchins, 2004), I have come to conceptualize a sequence of four distinct generations of Disney princess prototypes (see Fig. 1). Coincidentally, each generation has functioned in trios, ushering in a new archetype of princesses after every third feature film in the franchise. In this section, I provide an overview of each generation and explore why I believe the fourth to be the most promising stage of evolution for the Disney princess paradigm to date. Examining the thirteen Disney princesses back-to-back illuminates a promising trajectory and reason to hope for continued progress with room to grow.

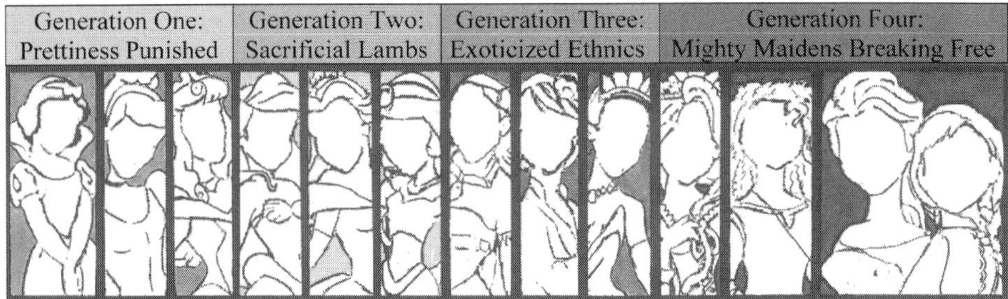

Fig. 1: Four Generations of Disney Princesses.
Sketches and classification courtesy of cole reilly.

Generation One: Prettiness Punished, Submissive Trophy Tropes Lacking Agency

In the first three movies, *Snow White and the Seven Dwarfs, Cinderella, and Sleeping Beauty,* we see the initial iconic prototype of a Disney princess: conventionally pretty maidens of Euro-descent who, when they're not in beloved ball gowns, tiaras, or castles, are minding their manners and doing a great deal of unpaid, domestic labor without complaint, all the while awaiting rescue by a handsome, unknown prince they will each "love" before knowing. Youth and beauty alone mark the only defining traits for each of these tragic innocents. These very qualities threaten the older women of power in their lives, inspiring spiteful wrath. However, these same traits save them by inspiring royal strangers to claim them as trophies. Indeed, these princesses' entire circumstances are steered by their innate, ageless beauty and by how others respond to it.

None of these young women exercises agency to overcome their unfortunate positions. Instead, they rely on fairy guardians and playboy princes to come to their rescue. In fact, two of the three are actually comatose and unable to consent to their suitor-stranger's advance. Ella, the lone first-generation princess not royal by birth, does meet the prince and dance with him, but he never catches her name and couldn't even recognize her in plain clothes and with loose hair. In each instance we see problematic messages about marriage having little to do with love (or even with knowing a person) and we see female characters with few options but to be domestic servants, lifeless mannequins awaiting resuscitation from a handsome stranger, and desirable visions of perfection—kiss-worthy trophies.

Generation Two: She Wants Adventure, But at What Cost? Sacrificial Lambs and Martyrs

More than thirty years passed between the end of the first trilogy of movies in the franchise and what establishes the second generation. With *The Little Mermaid*, *Beauty and the Beast*, and *Aladdin*, the princess image received a hip new makeover. From increased navel visibility on sexy figures to enormous eyes (Cohen, 2013), these princesses usher in a noticeably different aesthetic more akin to that of fashion models retouched for magazine covers. In terms of personality, second-generation Disney princesses offer more than vacant models for the male gaze; those enormous eyes take in the world as well. These young women are *doers*, or at least they mean to be. Ariel is a curious collector of odd treasures she finds on her journeys, and Belle is a voracious reader; both are adventure-seekers who with compelling voices belt out their frustrations about not fitting into their respective worlds. Jasmine is the most discerning of the three, turning down the advances of numerous suitors, wanting instead to be free of the shackles of a princess's sheltered life—to find love on her own terms. All three crave freedom and adventure.

Another feature that unifies second-generation princesses is their irrational sense of relational economy; each cedes a questionable quid pro quo arrangement. These maidens show tremendous heart and spirit but sacrifice themselves unreasonably for the men in their lives. At first, Ariel seems to be a defiant daredevil, yet she's willing to give up her voice for a chance to woo a handsome stranger. She changes her body drastically and surrenders her power of speech/song, so that he might notice her. Similarly, Belle willingly exchanges her own freedom for her father's. While this sacrifice is admirable, it leads her into an abusive relationship that is romanticized to the point that she seems to fall victim to Stockholm syndrome. She presumes to fall in "love" with her controlling captor and marries into the role of princess. Jasmine is first her restrictive dad's captive, then Jafar's slave, submitting to his desires for her affection, then a conquest by her disguised sweetheart. Thus, while these second-generation princesses have more complex personalities and aesthetics, each falls short of offering an image of empowered self-identity; all effectively martyr themselves for men.

Generation Three: Exoticized Ethnics Serve as Clumsy Caricatures/Apologies

What unites *Pocahontas*, *Mulan*, and *Tiana* (2009), the third-generation princesses, is their ethnic *otherness*; finally Disney introduces princesses of color.[1] By 1995, The Walt Disney Company had succumbed to widespread criticism of its Eurocentrism (Bell, Haas, & Sells, 1995). The intention of the third-generation princesses for the Disney princess franchise seems to have been (1) to provide a de facto apology for decades of seeming a "whites only" club and (2) to appeal to a broader audience of ticket-buying fans. Unfortunately, and this was particularly the case with *Pocahontas*, Disney failed on both counts. By neglecting to adequately research the story, much less indigenous culture, customs, or beliefs, the film clumsily perpetuates many stereotypes of indigenous cultures while leaving European imperialism and the effects of colonization largely unchallenged (Sacarangella, 2010).

These third-generation films arrive late to the Disney cotillion—as it seems their invitations must have been 'lost in the mail' for half a century (Bell, Haas, & Sells, 1995)—and so each tries to make up for lost time at the ball. As such, all three movies effectively overcompensate for their predecessors' white-centeredness, to the point of offensively exoticizing the ethnicities of these new princesses. Pocahontas, Mulan, and Tiana are positioned to *have to* represent a great deal to audiences—both to their respective ethnic/racial communities hoping to finally see themselves validated on screen, as well as to the presumably Western gaze that has served as Disney's default viewer. It is not enough for them to be young maidens with stories of their own; they are charged with being *the* Native American Disney princess (Sacarangella, 2010), *the* East Asian Disney princess (Limbach, 2013), and *the* Black Disney princess (Gregory, 2012). As such, their narratives are steeped in heightened levels of appropriated culture, custom, and geography.

Third-generation princesses seem so focused on their responsibilities and cultural obligations that their sense of humor, playfulness, and life are an afterthought when compared to the second-generation princesses. Pocahontas's task, for instance, is one of negotiating the tricky intersections of two races of people without a common language or understanding. Mulan risks her life for noble reasons—she must not only fight to honor her father and her family, but she must go to war to save her people. These are not the kinds of challenges any of their princess predecessors were expected to face. All three third-generation princesses exhibit remarkable resourcefulness and determination, achieving much, yet something about their stories falls short of feeling like *their own*. While not actually doing unpaid domestic labor per se, their narrative arcs suggest a discomforting metaphor—that these non-white princesses might be expected to clean up the messes of others. This comparison functions both in terms of the plots themselves, and as a larger metaphor for Disney needing to apologize for its history of white-centeredness and racial insensitivity. Ultimately, all three of these princesses of color are defined primarily by their race and ethnicity—more so than any of their more commercially successful princess predecessors. As such, it seems unsurprising that a capitalist company that did not find their efforts to include princesses of color particularly profitable or well received, would shift back to what they know best in the next generation.

Generation Four: Mighty Maidens Breaking Free—Independent Dreamers Resist Restraints

Not only is *Tangled* Disney's 50th animated motion picture, it also ushered in a fourth generation of the ongoing Disney princess evolution—arguably the most empowering princess generation yet in terms of balancing power and personality for feisty, fun, formidable females. Though all the fourth-generation princesses are white,[2] Rapunzel, Merida, Anna, and Elsa are a far cry from the shrinking violets of generation one. Each princess is ambitious and self-reliant, confidently believing in her abilities to realize her dreams. Furthermore, each learns to be skeptical of those who may seem to have her best wishes at heart yet truly wish to use her to serve their own interests. Each fourth-generation princess poses a challenge to the taken-for-granted notions of conventional fairytale love, drawing important distinctions between affection with an agenda versus genuine love.

Each of the fourth-generation princesses embraces philosophies and attitudes that can seem downright modern when compared to their princess predecessors. Her choices are to be her own, not predetermined for her by her kin, culture, or obedience to tradition. Rapunzel, Merida, Anna, and Elsa each exhibit qualities we should want for any empowered young person. In addition to evidencing wit, perspective, mercy, and humble aplomb, each shows initiative, resilience, agency, influence, and power. So undeniable is her power, in fact, that each fourth-generation princess quite literally *kicks ass*. These mighty maidens need no rescuing—they rescue others, themselves, and one another. What's more, these new fairytales provide an unabashed critique of the gendered confines of presumed *princess*ly obligation. Rapunzel, Anna, and Elsa resent feeling perpetually grounded like helpless children. Not held captive like her fellow fourth-generation peers, Merida embraces the freedoms her father allows, yet feels a confining corset of highly gendered expectations suffocating her when her perfectionist mother, Queen Elinor, nags her about her *princess*ly duties, which include everything from being knowledgeable about her kingdom, to being quiet, patient, cautious, and clean.

Although Queen Elinor's list of demands proves to be exhaustive, this is the first time in Disney history that we get to peek behind the curtain to see the grand production that goes into playing the conventional role of a royal lady. We see these qualities do not come naturally, not even to Elinor, but reflect hard work and intention that she too had to invest at one time, so they would eventually seem like second nature. *Brave* marks the first time that a princess figure is shown to have responsibilities beyond cleaning—namely, preparing nonstop to command respect and make informed choices when she reigns as queen someday. Prior to this, the franchise films do not mention ascending to the throne but in *Brave,* we see the juxtaposition of Elinor's and Merida's roles, coming to appreciate that Elinor was not born a queen; as a young princess once, she was groomed to become one. As such, she *can* relate to Merida's struggles to prepare for such a day. *Frozen* takes this progression of roles and responsibilities a step further as, midway through the film, Elsa transitions from princess to queen and is expected to rule all of Arendelle.

ANALYZING THE FOURTH GENERATION FURTHER AS WELL AS ITS PRAISE AND SCRUTINY

Although some contend the most recent Disney princesses suggest a post-feminist backlash (Cohen, 2013; Colman, 2014; McRobbie, 2004; Rogers, 2014; Wilde, 2014), undermining feminist gains with a return to reductive gender stereotypes, I maintain that reading *otherways* (Paul, 1998) reveals evidence that generation four narratives function as pointed critiques of outdated princess archetypes. True, the vague *once upon a time* settings harken back to the first two generations, as do the persistently problematic notions of unrealistic beauty and body image. However, I see these newer characters and their narratives as boldly revisiting a familiar formula as the backdrop but playing out the scenes in markedly different ways that function as critique.

All of the fourth-generation princesses satisfy with flying colors both the Bechdel (1985) and Mako Mori (Romano, 2013) criteria used for quantifying how females in film are represented—but *how* their narratives arc is particularly noteworthy. In *Tangled*, both Rapunzel and Mother Gothel are flawed, albeit fully developed female characters. Although Gothel proves vainly obsessed with looking young and beautiful, she seems happy to live a life that is independent of men. She exploits the kidnapped princess, wavering between a possessive and sadistic nature, yet there are also signs of affection in their relationship. Provided she gets to use and control Rapunzel, life for Mother Gothel would be ideal. By contrast, Rapunzel initially knows only to respect and care for the woman who raised her. However, the devotion she feels to respect Gothel's feelings and wishes does not usurp her own sense of certainty to get out and see the world (Wilde, 2014). True, Gothel provides a vain villainess whose mean-spirited manipulation mirrors that of the evil queen from *Snow White*, encapsulating the ugliest of stereotypes associated with women regarding age and beauty. Yet, Rapunzel provides a female foil to Gothel, reminding us to prioritize freedom, family, friendship, adventure, agency, and, most of all, love.

Her relationship with Flynn Rider/Eugene Fitzherbert begins with suspicion. She fears he will take advantage and use her (for her magical hair), but it is clearly she who is the stronger of the two and she *uses him* as a tour guide to inform her capable, albeit emotional escape. Nearing the story's conclusion, she independently deciphers all of Gothel's wicked deception and refuses to continue being her enslaved prop. When the enraged Gothel retaliates by mortally wounding Eugene, the mighty maiden is willing, like Belle before her, to surrender her freedom for the chance to save him. Unlike Belle's father or the beast, however, Eugene insists she must not do this, and he willingly dies rather than allow her to make such a sacrifice. It all works out in the end, for even without her powerful blond hair, she has just enough magic within her left to save him one last time by bringing him back from the dead. The story ends with the promise of a more equitable marriage arrangement—the *happily ever after* staple of heteronormativity—than the franchise has yet explicitly shown (Wilde, 2014).

In *Brave,* Merida and Elinor offer strong-willed, counter-narratives as a mother and daughter who feud at times but who love one another intensely. Their stances on Merida's gender performance seem to be directly at odds with one another, but to Disney's credit, neither is represented as entirely unreasonable in this regard. Furthermore, for the first time, we see a parent acknowledge that she was wrong to insist upon conformity in the face of a child's gender wishes. The fact that Queen Elinor comes to respect and to agree with her daughter's position is nothing short of groundbreaking. Merida, too, comes to appreciate her mother's flawed logic as not that of a tyrant, but of a mother bear protectively advising her young to brave the world as she understands it.

Theirs is a complicated relationship: when it seems that her mother simply will not listen, Merida turns to magic in the hope of changing her fate. Merida just wants to be heard; she feels that she has tried everything else in her power. Though not intended, Elinor's transformation into bear form effectively allows her to surrender her perfectionist ideas about her own gender performance, and mother and daughter have a chance to finally see one another anew. When she transforms back into her human form, Queen Elinor is seen as vulnerable and real, remaining dignified and deserving of respect, yet displaying a humbler, less harsh edge. The range of femininities offered by the pair of protagonists suggests an expanding flexibility in the Disney princess franchise and we see that Merida needn't marry by the film's end. If she decides to marry, it will be a person *she* alone chooses. Choice is undoubtedly a feminist ideal (hooks, 2000), and this makes for a promising redefinition of what a fairytale ending might entail.

Where *Brave* leaves off, improving upon the dynamics of complex mother-daughter relations featured less healthily in *Tangled*, *Frozen* carries the torch of exploring feminist familial bonds—an ongoing theme uniquely present in all of the fourth generation films. Sisters Elsa and Anna offer an interesting pairing, for their particular character juxtaposition is one not familiar to the franchise. They provide a unique pair of princess partners, neither competing over a man nor constructed as one good and the other evil. They possess distinctly different talents, outlooks, insights, needs, and even upbringings, given that their parents raised them so differently and separated them from each other for much of their childhood and adolescence.

Ignorant of what to do, yet riddled with parental guilt after young Anna's near-death experience, the king and queen shift into a mode of self-preservation, cloaking what happened in secrecy and seeking to isolate the problem. The trouble is, they construct Elsa *as* the problem, quarantining her from her beloved sister and best friend, as well as from the rest of the kingdom, shrouding her coming of age years in shame, blame, and isolation. Anna is robbed not only of her sister, but also of the dignity of an honest explanation as to what happened. She is frozen out of her older sister's world for thirteen years without explanation, and led to believe that this is all Elsa's choosing. When the girls' parents die, the pair are positioned to pick up the pieces, inheriting not only the adult responsibilities as reigning royals but also the consequences and resultant confusion associated with the poor choices their parents made for them as a family and for the entire kingdom.

Introverted Elsa feels such pressure to conceal her magical powers from all of Arendelle on the day of her very public coronation as queen that her anxiety gets the best of her and she loses control, storming from the kingdom in an icy mixture of fear and confusion. Whereas others wish to brand the new queen an evil witch, chasing her our of town and angling for an opportunity to somehow usurp the crown themselves, Princess Anna shows unwavering faith in her sister, defending Elsa's honor and insisting that there is an explanation, even if she cannot yet imagine what that would be. She will not stand for the gossip of others who wish to tarnish her sister's reputation.

Similarly, Elsa goes to bat for her younger sister, looking out for her interests. Despite thirteen years of separation making it difficult for her to fully know adult Anna, Queen Elsa refuses to endorse Prince Hans's plans to become engaged to Anna the very day they meet. To be clear, this is not about suggesting young Anna is hopelessly naïve; Elsa's cool insistence that the couple get to know one another better before seriously considering marriage is not reflective of an older sister figuring it all out. The fact that Hans turns out to be a scheming wolf in prince's clothing is more or less irrelevant to her cautionary advice. She believes Anna deserves better than to wed the first guy she meets. They may not yet know one another well, but the sisters instinctively look out for one another as family, though this was not a lesson their parents taught them.

Tucked away in the mountains a good distance from Arendelle, where she need not fear hurting others, Elsa finally feels safe to explore the seemingly endless possibilities of her magic gifts—to be playful again even, for not since childhood has she been able to see this facet of herself with joy.[3] Once Elsa is able to take her magic capabilities for a test-drive, she and the audience are in awe. It is clear that she is capable of amazing feats—running across still water, raising impressive castles from the ground, creating blizzards without end, and even fashioning outfits that would rival those on any runway.[4] While her sister, Anna, may not have magical powers, she is passionate, brave, trusting, and outgoing. Nothing can stop her when she commits to something, not even an abominable snow-monster. She is unafraid of her sister, even when Elsa herself fears she may hurt Anna. It is this sisterly trust that inspires Elsa to love and trust herself, too. *Frozen*'s idea that true love's kiss could be sisterly and not romantic is groundbreaking for Disney (Rogers, 2014). Not only does neither princess marry a man by the end of the movie, but their sisterly love is held to be on par with the great loves of all time.

Some (Colman, 2014; Rogers, 2014) downplay the significance of *Frozen's* non-wedding ending. While people do overestimate the percentage of films in the Disney princess franchise that end with a wedding or formal engagement (Colman, 2014), all three first-generation movies do, as does at least one of the films in every generation since, including *Tangled*. However, *Frozen* offers a courageous critique of marriage as *not* being something one needs in a happily ever after. Elsa discourages

Anna from rushing into an engagement with Hans earlier in the film—too naïve and enthusiastic in the moment to take stock of really knowing him, as opposed to just a first impression of him. Furthermore, Elsa herself never expresses any need for romance of her own. One might imagine any number of reasons why this is the case, but I, for one, am relieved that it doesn't get an explanation, because it doesn't *need* one.

CONCLUDING INSIGHTS AND IMPLICATIONS

Reframing Disney's iconic princess archetype through these four generations offers promising patterns of evolution in the franchise. To be clear, these characters are still fairytale princesses, privileged protagonists constructed by design to fulfill certain marketing formulas. If this newly empowered image of a princess wasn't profitable to the Disney Corporation, she would likely be hidden away somewhere in a far-off tower. Fortunately, however, the three most recent films in the Disney Princess franchise have surpassed all of their predecessors handily in terms of commercial success. I believe this success is fortunate not because I am looking to line the pockets of Disney executives, but because I recognize that what proves to be profitable to a capitalist corporation is bound to continue. If the boulder of change has started to even budge in favor of something more progressive, such gains stand to continue. The success of these newer films, and especially *Frozen*, dispels any argument that audiences do not want to see empowered young women such as these. The time is now to push Disney for continued improvements while marketing momentum is on our side.

What might this look like? To begin, we can advance the conversation by insisting that we are *all* a part of it. We can discuss this ourselves with the children in our lives as well as with their caregivers. Those of us who teach can also discuss this with our colleagues and encourage discussion among our students as well as with students' parents and guardians. Children, in particular, have tremendous insights to share if we don't presume to speak for them or to tell them what they should think. In some ways, theirs are the voices that perhaps are the most powerful in all this. In terms of whom Disney actually wants to listen to and please, it's the child-consumer who is likely to influence parental purchases. Disney wants to generate products that children will want to consume, but perhaps they sell kids short with their estimations. Maybe they don't realize that children want *more*—that the *Merida*s of the world might in fact have a better read of the pulse of what is in their interest than the *Elinor*s among us; certainly they have a perspective we must not sacrifice—how might we instead help nurture, empower, and amplify it?

Research is another viable way to advance this conversation, and that could emerge in a variety of forms and forums, utilizing a broad range of perspectives and methodologies. Collecting and analyzing empirical data with children, parents, and teachers, may prove to be both empowering and influential. All too often, the extant research is largely theoretical and does not always prove to be as persuasive to some audiences as we might hope. Publishing this new work might take the form of student newspapers, blogs, podcast interviews, petitions, boycotts, and protests, or as letters drafted and directed to people of influence from Disney to the White House.

As we engage in this research, it is important to continue to critique where critical shortcomings continue to exist. For instance, Disney still struggles with matters of ethnic diversity and race representation and perpetuates problematic notions of beauty and body image. These are important observations and countless others await. I contend, however, that we need to watch just as doggedly for sparks of growth as we do for missteps. Pedagogically, we know that if feedback only sounds like complaints, people stop listening. If Disney executives do not know how better to address such matters, if their progress reports make no gesture to recognize improvement, why should they try? We must indicate when we see progress as well as regression, constructively clarifying how and why, not just offering criticism. I am not suggesting we simply celebrate where we are already as "good enough." We ought to continually ask more of Disney, just as we should our elected officials—that's a practice of citizenry that has historically brought about positive change. A mindful, coordinated effort can make a bigger impact than one might imagine.

DISCUSSION QUESTIONS

1. Who ought the next protagonists in the Disney princess franchise be? How might they differ from their predecessors? Should Disney extend upon the fourth generation or begin a fifth? Storyboard some ideas and pitch them to your classmates as if they are Disney executives, trying to decide which films(s) to make next.
2. Given that all of these films are mass-marketed to children, consider some counter-narratives (from books, films, or human history) that may prove to be illustrative in helping children, parents, or teachers become more critical consumers of such fairytale storylines. How might you pair some of these Disney feature films with other existing texts to encourage and facilitate rich discussions that expand conventional notions of gender, race, age, class, beauty, love, or family?
3. In light of the idea that an evolution of princess character archetypes potentially provide powerful opportunities for exploring a range of femininities one might embrace, what, if any, equivalent notions of a continuum of masculinities

might be made available by the following twelve male protagonists from Disney films: Pinocchio (1940), Peter Pan (1953), Arthur/Wart (1963), Mowgli (1967), Tarzan (1985), Aladdin (1992), Quasimodo (1996), Hercules (1997), Tarzan (1999), Llama Man (2000), Flynn/Eugene (2010), and Ralph (2012)? What, if any, patterns exist between or across generational groupings?

NOTES

1. While Jasmine (1992) is Arabic, American children watching the movie at the time did not necessarily recognize her as anything but another white girl with a tan and some alluring attire. Prior to 9/11/2001, many non-Arab Americans may have neglected to recognize Arab as a race category.
2. Indeed, the white, wealthy, and wide-eyed (Cohen, 2013) aesthetic of generation two appears again with *Tangled* and with *Frozen*.
3. Many draw parallels between Elsa's anthemic delivery of "Let It Go" as a torch song for "coming out" in any number of ways. Elsa decided to no longer conceal this part of her, but to embrace it instead. This facet of her, which she was told was horrible, dangerous even, can finally be appreciated as beautiful, special, and liberating. Whatever the metaphor, the song rejects notions of shame to celebrate self-love and empowerment.
4. Much conservative and/or post-feminist criticism is made of the "sexy" saunter to Elsa's walk near the end of "Let It Go" as her dress has a significant slit, accentuating her legs and hips. I won't slut-shame Elsa, or suggest there is anything inappropriate about her gender expression here. This dress reflects her choosing—she made it, and she appears to move comfortably in it. No one else is in the castle with her, so she's not trying to impress anyone else. She is not doing this for the male gaze but for herself. It seems to be a healthy metaphor for expressively rebelling against others' restraints.

REFERENCES

Bechdel, A. (1985). "The rule" & "Testy" comic strips, *dykes to watch out for*. Available at: http://dykestowatchoutfor.com/wp-content/uploads/2014/05/The-Rule-cleaned-up.jpg

Bell, E., Haas, L., & Sells, L. (1995). *From mouse to mermaid: The politics of film, gender, and culture.* Indianapolis: Indianap University Press.

Clements, R., & Musker, J. (Co-producer/director). (1992). *Aladdin* [Motion Picture]. United States: Walt Disney Pictures.

Coats, P. (Producer), Bancroft, T., & Cook, B. (Co-directors). (1998). *Mulan* [Motion Picture]. United States: Walt Disney Pictures.

Cohen, P. (December 17, 2013). "Help, my eyeball is bigger than my wrist!": Gender dimorphism in *Frozen*. *Sociological Images*. Available at: http://thesocietypages.org/socimages/2013/12/17/help-my-eyeball-is-bigger-than-my-wrist-gender-dimorphism-in-frozen/

Colman, D. (2014). The problem with false feminism: Why "*Frozen*" left me cold. Retrieved from: https://medium.com/@directordanic/the-problem-with-false-feminism-7c0bbc7252ef

Conli, R., Lasseter, J., & Keane, G. (Co-producers), Greno, N., & Howard, B. (Co-directors). (2010). *Tangled* [Motion Picture]. United States: Walt Disney Pictures.

Davis, A. M. (2006). *Good girls and wicked witches: Women in Disney's feature animation*. Eastleigh, UK: John Libbey Publishing.

Del Vecho, P. (Producer), Buck, C., & Lee, J. (Co-directors). (2013). *Frozen* [Motion Picture]. United States: Walt Disney Pictures.

Del Vecho, P., & Lasseter, J. (Co-producers), Clements, R., & Musker, J. (Co-directors). (2009). *The princess and the frog* [Motion Picture]. United States: Walt Disney Pictures.

Disney, W. (Producer), Geronomi, C., Clark, L., Larson, E., & Reitherman, W. (Co-directors). (1959). *Sleeping beauty* [Motion Picture]. United States: Walt Disney Pictures.

Disney, W. (Producer), Geronomi, C., Jackson, W., & Luske, H. (Co-directors). (1950). *Cinderella* [Motion Picture]. United States: Walt Disney Pictures.

Disney, W. (Producer), Hand, D. (Director). (1937). *Snow White and the seven dwarfs* [Motion Picture]. United States: Walt Disney Pictures.

Giroux, H. A. & Pollock, G. (2010). *The mouse that roared: Disney and the end of innocence*. Lanham, Boulder, New York, and Oxford: Rowman & Littlefield,

Gregory, S. M. (2012) Disney's improvisation: New Orleans' second line racial masquerade and the reproduction of whiteness in *The Princess and the Frog*. In M. Mask (Ed.), *Contemporary black American cinema: Race, gender, and sexuality at the movies* (pp. 175–199). New York: Routledge.

Hahn, D. (Producer), Trousdale, C., & Wise, K. (Co-directors). (1991). *Beauty and the beast* [Motion Picture]. United States: Walt Disney Pictures.

hooks, b. (2000). *Feminism is for everybody: Passionate politics*. Cambridge, MA: South End Press.

Limbach, G. (2013). "You the man, well, sorta": Gender binaries and liminality in *Mulan*. In B. Cheu (Ed.), *Diversity in Disney films: Critical essays in race, ethnicity, gender, sexuality, and sisability* (pp. 175–199). Jefferson, NC: McFarland.

McRobbie, A. (2004). Post-feminism and popular culture. *Feminist Media Studies, 4*(3), 255–264.

Musker, J. (Co-producer/-director), Ashman, H. (Co-producer), Clements, R. (Co-director). (1989). *The little mermaid* [Motion Picture]. United States: Walt Disney Pictures.

O'Brien, P. C. (1996). The happiest films on earth: A textual and contextual analysis of Walt Disney's *Cinderella* and *The little mermaid*. *Women's Studies in Communication,19*(2), 155–183.

Paul, L. (1998). *Reading otherways*. Portland, ME: Calendar Island.

Pentecoste, J. (Producer), Gabriel, M., & Goldberg, E. (Co-directors). (1995). *Pocahontas* [Motion Picture]. United States: Walt Disney Pictures.

Rogers, M. (2014). Is Disney frozen in time, or moving forward? *Feminist Disney*. Available at: http://feministdisney.tumblr.com/post/72728984022/is-disney-frozen-in-time-or-moving-forward

Romano, A. (August 18, 2013). The Mako Mori test: 'Pacific Rim' inspires a Bechdel test alternative. Available at: http://www.dailydot.com/fandom/mako-mori-test-bechdel-pacific-rim/

Sacarangella, L. (2010). Indigeneity in tourism: Transnational spaces, pan-Indian identity, and cosmopolitanism. In M. C. Forte (Ed.), *Indigenous cosmopolitans: Transnational and transcultural indigeneity in the twenty-first century* (pp. 165–188). New York: Peter Lang.

Sarafian, K. (Producer), Andrews, M., & Chapman, B. (Co-directors). (2012). *Brave* [Motion Picture]. United States: Walt Disney Pictures/Pixar Animation Studios.

Wilchins, R. (2004). *Queer theory, gender theory: An instant primer*. Los Angeles: Alyson Publications.

Wilde, S. (2014). Repackaging the Disney princess: A post-feminist reading of modern day fairy tales. *Journal of Promotional Communications, 2*(1), 132–153.

PART TWO

Teaching Race

CHAPTER FIVE

Disney's (Post?)-Racial Gaze

Film, Pedagogy, and the Construction of Racial Identities

JESSICA BAKER KEE AND ALPHONSO WALTER GRANT

Disney's films have been subject to multiple political critiques over the past 40 years, while The Walt Disney Company itself has been enmeshed in politics since at least the 1930s. Budd and Kirsch (2005), for example, document the corporation's historical alignment with right-wing ideologies, from the 1941 cartoonists' strike brought on by charges of labor exploitation, to Walt Disney's own reactionary McCarthyism. While Disney animated films are renowned for their Technicolor visual pleasures and nostalgia-inducing depictions of childhood innocence, the viewing public has become increasingly aware that "behind all those cute characters, that family fun, and that nearly impenetrable aura is another avaricious multinational corporation" (Budd & Kirsch, 2005, p. 3). While the Disney brand persists as a pervasive and ubiquitous force in children's visual cultures around the world, it has recently come under fire for the conservative and reactionary subtexts of its films and products (Byrne & McQuillan, 1999; Giroux & Pollock, 2010).

Critics and social theorists have also described Disney films as racially problematic, working as visual texts to both mask and to reinforce institutional White hegemony (Benhamou, 2014; Byrne & McQuillan, 1999; Giroux & Pollock, 2010; King, Lugo-Lugo, & Bloodsworth-Lugo, 2010; Tavin & Anderson, 2003; Willetts, 2013). In this chapter, we address and extend these critiques while also suggesting that Disney's animated films remain complex discursive spaces providing openings for alternative and oppositional pedagogies due to their ability to be read through—and complicated by—multiple racial gazes. We ask how Disney films have addressed questions of racial identity and politics and how they have elided or avoided such questions. We also seek to understand what critical readings of these films as visual texts reveal about their power to teach viewers about diverse racial identities. Finally, we explore how viewers might employ racial counter-gazes to disrupt hegemonic readings of these films.

We explore these questions through both an overview of critical scholarship addressing racial diversity in Disney's filmography, and through a case study of two animated films from different historical eras. *Song of the South* (Disney, Foster, and Jackson, 1946), and *The Princess and the Frog* (Del Vecho, Clements, & Musker, 2009) that have each received praise and criticism for their complicated racial content, and both deal (both explicitly and implicitly) with the onscreen representation of Black identities within White supremacist power structures. Incidentally, both films also draw on Black narrative and spiritual traditions for their characteristic Disney 'magic.' We hope our analysis here will also serve as a pedagogical engagement, offering multiple questions, provocations, and entry points for discussing these films both in formal and informal learning contexts.

HISTORICAL CONTEXT: DISNEY FILMS AS RACIAL PEDAGOGY

Although race is implicated throughout the history of Disney filmmaking, this may not be immediately recognizable to casual viewers. As Bloodsworth-Lugo and Flory (2013) explain, "for most moviegoers … racial matters function at the level of unexamined presumption rather than thoughtfully considered judgment" (p. 1). Early Disney films explicitly promoted a White supremacist ideology, representing non-White characters as comical, inferior, or dangerous when they were not erased altogether. The 1990s saw a new wave of 'multicultural' films: *Pocahontas* (Pentecost, Gabriel, & Goldberg, 1995), *The Hunchback of Notre Dame* (Conli et al., 1996), and *Mulan* (Coats, Bancroft, & Cook, 1998), ushered in by a more liberal Clinton-era social and political climate. While these films included less offensive and more humanizing depictions of non-White characters, they tended to avoid addressing racial politics directly and instead presented romanticized "composites based on images, stereotypes, and fantasies of the Other" (Benhamou, 2014, p. 157). Disney films in the 21st century also echoed contemporary racial discourse by addressing racial hybridity more directly, while also reinforcing 'color-blind' ideologies and middle-class American values of individualism and cultural exceptionalism. As the treatment of diversity in Disney films has evolved to address the social politics of each era, a body of critical academic scholarship has arisen concurrently (e.g., Barker, 2010; Byrne & McQuillan, 1999), much of it based in postmodern identity politics and neo-Marxist social analysis. These critiques implicate Disney films in reinforcing White institutional power by framing non-White racial identities as 'Other' through racial binarism and primitivism, reinforcing negative racial stereotypes through anthropomorphic representation, and at times erasing non-White perspectives entirely.

As early as *Fantasia* (Disney, Sharpsteen, Ferguson, and Algar, 1940), in which a Black female 'pickaninny' centaur subserviently polished the White centaurs' hooves, Disney's 'magical' visual world has been characterized by racial binarism. Black characters were framed in ways that "emphasized and naturalized the desirability of 'civilized' whiteness as opposed to the objectionable 'primitiveness' of blackness" (Barker, 2010, p. 484). Even in earlier films that did not directly address race such as *Snow White and the Seven Dwarfs* (Disney & Hand, 1937) and *Sleeping Beauty* (Disney & Geronimi, 1959), critics found evidence of a binary system associating 'whiteness' with good, and 'blackness' with evil (Hurley, 2005). Critiques of early Disney films (*Dumbo* [1941], *The Jungle Book* [1967], and *Song of the South* [1946]) also focused on their representation of Black identities as racially stereotyped, comically naïve animal characters (Byrne & McQuillan, 1999, p. 97). Other non-White identities fared no better in the Disney canon: *Lady and the Tramp* (Disney et al., 1955) featured dishonest, avaricious "Oriental" cats in addition to other ethnically stereotyped animals, while *Peter Pan* (Disney et al., 1953) depicted Native Americans as "savages" who possessed "red" skin due to a state of perpetual sexual arousal.

Black human representations have mostly been invisible in Disney films: Black men have only appeared in human form in the two films discussed in this chapter, and Black women only in *Hercules* (Clements and Musker, 1997) and in *The Princess and the Frog*. Other films, such as *The Lion King* (Hahn, Allers, & Minkoff, 1994) and *Tarzan* (Arnold, Buck, & Lima, 1999) are set in Africa yet contain no African humans at all. King, Lugo-Lugo, and Bloodsworth-Lugo (2010) contextualize this erasure within histories of Western colonialialism in Africa and characterize it as "a violent act, a symbolic clearing allowing for yet more stereotypical representations of 'Africanized' animals" (p. 59). The consistent practice of reducing non-White characters to animals while erasing their humanity served to 'domesticate' them and thus to render them non-threatening to White hegemony while simultaneously reinforcing their social positioning as primitive Others.

Disney films have also been critiqued for normalizing dominant racial perspectives; traditionally created by White filmmakers for a majority-White audience, they have often portrayed protagonists with Americanized accents and with Caucasian facial features while coding antagonists and other peripheral characters as Other with ethnically stereotyped features and accents (King, Lugo-Lugo, & Bloodsworth-Lugo, 2010). Through these films, as Henry Giroux and Pollock (2010) argue, "whiteness is universalized through the privileged representation of middle-class social relations, values, and linguistic practices" (p. 106). Through the normalization of White language, culture, and beauty standards, these films serve as *racial pedagogies* that both reinforce structural and institutional racism and maintain status quo ideologies. Negative depictions of non-White identities in earlier Disney films were particularly damaging because alternative representations were so rare. For generations, children of color were offered no positive representations from the primary arbiter of children's visual culture; instead their identities were either lampooned by negative stereotypes or rendered invisible altogether.

As ideological and pedagogical texts, Disney films provide multiple entry points for critical discussions about how race is represented in the media. However, these discussions are often emotionally complicated by the realization that these films have been treasured sources of knowledge construction, visual pleasure, and the ephemeral 'magic' of childhood nostalgia for even their harshest critics. As Budd and Kirsch (2005) note, "Disney critics implicitly had to try to understand why people, perhaps including at least part of themselves, actually liked, even needed Disney—without attacking, demonizing, or condescending to those people" (p. 12). Thus, participants in any critical discussion must acknowledge that the problematic racial politics of Disney films do not necessarily preclude these films' affective and emotional pleasures, or even the more positive and wholesome messages they may convey on other levels; indeed, the coexistence of all these elements reveals Disney films as complex discursive spaces with multiple possibilities for pedagogical engagement.

THEORETICAL CONTEXT: DECODING DISNEY'S RACIAL GAZE

One theoretical lens through which we can acknowledge multiple perspectives while viewing Disney films is *gaze theory*, introduced by the feminist film theorist, Laura Mulvey (1975), in her essay, "Visual Pleasure and Narrative Cinema." Mulvey employed Lacanian psychoanalysis to explain how a film's viewer (or subject) is implicitly constructed as male, while the woman's image is presented as the eroticized object of his viewing pleasure. The gaze is innately enmeshed in social and institutional power structures through the politics of looking relations (Kaplan, 1997). Black feminist scholars later argued that gaze theory relied on an overdetermined gender politics while failing to address ways in which race, class, and other forms of difference were also implicated in looking relations (Gaines, 1988). bell hooks (1992) addressed the relative rarity of Black women in mainstream cinema, noting that the "woman as object of scopophilic pleasure" primarily referred to *White* women on screen, leaving Black women to "create a critical space where the binary opposition Mulvey posits … was continually deconstructed. As critical spectators, black women looked from a location that disrupted" (pp. 122–123).

This disruption suggests the existence of multiple racial gazes enmeshed in unequal social power relations. In addition to the White hegemonic gaze that Fanon (2008) and others argue constructs the non-White subject as a colonized

Other, theorists have posited the existence of a *Black counter-gaze* that serves to destabilize White hegemonic assumptions and to open up spaces of agency. Kaplan (1997) argues that "white subjectivities ... can also be destabilized when exposed to the gaze of the Other, since this is a gaze to which such subjects have not traditionally been subjected" (p. xix). bell hooks (1992) characterizes the racial counter-gaze as a "site of resistance" (p. 116) for colonized people; while Yancy (2013) argues that the counter-gaze "enables a more complex epistemic field in terms of which whiteness becomes recognizable in its daily manifestations and thereby reveals the complex and subtle ways in which whiteness is a socially embedded phenomenon" (p. 135). In this way, discussing Disney films only in terms of how they perpetuate *hegemonic* racial gazes fails to address how non-White and oppositional viewers resist this gaze and enable counter-hegemonic readings of visual texts:

> Reception is never a matter of passive acceptance but always a process of creative adaptation and unintended consequences. Meanings constantly shift and are subject to multiple interpretations. It is in this process of negotiation that different, alternative, and even oppositional readings are possible. (Pack, 2008, p. 141).

Throughout our analysis of racial representations in Disney films, we acknowledge that viewers also possess the agency to affirm, to deny, or to creatively reinterpret such messages through their own diverse gazes, and that the 'meaning' of racial representation on screen is in fact a complicated matrix of contested and negotiated meanings. Nevertheless, any comprehensive critique of these films must also acknowledge their place within power structures that may reinforce and reinscribe particular racial gazes while denying the legitimacy of others.

RACIAL IDENTITY AND NOSTALGIC TENSION IN *SONG OF THE SOUTH*

Disney's most controversial film was produced in the midst of post-war financial struggles. As the studio's first full-length live feature, it utilized beautiful color-saturated cels and cutting-edge technology that allowed the actors to interact directly with animated animal characters. The film adapted the highly popular tales of Uncle Remus, Black oral folk narratives collected and transcribed by Joel Chandler Harris in 1876, and told "the story of a wise old ex-slave who recounted to children entertaining parables about fictional animals in the nearby woods" (Sperb, 2005, p. 929). Walt Disney had heard these tales as a child and had a lifelong dream of filming them, as they "impressed him as authentic American folklore" (Inge, 2012, p. 219).

The resulting film represented both a financial and political risk by the studio. It appears that Disney was at least somewhat aware of the racial implications of filming traditional Black slave tales. The script was sent in advance to noted Black intellectual Alain Locke, and NAACP president Walter White was offered (and declined) a consulting position on the script. Since the literary version of Uncle Remus was already controversial due to public perceptions that he represented a sanitized characterization of American slavery, Disney changed the film's name from *Uncle Remus* to the vague *Song of the South* (Sperb, 2005). Despite these preemptive gestures toward political correctness, the film was problematic from its inception. Disney was unfamiliar with Southern history and culture, and his cinematic interpretation largely relied on sanitized Hollywood depictions such as *Gone with the Wind* (Selznick et al., 1939), which had already come under fire for romanticizing slavery and plantation life (Inge, 2012). Although the film was set in the post-Civil War Reconstruction era and its Black characters were technically freed laborers or sharecroppers, the film never makes this clear, merging antebellum and postbellum cultures together and constructing

> a nonexistent South of fantasy and romance where the tensions of slavery and racism have not entered or been resolved…in accordance with a mythic social structure of tolerance and civility that bears no relationship to the harsh history and experience of slavery. (Inge, 2012, p. 225)

In spite of these concerns (and mixed critical reviews) the film was commercially successful, grossing $3 million domestically and winning several Academy Awards (Bernstein, 1996). However, its racial controversy was the subject of scrutiny in the national media. The NAACP released a statement praising its artistic merits but accusing it of glorifying the Old South and slavery; the National Negro Congress picketed the film, while Harlem congressman Adam Clayton Powell Jr. publicly denounced it. Subsequent releases downplayed the film's live actors in promotional materials while focusing solely on its more innocuous cartoon animal characters, and Disney stopped re-releasing it entirely in 1986. Due to the ongoing controversy, *Song of the South* remains the only feature-length Disney film that has never been released domestically in cinemas or on video since the mid-1980s (Bernstein, 1996; Sperb, 2005).

The film opens with a young White boy named Johnny (Bobby Driscoll) arriving at his grandmother's plantation in rural Georgia with his father, his mother, and his Black nanny, Aunt Tempy (Hattie McDaniel). Johnny's father immediately abandons the family to find work in Atlanta, leaving Johnny distraught. As Johnny runs away to find his father, he meets Uncle Remus, an elderly Black employee living on the plantation. Uncle Remus takes Johnny under his wing and shares his stories of Bre'r Rabbit, Bre'r Fox, and Bre'r Bear, traditional animal characters who illustrate life lessons of cleverness and survival. The plot eventually leads to a tragic accident, which culminates in Uncle Remus healing the fractured White nuclear family through the power of his storytelling and finally walking away over an animated landscape, hand in hand with the Black and White child characters, flanked by singing cartoon animals.

We posit Uncle Remus as a complex figure whose implications for Black racial representation in Disney films can be addressed through multiple readings. The filmed version of Uncle Remus was widely condemned by film critics as a negative stereotype of Black servitude (Bernstein, 1996). His placid, conciliatory responses to White hegemony are frustrating; although he is portrayed as a Black elder of great wisdom and moral dignity, he apologizes profusely to his White employers if he offends them and becomes inconsolably distraught when they refuse his repeated offers of help. Many critics considered him "a controversial figure who suggests that blacks lived in extreme poverty, but were nonetheless happy and content alongside their former owners" (Sperb, 2005, p. 932). Peggy A. Russo (1992) dismisses him as "a spectre haunting our land for the last forty-five years" who caused "generations of readers, especially African-Americans…[to] eschew the original printed text because, based on the Disney image, they see it only as an example of black stereotyping" (p. 29). Russo argues that Disney has minimized Harris's Uncle Remus, a traditional shamanic or 'wise man' figure who preserves and transmits folk wisdom to the youth, into a harmless, White-friendly entertainer. Other critics connect Disney's Uncle Remus to the minstrelsy tradition, which incorporated kindly Black parental stereotypes to evoke the pleasures of pastoral nostalgia in White viewers (Terry, 2010).

Others have read more ambiguous or even positive traits into Disney's Uncle Remus as "the moral center of the film [who] has deeper insights into human nature and the psychology of the child than either of Johnny's parents" (Inge, 2012, p. 226). Kheli R. Willetts (2013) laments that Disney's "offensive" reinterpretation caused viewers to deny Uncle Remus and the Br'er animals' previous legacies as keepers of Black oral narrative, explaining that "centuries-old characters, born in ancient Africa as animal metaphors for crafty, sage survivalists, have been silenced and are no longer an active part of African American folklore and culture" (p. 20). Uncle Remus himself laments his fractured narrative in the film when he leaves the plantation after Johnny's mother forbids him to continue telling stories to the children: "I'm just a worn-out old man what don't do nothin' but tell stories. But they ain't never done no harm to nobody. And if they don't do no good, how come they last so long?" (Disney, Foster, & Jackson, 1946). If Uncle Remus is a character whose "time had run out" by 1946, what does this imply for the ancient pedagogies of Black survival represented by his tales?

The ongoing controversy of Uncle Remus positions this film as a microcosm of broader cultural debates around the preservation of traditional Black folklore that began in the late 1900s and continued throughout the first half of the century. Some Black historians cautioned against forgetting such 'conjure stories,' defending them as historical artifacts of great pedagogical value in understanding how slaves managed to preserve African cultural and spiritual knowledge in coded forms; others cautioned that Southern Blacks were "jeopardizing their own survival" by clinging to such outmoded and stereotypical forms of narrative (Chireau, 2003, p. 132). As a visual culture artifact, *Song of the South* allows for multiple racial gazes through which this nostalgic tension can be engaged, critiqued, and discussed (Sperb, 2012).

For example, *Song*'s 'happy' ending becomes much more ambiguous when viewed through a historical lens. It can be argued that Uncle Remus is not simply disappearing into an animated pastoral realm surrounded by adoring children and wildlife, but symbolically retreating into a tragic and dying past along with other traditional Black folklore. In this way, Uncle Remus remains a complex and troubling character worthy of contemporary re-examination. While such 'nostalgic' racial identities have long been erased from Disney's filmography after a series of damaging public relations controversies, they raise the persistent spectre of other forms of Black knowledge marginalized by stereotyping, racial overdetermination, and institutional racism. Perhaps the subsequent banning and erasure of this film from popular visual culture, rendering it as a piece of offensive and unredeemable antebellum nostalgia, may itself become the subject of broader critical examination and discussion in the future.

Hybridity and Colorblindness: Racial Representations in *The Princess and the Frog*

Over half a century after *Song of the South's* controversy, the studio produced its second representation of Black racial identity with *The Princess and the Frog*. The film also marked a return to traditional hand-drawn animation after nearly a decade of CGI features. Once again Disney attempted to mitigate racial controversies ahead of time, reaching out to the NAACP, Oprah Winfrey, and African American focus groups for consultation. This feedback caused Disney to drop its central character, a chambermaid named Maddy (consultants pointed out her stereotypical social positioning and her name's phonetic resemblance to "mammy") and replace her with an ambitious, pragmatic waitress named Tiana (Benhamou, 2014). Although the film underperformed at the box office, grossing only $104 million domestically by April 2010, its promotional line of toys sold very well and quickly became collectors' items (Lester, 2010).

Similar to its predecessor, the film received both widespread praise and criticism upon release. While audiences reacted warmly to the film's positive portrayal of a Black nuclear family and of Tiana's increased ingenuity and agency in relation to earlier gender-stereotyped Disney princesses, others pointed out its troubling erasure of Jim Crow-era racial politics (Bloodsworth-Lugo & Lugo-Lugo, 2013; Gehlawat, 2010; Gregory, 2010; Terry, 2010). The film is set in New Orleans in the 1920s, and tells the story of a young Black waitress who dreams of opening her own restaurant. After a confrontation with an evil voodoo priest, Dr. Facilier, who turns both Tiana and the visiting Prince Naveen into frogs, they venture into the bayou to entreat the benevolent voodoo priestess, Mama Odie, to break the spell. Along the way they encounter many other colorful animated characters, debate the value of hard work versus leisure, and eventually fall in love.

Although critical interest in *Song of the South* has primarily focused on its status as a 'nostalgic' historical artifact, we position *The Princess and the Frog* as a postmodern film that reflects contemporary political discourse and takes up current questions of racial hybridity, colorblindness, and respectability politics. The film's visual world has replaced the harsh segregation of the Jim Crow South with a colorful, raucously diverse 'Jazz Age,' a "utopian vision of a colorblind New Orleans which blends individuals from different cultures, races, and classes who are able to live and play together" (Gregory, 2010, p. 438). Although this hybridity reflects a more egalitarian approach to racial identity than previous Disney films, critics have suggested this approach avoids addressing race directly in the service of a more hegemonic doctrine of 'colorblindness' (Barker, 2010; Bloodsworth-Lugo & Lugo-Lugo, 2013; Turner, 2013). While race is visually apparent in the film, it curiously remains both unmarked and unremarked upon. While 'cultural Blackness' (e.g., music, cooking, and family life) is celebrated, 'political Blackness' (e.g., the persistence of racism and the ongoing struggles for equality in the face of institutional oppression) is either erased or coded more vaguely as class struggle. The racial politics of Whiteness are also folded into a more innocuous class politics; the film characterizes its wealthy White oligarchs Charlotte and 'Big Daddy' La Bouff as harmless and benevolent, even as New Orleans society operated under a strict racial caste system reinforced by anti-Black violence. Tiana spends most of her screen time as an enchanted frog, allowing the film to skirt the grim racial and sexual politics of its setting; her whimsical greenness "does not really move us beyond the stereotypical image of black women as invisible or as solely attached to labor" (Gregory, 2010, p. 433).

The film's colorblindness and failure to address structural racism also evoke a contemporary respectability politics; as Turner (2013) explains, "according to a color-blind ideology, race has nothing to do with success or failure; those who fail to succeed do so at the level of the individual, thus exonerating the hegemonic culture" (p. 91). Tiana's defining character trait is her tremendous work ethic; she repeatedly asserts that hard work is the only means to success and even eschews social dancing, a well-established source of Black community solidarity in historical New Orleans. She is positioned as a Black working-class character with solidly White middle-class values; her eventual success serves to reaffirm the capitalist ethos of hard work and individualism while eliding the unequal racial politics and institutional power structures conscribing her opportunities (Turner, 2013).

Disney's hesitancy to fully address Tiana and the other characters' racial identities reflects the hidden complications of Obama-era social politics. As Turner (2013) asserts, "this film represents a complex moment in a culture steeped in political correctness and an adherence to the politics of colorblindness" (p. 83). An analysis of *Song* and *Princess* reveals both admirable progress in presenting more positive and uplifting portrayals of racial diversity, and a persistent stubborn denial of the more complex and troublesome aspects of American racial identity, evinced by Disney's ongoing tendency to romanticize the cultural and narrative trappings of its Black characters while erasing their historical struggles for social and political equality.

WHAT DISNEY TEACHES ABOUT RACE: CURRICULAR AND PEDAGOGICAL IMPLICATIONS

As visual texts, Disney's animated films have served to mask the institutional entrenchments of racism while silently reinforcing them through a history of stereotyped and Othered representations of non-White identities. At the same time, these films have shown a remarkable political pliability over the years, reflecting the overtly nostalgic racism of the past, the postmodern shift toward a hybridized multiculturalism, and the contemporary respectability politics of the Obama era. This suggests that while these films have the potential to continue evolving toward more progressive depictions of diversity, they also contain the ever-present threat of the sanitization and erasure—indeed, the 'Disneyfication'—of complex racial identities. Barker (2010) expresses the unlikelihood that Disney will ever address issues of inequality and oppression directly when he argues that "the sanitized aesthetic…necessary to appeal to broad markets is fundamentally incompatible with a realistic representation of history" (p. 483).

Thus, Disneyfied depictions of racial identities removed from the social and political contexts that constructed them may be inevitable, but they remain problematic and call for an ongoing and vigorous critical discourse. Although both Uncle Remus and Tiana inhabit historical periods marked by pervasive anti-Black violence and repression (the Reconstruction and Jim Crow eras, respectively), their interactions with White characters remain innocuous, benevolent, and paternalistic, allowing the more troublesome aspects of White racial identity to remain uninterrogated as well. Characters like Tiana and Uncle Remus are overburdened with criticism precisely due to the *scarcity* of other representations of Black identity in Disney's filmography. White characters, on the other hand, are plentiful but have continued to escape such racialized scrutiny. There is a need for more robust critical interrogations of White subjectivities within these films. What can Johnny and his parents, Charlotte and Big Daddy LaBouff, portrayed as kindly if ineffectual benefactors to non-White characters, tell us about the ways in which Whiteness has been socially and politically constructed over the years in visual media? The tendency to overdetermine non-White identities with racial signifiers while coding (and masking) Whiteness appears throughout Disney's animated films and is also addressed by gaze theory, which helps us to understand how multiple racial gazes enable diverse interpretations of visual culture while themselves being caught up in institutional power structures which reify some interpretations while marginalizing others. The intense critical scrutiny around Disney's few existing Black representations and the concurrent tendency to avoid racialized critiques of its abundance of White representations, itself suggests the need for more discussion on how race is represented and encoded within its filmography.

As complex texts that accrue multiple meanings through engagements with a broad and diverse public audience, these films contain the potential for racial counter-gazes and counter-hegemonic readings. Disney films reveal an excess of potential interpretations and understandings within their rich visual imagery, narrative, and subtext; even dominant readings may contain elements that do not 'fit' and may serve as fertile ground for subversive and even oppositional interpretations. The racial pedagogy of both films discussed in this analysis, as well as in other Disney films representing diverse racial identities, remains complicated and open to multiple readings: as barometers of the racial tensions and anxieties of their eras, as well-intentioned yet risk-laden attempts to diversify Disney's animated filmography, and/or as cynically politicized attempts to rewrite American history by romanticizing or erasing centuries of institutional racial oppression.

DISCUSSION QUESTIONS

1. How have representations of non-White racial identities in Disney animated films changed and/or remained static throughout the years? How have representations of White racial identities changed and/or remained static?
2. What is the power of the *counter-gaze* in relation to viewing Disney films? How do viewers already employ gazing and counter-gazing in their relationships with visual culture?
3. What can the character of Uncle Remus tell us about the survival of traditional Black narratives in mainstream visual culture? What are some similarities and differences between the film, *Song of the South* and its source material?
4. How is racial representation handled in *The Princess and the Frog*? What are the responsibilities of films set in specific historical periods to represent their settings with historical accuracy?

REFERENCES

Arnold, B. (Producer), Buck, C., & Lima, K. (Directors). (1999). *Tarzan* [Motion Picture]. United States: Walt Disney Pictures.

Barker, J. L. (2010). Hollywood, black animation, and the problem of representation in *Little old' Bosko* and *The princess and the frog*. *Journal of African American Studies, 14*(4), 482–498.

Benhamou, E. (2014). From the advent of multiculturalism to the erasure of race: The representation of race relations in Disney animated features (1995–2009). *Exchanges: The Warwick Research Journal, 2*(1), 153–167.

Bernstein, M. (1996). Nostalgia, ambivalence, irony: 'Song of the South' and race relations in 1946 Atlanta. *Film History, 8*(2), 219–236.

Bloodsworth-Lugo, M. K., & Flory, D. (Eds.). (2013). *Race, philosophy, and film*. New York: Routledge.

Bloodsworth-Lugo, M. K., & Lugo-Lugo, C. R. (2013). Elisions of race and stories of progress: *Planet 51* and *The princess and the frog*. In M. K. Bloodsworth-Lugo & D. Flory (Eds.), *Race, philosophy, and film* (pp. 181–193). New York: Routledge.

Budd, M., & Kirsch, M. H. (Eds.). (2005). *Rethinking Disney: Private control, public dimensions*. Middletown, CT: Wesleyan University Press.

Byrne, E., & McQuillan, M. (1999). *Deconstructing Disney*. London, UK: Pluto Press.

Chireau, Y. P. (2003). *Black magic: Religion and the African American conjuring tradition*. Berkeley: University of California Press.

Clements, R., and Musker, J. (Producers), Clements, R., & Musker, J. (Directors). (1997). *Hercules* [Motion Picture]. United States: Walt Disney Pictures.

Coats, P. (Producer), Bancroft, T., & Cook, B. (Directors). (1998). *Mulan* [Motion Picture]. United States: Walt Disney Pictures.

Conli, R., & Hahn, D. (Producers), Trousdale, G., & Wise, K. (Directors). (1996). *The hunchback of Notre Dame* [Motion Picture]. United States: Walt Disney Pictures.

Del Vecho, P. (Producer), Clements, R., & Musker, J. (Directors). (2009). *The princess and the frog* [Motion Picture]. United States: Walt Disney Pictures.

Disney, W. E. (Producer), Foster, H., & Jackson, W. (Directors). (1946). *The song of the South* [Motion Picture]. United States: Walt Disney Pictures.

Disney, W. E. (Producer), Geronimi, C. (Director). (1959). *Sleeping beauty* [Motion Picture]. United States: Walt Disney Pictures.

Disney, W. E. (Producer), Geronimi, C., Jackson, W., & Luske, H. (Directors). (1995). *Lady and the tramp* [Motion Picture]. United States: Walt Disney Pictures.

Disney, W. E. (Producer), Geronimi, C., Jackson, W., & Luske, H. (Directors). (1953). *Peter Pan* [Motion Picture]. United States: Walt Disney Pictures.

Disney, W. E. (Producer), Hand, D. (Director). (1937). *Snow white and the seven dwarfs* [Motion Picture]. United States: Walt Disney Pictures.

Disney, W. E., & Sharpsteen, B. (Producers), Ferguson, N., and Algar, J. Directors (1940) *Fantasia* [Motion Picture]. United States: Walt Disney Pictures.

Fanon, F. (2008). *Black skin, white masks*. New York: Grove Press.

Gaines, J. (1988). White privilege and looking relations: Race and gender in feminist film theory. *Screen*(4), 12–27.

Gehlawat, A. (2010). The strange case of 'The princess and the frog': Passing and the elision of race. *Journal of African American Studies, 14*(4), 417–431.

Giroux, H. A., & Pollock, G. (2010). *The mouse that roared: Disney and the end of innocence.* Lanham, MD: Rowman & Littlefield Publishers.

Gregory, S. M. (2010). Disney's second line: New Orleans, racial masquerade, and the reproduction of whiteness in *The princess and the frog. Journal of African American Studies, 14*(4), 432–449.

Hahn, D. (Producer), Allers, R., & Minkoff, R. (Directors). (1994). *The lion king* [Motion Picture]. United States: Walt Disney Pictures.

hooks, b. (1992). *Black looks: Race and representation.* Boston: South End Press.

Hurley, D. L. (2005). Seeing white: Children of color and the Disney fairy tale princesses. *Journal of Negro Education, 74*(3), 221–232.

Inge, M. T. (2012). Walt Disney's *Song of the South* and the politics of animation. *The Journal of American Culture, 35*(3), 219–230.

Kaplan, E. A. (1997). *Looking for the other: Feminism, film, and the imperial gaze.* New York: Routledge.

King, C. R., Lugo-Lugo, C. R., & Bloodsworth-Lugo, M. K. (2010). *Animating difference: Race, gender, and sexuality in contemporary films for children.* Lanham, MD: Rowman & Littlefield Publishers.

Lester, N. A. (2010). Disney's *The Princess and the Frog*: The Pride, the Pressure, and the Politics of Being a First. *Journal of American Culture, 33*(4), 294–308.

Mulvey, L. (1975). Visual pleasure and narrative cinema. *Screen, 16*(3), 6–18.

Pack, S. (2008). 'I hate white people!' Subverting the televisual gaze. *Visual Anthropology, 21,* 136–150.

Pentecost, J. (Producer), Gabriel, M., & Goldberg, E. (Directors). (1995). *Pocahontas* [Motion Picture]. United States: Walt Disney Pictures.

Russo, P. A. (1992). Uncle Walt's Uncle Remus: Disney's distortion of Harris's hero. *Southern Literary Journal, 25*(1), 19–32.

Selznick, D. O. (Producer), Fleming, V., Cukor, G., & Wood, S. (Directors). (1939). *Gone with the wind* [Motion Picture]. United States: Selznick International Pictures.

Sperb, J. (2005). 'Take a frown, turn it upside down': Splash Mountain, Walt Disney World, and the cultural de-rac[e]ination of Disney's *Song of the south* (1946). *Journal of Popular Culture, 38*(5), 924–938.

Sperb, J. (2012). *Disney's most notorious film: Race, convergence, and the hidden histories of* Song of the South. Austin: University of Texas Press.

Tavin, K. M., & Anderson, D. (2003). Teaching (popular) visual culture: Deconstructing Disney in the elementary art classroom. *Art Education, 56*(3), 21–24, 33–35.

Terry, E. L. (2010). Rural as racialized plantation vs. rural as modern reconnection: Blackness and agency in Disney's *Song of the south* and *The princess and the frog. Journal of African American Studies, 14*(4), 469–481.

Turner, S. E. (2013). Blackness, bayous and gumbo: Encoding and decoding race in a colorblind world. In J. Cheu (Ed.), *Diversity in Disney films: Critical essays on race, ethnicity, gender, sexuality and disability* (pp. 83–98). Jefferson, NC: McFarland & Company.

Willetts, K. R. (2013). Cannibals and coons: Blackness in the early days of Disney. In J. Cheu (Ed.), *Diversity in Disney films: Critical essays on race, ethnicity, gender, sexuality and disability* (pp. 9–22). Jefferson, NC: McFarland & Company.

Yancy, G. (2013). 'Now imagine she's white': The gift of the black gaze and the reinscription of whiteness as normative in A *time to kill.* In M. K. Bloodsworth-Lugo & D. Flory (Eds.), *Race, philosophy, and film* (pp. 134–148). New York: Routledge.

CHAPTER SIX

"I don't think Disney has anything to do with it"

Unsettling Race in a White English Classroom

CHRISTINA BERCHINI

Several years ago, I presented to my secondary English education students a short clip from *Mickey Mouse Monopoly* (Picker & Sun, 2001),[1] a documentary in which noted scholars and educators deconstruct racialized representations in some of the highest-grossing Disney films (e.g., Tito the chihuahua in *Oliver & Company* [1988], the hyenas in *The Lion King* [1994], crows in *Dumbo* [1941], and orangutans in *The Jungle Book* [1967], just to name a few). Several students told me that the clip made them "angry." Most others remained silent, seemingly unwilling to engage in a discussion about the racism that is articulated and reinforced by the universally beloved Disney films depicted in this documentary.

In a teacher education course in which students are asked to engage issues of race and diversity, I was admittedly surprised by their responses (and lack thereof). However, such responses are perhaps to be anticipated. As Giroux (1995) reminds readers with what he has termed the "Disneyfication" of children's culture, "any attempt to take up Disney films critically rubs against the grain of American popular opinion" (p. 66). Likewise, for several of my students (White, pre-service English teachers), Disney is a sacred staple of their childhood. You simply do not critique Disney. To borrow from Marisa Peralta of the Rafael Hernandez School and contributor to this powerful documentary, "If it weren't so tragic, it would be comical" (Picker & Sun, 2001).

Classroom discourses around Disney and racism raise questions about how to encourage teachers to engage the difficult knowledge (Britzman, 2003) of pedagogies that seek to disrupt "the deep investments students hold in the ready-made discourses that live in schools and in the larger social world" (Britzman, 1991, p. 79). To deconstruct Disney is to attempt to disrupt an authoritative discourse (Bakhtin, 1981) about racialized representations. It is, as Britzman (1991) asserts, to offend sensibilities; it is to "challenge the comfort of clear boundaries" (p. 64). Here, to illustrate the challenges presented by such critical pedagogical approaches, I explore how one English teacher—Mr. Kurt—draws on racialized representations in Disney films to "open [his students'] eyes to the world" (Mr. Kurt,[2] interview).

This chapter draws on Giroux's (2014) notion of an "unsettling pedagogy," a critical approach to teaching that is evident in Mr. Kurt's attempts to disrupt his students' emotional investments in Disney films in order to deconstruct the racialization of popular cartoon characters. For Giroux, an "unsettling pedagogy" encourages students to not only understand but to "[engage] with the deeper affective investments that make them complicit with oppressive ideologies" (p. 35). On one hand, deconstructing Disney imagery and pedagogy is considered a "subversive" act (Giroux, 1998) that is often met with resistance. On the other hand, as Britzman (1991) points out, "to act as if meanings are stable is to already undermine the more difficult work of social change" (p. 63). My own experiences using Disney to teach White students about racialized representations in media inspired my work with Mr. Kurt, the novice English teacher on whom I focus in this chapter.[3] Specifically, I ask: What happens when a new teacher uses Disney texts to teach issues of race, Whiteness, and social justice to a predominantly White, rural student population, and how might that experience inform pedagogies that "unsettle" race through Disney texts?

Critical theorists have argued how Disney, as a cultural force, constructs and defines the Western ideal, "while also attempting to define the non-western 'other'" (Belkhyr, 2013, p. 1366; see also Cheu, 2013). Numerous critical cultural studies have examined the racialized cultural messages expressed through Disney characters (Hurley, 2005; Pewewardy, 1996), song lyrics (Belkhyr, 2013), and voiceover casting (Neff, 1996; Wright, 2013), pointing to the myriad ways Disney films promulgate a Eurocentric curriculum (Shohat & Stam, 2014; Wright, 2013) that frames and idealizes White identity at the expense of the identities of people of color and non-Western communities. The resounding message in these critical studies is that Disney is a pedagogical and curricular vehicle where Whiteness is held as the standard through which stories are told (Belkhyr, 2013; Pewewardy, 1996; Wright, 2013). For example, in an analysis of the impact of Disney's fairy princesses on the racial identities of children of color, Hurley (2005) points out that "[t]he implications that most if not all children, including children of color, see 'White' as good, living happily ever after, and pretty, are disturbing" (p. 222). Such studies illustrate that Disney is a global media force with ideals rooted in Whiteness and a cultural impact that makes critical pedagogy and critical awareness all the more necessary (Horn, 2003). As such, the implications of employing Disney as a pedagogical tool are many, and should not be ignored. To this point, Giroux (1998) advocates for Disney as a critical space for learning, emphasizing that, given Disney's dominance as a cultural and educational force, it only makes sense that teachers—and in turn, students—learn to critically consume and analyze Disney's textual messages and values.

The arguments put forth by critical Disney studies, as well as the story I tell in this chapter, suggest that it might be considered irresponsible—in a pedagogical sense—to reduce Disney texts to mere innocent entertainment. Children view Disney films (and other texts) and acquire its merchandise; these engagements have the very real impact of entrenching children's sensibilities and understandings of their identities in relation to that of their peers (Giroux & Pollock, 2010). Disney's social and curricular impacts are precisely why, in Giroux's (1995) words, "[p]opular audiences tend to reject any link between ideology and the prolific entertainment world of Disney" (p. 67). Likewise, according to Britzman (1991), "Concepts that threaten to throw students into emotional and social disarray are likely to be unpopular" (p. 63). In this chapter, I illustrate the "emotional and social disarray" that arises when Mr. Kurt, a White high school English teacher in a rural Midwestern town, teaches with Disney in an attempt to enact anti-racist and multicultural education in his predominantly White classroom.

Using data from a lesson I observed in Mr. Kurt's classroom, I draw on classroom discourse to expose problems, tensions, and opportunities embedded in using Disney to engage students in difficult conversations around race and other social issues. This study employs qualitative case study methodology, an approach that "usually means finding good moments to reveal the unique complexity of the case" (Stake, 1995, p. 63). Data for this study were gathered from three main sources: four individual interviews, classroom observations, and what I call, school "shadowing" informed by ethnographic methods (Heath & Street, 2008; Spradley, 1979). The data I feature in this chapter are the product of one classroom observation and the discourse that emerged from those observations, as well as from my general experience shadowing Mr. Kurt during the course of this study. I also draw from interview data to illuminate how Mr. Kurt contextualized his critical work with his students. These data reveal the complexities of engaging students in critical conversations about Disney and offer insight into pedagogical practices that may help teachers and students "unsettle" racialized narratives presented in Disney texts.

UNSETTLING DISNEY IN MR. KURT'S CLASSROOM

Mr. Kurt has taken on the responsibility of addressing racism in his classes with a critical lens. He does this with literature, but he does not rely solely on literature to achieve these ends; I witnessed Mr. Kurt seize several opportunities to address institutional racism in classroom discussions, in student work, and, to the point of this chapter, in racialized representations in Disney films. As such, he located his White high school and 9th grade English classroom as a space in which to do critical work. Mr. Kurt explained what it looks like to employ a critical approach to teaching his predominantly White students about racism by using Disney's texts. He explained:

> A problem that I think I just realized that I have with this district is, since they talk about racism so much, [in the] 8th, 9th, 10th grade[s], the students hear it every year. Through the books they read, the topic is always brought up. So my *worry* is that when we talk about it, like [he mocks an irritated grunt, here], I get the eye-roll. And it's like, "Here we go again." And they might check out, because it's like, "we've heard this a million times." So I think that what needs to happen, or what *should* happen, is, we need to talk about racism, and it needs to be in a meaningful … way, instead of like, this on the surface [in a singsong voice], "Don't be mean to Black people" type of thing. Because *that's* when you get the eye-roll, and it's like, "Alright, I get it; I'm not going to be mean to a Black person. I'm not part of the KKK"; that's what they're all gonna think. Whereas, to toot my own horn, if we talk about White privilege, and we talk about how it's in Disney movies, they get *mad*, and they get *riled up*. *That's* like a meaningful, productive discussion. Even if they don't start thinking differently right *now*, that's *productive*, because they've had an emotional attachment to it, and they got into it. But if like, since 8th grade, they hear the same old, same old, they're gonna be checking out by the time they get to 10th grade.

By taking up "White privilege" in his class discussions, Mr. Kurt refers to the privilege of not seeing, or "dealing with" (Frankenberg, 1993) race and racialized representations in film (Hurley, 2005). As Hurley points out in relation to Disney's fairytale princesses, for *all* children, "[t]he problem of pervasive, internalized privileging of Whiteness has been intensified by the Disney representation of fairy tale princesses which consistently reinforces an ideology of White supremacy" (p. 223). Part of the insidiousness of Whiteness, White privilege, and White identity development is that it is part of a discourse of blindness—of not having to think about it (Berchini, 2014).

As such, Mr. Kurt's struggles are myriad and complex. He is faced with a number of structural barriers, not the least of which consists of a resistant White student population. To address these challenges, Mr. Kurt often used themes in literature to teach his students about White privilege, race, and social justice. In his words, "literature [provided] the best segue for that." However, Mr. Kurt also desired to "forget about the book" and "go off on a tangent" as appropriate; he often located dissonance between what he is required to teach and his larger, critical goals. In fact, forgetting about the book and other aspects of the required English curriculum in order to address larger social issues was a practice that Mr. Kurt employed repeatedly throughout the school year, in a variety of ways.

During my initial visits to Mr. Kurt's classroom, he was in the early stages of teaching the district-sanctioned text, *The Mississippi Trial' 1955* by Chris Crowe (2002), a White male novelist who explores the thoughts, actions, and racialized experiences of a White boy, Hiram Hillburn, against the backdrop of the murder trial of Civil Rights icon, Emmett Till. By the time this particular lesson occurred, Mr. Kurt had also presented to his students the same ten-minute clip of *Mickey Mouse Monopoly* that I describe at the beginning of this chapter. The clip, which he used to supplement discussions of racism in the novel, focused on representations of Latino, Black, Chinese, and Middle Eastern characters in selected animated Disney films.

Like all teachers, Mr. Kurt has to address institutional demands to teach the national Common Core Standards for the English Language Arts. In an effort to meet his district's expectations that English teachers address literacy standards for informational and nonfiction texts, he developed a regular "Article of the Week" segment of his curriculum to help supplement his anchor texts. Mr. Kurt assigned an opinion piece by Pulitzer Prize winner, Leonard Pitts Jr. (2012), "Don't Lower the Bar on Education Standards," as a supplemental text to *The Mississippi Trial, 1955*. During one classroom observation, I witnessed him using these texts in an attempt to address institutionalized racism with his students.

As I describe after the following exchange, the "Article of the Week" and the *Mickey Mouse Monopoly* clip acted as springboards into a whole-class discussion about racism and White privilege. In this exchange, students do not seem to have trouble deconstructing the educational policies described by Pitts (2012) as "racist"[4]; however, when Mr. Kurt brings an analysis of Disney characters into the discussion about racism and White privilege, it is quite another story. Mr. Kurt asked one particularly demonstrative student, Adam, to read the "Article of the Week" aloud to the class; when Mr. Kurt interjected and repeated a portion of the article for emphasis, "So yes, it touches me in a raw spot, this news that two states—Florida and Virginia—have adopted new education standards under which they would set different goals for students, based on race, ethnicity and disability. …," the following exchange took place:[5]

1. Adam: Isn't that kind of a bit racist?
2. Mr. Kurt: What makes you say so?
3. Adam: Making the goal lower because the person's Black?
4. Shane: Racism is pretty much discriminating against you because of the color of your skin, and this is exactly that. They are setting different goals for kids based on race. …
5. Mr. Kurt: What do you guys think of that; is that okay?
6. [A few students chime in with a choral, drawn out "Noooo."]

7. Meg: It also said that they have different goals for kids with disabilities, because they have problems that prevent them from learning.
8. Mr. Kurt: So you're saying that it's tougher for kids who may have a disability?

On one hand, Adam seemed to recognize the racist structure within which educational standards and goals in Florida and Virginia were enacted (line 1), according to the article. His response, as well as Shane's (line 4) and also the choral "Noooo" (line 6) marked the beginnings of a discussion about institutionalized racism. However, as Meg's response revealed, it is not difficult for White students to shirk the topic of race and racism by deflecting the issue, a strategy discussed in several critical studies of Whiteness (Flynn, Lensmire, & Lewis, 2009; Haviland, 2008; Picower, 2009). For instance, Meg's response seems to suggest that the education policies described in the article might be targeting disabilities, rather than race. This act of deflection has been cited in Critical Race Theory and Critical Whiteness Studies as an "ideological tool" (Picower, 2009) that Whites use to displace responsibility for developing an understanding about, and acknowledging the presence of, racialized discourses, texts, settings, and situations.

The purpose of highlighting the above exchange is two-fold: First, as the discussion reveals, Mr. Kurt's students readily deconstruct education policies in Florida and Virginia as "racist," a detail worth noting. Moreover, the article acts as a springboard into a whole-class discussion about White privilege, using cultural artifacts such as Band-Aids and examples from Disney films. While Mr. Kurt acknowledged Meg's response (line 7) he did not push her to elaborate on her point. Instead, he directed his next question to the entire class, and the following exchange took place (italics have been applied in lines where words were dramatically emphasized):

10. Mr. Kurt: Do you know what the term *white privilege* means? [Students collectively indicate that they are not familiar with this term.]
11. Mr. Kurt: I can give you a very small example: What color are flesh-colored Band-Aids?
12. Cabe: [incredulous in tone] You're comparing this to *Band-Aids*?![6] [Meanwhile, in the midst of Cabe's outspoken resistance, it is as though the metaphorical light bulb "goes off," as a handful of other, seemingly less resistant students exclaim, "Ohhhh yeaaaaaaaa!"]
13. Jay: Nobody says, "Is it because I'm White?" But people do say, "Is it because I'm Black?"
14. Mr. Kurt: [Referencing *Mickey Mouse Monopoly*] What color skin does every Disney character have, except for one?
15. Cabe: [Dramatically slams both fists on his desk and leans forward indignantly] Now you're comparing it to *Disney*?!

16. Adam: The thing about Disney, I honestly, like, Mr. Kurt, you're an awesome teacher, but I don't think Disney has anything to do with it.
17. Mr. Kurt: Really? Did you notice how every evil character has darker skin? Did you notice how the crows sound Black? The hyenas [in *The Lion King*] sound Black?
18. [One female student laughs during this exchange.]

Mr. Kurt's attempted deconstruction of Disney characters' appearance and vocal characterizations is consistent with what has been argued in several media studies that address racial representation in Disney films. For example, Neff (1996) points out how the voice-overs of *The Lion King*'s "heroes" (p. 58) were assigned to White actors, while "the non-whites were relegated to secondary roles" (p. 58). Similarly, Giroux and Pollock (2010) describe "racially coded representations and language" seen in the film: "Scar, the icon of evil, is physically darker than the good lions. Shenzi and Banzai, the despicable hyena storm troopers … speak in the jive accents of decidedly urban black or Hispanic youth" (p. 110).

These critical perspectives of the racialized representations in Disney films are consistent with the analyses presented in the *Mickey Mouse Monopoly* clip; Mr. Kurt's analysis appears to be grounded in cultural critiques of racialized representations in Disney films. However, Mr. Kurt seemed to sense that his students were not on board with critical interpretations of Disney characters. The class discussion ensued as follows:

19. Mr. Kurt: [Not directing this response to anyone in particular] Before you say that my Disney references are not valid, you should educate yourself.
20. Cabe: I think the Band-Aid thing is stupid. If it really matters that much, send a letter. And Disney, really? It's a cartoon.
21. Meg: I have a lot of friends who are Black. I am not racist toward them at all. I think it's strange that they have the BET [Black Entertainment Television] channel. … I think it's stupid how certain people think that certain shows are for certain races.[7]
22. Cabe: There is a Black History Month; why is there no *White* History Month?
23. Mr. Kurt: [somewhat deadpan in tone] Because every *other* month is White History Month?
24. Brad: I always thought that, you know how kids are afraid of the dark? They make characters darker so people would be afraid of them.
25. Aubrey: Black has always been associated with scary things, for me. Like EMO, Goth. …

This excerpt reveals a range of responses to the notion that Mr. Kurt's students' experiences of White privilege are likely expressed through their investments in

Disney texts. Brad seems open to the idea of deconstructing Disney, while Cabe flatly rejects Mr. Kurt's efforts. Meg's response, however, represents an explicit "tool of Whiteness" (Picower, 2009). Picower defines tools of Whiteness as the negative or dismissive reactions to discussions in which Whites' complicity in racist structures and institutions is centered; moreover, tools of Whiteness "facilitate in the job of maintaining and supporting hegemonic stories and dominant ideologies of race" (pp. 204–205). Picower explains how tools of Whiteness, and emotional tools in particular, "are tools based upon participants' feelings" (p. 205). As the classroom discourse reveals, by claiming to "have Black friends" and that she is "not racist toward them at all," Meg negates Mr. Kurt's argument that Disney's representation of characters can be viewed through a critical lens.

The excerpt of classroom discourse examined here reflects the findings of cultural studies about the range of ways in which students respond to critiques of Disney. For example, as King (2006) points out, "[w]hile some students will enthusiastically embrace [critiques of Disney]...others will passionately defend Disney as harmless, magical fun, and denounce critical perspectives as 'reading too much into it'" (p. 11). The students' resistance to critiques of Disney reveals a by-product of the corporation's impact as a pedagogical and curricular force or, as Giroux and Pollock (2010) put it, the product of a "teaching machine [which] now shapes the identities of youth from infancy to the teenage years" (p. 92). Their passionate resistance to Mr. Kurt's critiques of Disney reveals their strong emotional attachment to Disney's narratives and characters, and as such, the complexities embedded in attempting to "unsettle" race through Disney texts.

Considering the students' strong attachments to Disney, their attempts to dismiss and to silence Mr. Kurt (e.g., lines 15–16) are not surprising. According to Britzman (1991), "Unpopular narratives unleash ambiguous effects. A story may be deemed unpopular if it goes against the grain of the acceptable in ways that either offend sensibilities or challenge the comfort of clear boundaries. ... [Unpopular narratives set] loose unanticipated and rebellious meanings that throw into question our very agency." (p. 64)

As I mentioned at the outset of this chapter, to deconstruct Disney is to commit to "unleashing" an unpopular narrative. Mr. Kurt's students seemed more willing to engage the narrative of institutionalized racism in Pitts's (2012) article than they were the racialized representations in Disney films. This may be because, with the article, students were able to interpret racism as outside of themselves (and perhaps even geographically distant, insomuch as the policies pertained to Florida and Virginia). Disney and Band-Aids, however, are more likely to directly represent a feature of their lived experiences.

Mr. Kurt was not deterred by his students' resistance to his efforts; rather, he persists in pursuit of his critical pedagogical goals. In the exchange that follows,

Mr. Kurt resists his students' efforts to silence his larger goal of teaching them about White privilege:

26. Cass: The thing about the Band-Aids, I think they're over thinking it, because I never thought. …
27. Mr. Kurt: [Dramatically leans toward Cass and responds to her in a mock whisper]: *Psssst … Because you're White!*
28. Mr. Kurt: What if the Band-Aids were black, and we called it "flesh-colored Band-Aids"?
29. Cass: Well yea, then we would think about it.
30. Mr. Kurt: I wonder, that those [Disney] characters often have a Black dialect…do you not learn something about people who are darker if that's what you're brought up with?
31. Aubrey: Black people think that because they were enslaved once, that the world owes them something.
32. Mr. Kurt: It's easy for a group of white kids to say this. If we were in Detroit, they might say, "Yea, I know what you're saying."
33. Meg: [References racialized representations in a Crest Toothpaste commercial]…checking peoples' mouths for germs. The Black girl's mouth is dirtier than the White person's mouth.
    [A male student presents an actual Band-Aid and says, "To me, that's not flesh-colored."]
34. Cabe: [Takes the Band-Aid and makes a dramatic display of delivering it to Mr. Kurt] Mr. Kurt, can I see your skin for a minute?
35. Vito: Now it's gonna bug me any time I put on a Band-Aid.
36. Mr. Kurt: [Allowing Cabe to hold the Band-Aid up to his skin] For homework, finish chapter 2 and chapter 3.

At the end of the discussion, there appeared to be several shifts in the way in which students talked about the issue of institutionalized racism. For example, in Meg's case, she moves from "think[ing] it's stupid how certain people think that certain shows are for certain races," to offering her own example of media which perpetuate harmful racialized representations, as with a Crest Toothpaste commercial. I argue that this shift would not have occurred without Mr. Kurt's persistence (e.g., "*Psssst … Because you're White!*"/"It's easy for a group of White kids to say this").

TOWARD AN "UNSETTLING PEDAGOGY" OF DISNEY

The classroom conversations featured here reveal some of the challenges faced by teachers like Mr. Kurt, who resist the stereotypical depiction of the White teacher who "avoids" (Haviland, 2008; Picower, 2009) foregrounding topics related to racism and to White privilege. Mr. Kurt recognizes and is openly frustrated with his White students' apathy toward racism. In his words,

> Especially because of the population I'm teaching now, it's very, very White. Seeing their close-mindedness, because of the lack of, not just race, but sexuality, all that stuff. Just seeing how close-minded the community is there, is very frustrating. They [do not] seem to understand the *problem*. ... They're like, 'yeah, race is still a problem today but I think they [people of color] need to get over it' is what they [his students] say.

Rather than accepting his students' apathy, Mr. Kurt challenges it by encouraging his students to consider the extent to which their own White privilege has rendered them complicit in their unquestioned consumption of racialized representation in Disney films (lines 14, 17, and 19). Yet, not only were several students resistant to Mr. Kurt's efforts, but some responses sought to dismiss—and perhaps silence—his efforts.

Mr. Kurt's conversations with his students in the secondary English classroom, while offering only a narrow glimpse into the intricacies of using Disney to teach about race, reveal the complexities embedded in "unsettling pedagogies." The emotional attachments students have to Disney's texts; the denial of, and resistance toward, Mr. Kurt's "unexpected vantage point" (Giroux, 2014) from which he invites students to deconstruct this powerful staple of their childhood; and the students' immediate desire to dismiss and to silence Mr. Kurt all combine to reveal the very real challenges a teacher might face when attempting to unsettle race using Disney's texts.

On the other hand, the classroom discourse in which Mr. Kurt encourages his students to deconstruct the racialization of Disney characters also reveals possibilities for "unsettling pedagogies." Such pedagogies expose unquestioned assumptions about race and privilege by troubling Disney texts, which provided Mr. Kurt with a way to problematize surface-level engagements with race and racism in his rural, predominantly White context—a way which, in his words, "gets [students] *mad*" and "*riled up*." The students' resistance and Mr. Kurt's persistence show promise for the possibilities embedded in teaching with Disney's texts. To borrow from Britzman (1991), the vignette featured in this chapter reveals how "pedagogy is not just about encountering critical knowledge. The focus is on both producing knowledge and constructing ... social relations that recognize the power of lived experiences and of ideology" (p. 62). Mr. Kurt's pedagogies reveal the possibilities embedded in using Disney to help his students recognize how their lived experiences as White youth have shaped their ideologies toward race and racialized representations. An unsettling pedagogy also reveals the importance of encouraging students to get angry about critiques of Disney and race. Angry resistance, as we saw in Mr. Kurt's classroom, opens up space for dialogue.

Moreover, Mr. Kurt's classroom also reveals how Disney texts might be used as a means to depart from trite discussions about race and racism in education. In the area of multicultural education, extant research tends to emphasize the preparation of teachers for work in urban settings. I am not downplaying the importance of preparing teachers for important work in these settings; however, as Nieto (1999) points out, "multicultural education is consequently as important for middle-class White suburban students as it is for the students of color who live in the inner city" (p. x). The case of Mr. Kurt provides insight into what unsettling pedagogies using Disney texts might look like in a predominantly White school, as such schools are also positioned within a racialized society.

DISCUSSION QUESTIONS

1. Consider the vignette featured in this chapter: What are your concerns? Fears? Skepticisms? Based on the discourse that took place in Mr. Kurt's classroom, what sorts of possibilities does the deconstruction of Disney texts present for teachers who are interested in teaching about race in general?
2. Britzman (1991) emphasizes that creating an atmosphere in which "unpopular" (p. 65) topics are explored is both necessary and difficult. How might we encourage pre-service and in-service teachers to responsibly "unleash unpopular things" (Britzman, 1991)? Likewise, how might we encourage students to grapple with topics (e.g., White privilege) that might disrupt their worldviews?

NOTES

1. I encourage readers to view this documentary in whole or in part, as it provides a backdrop to the points made in this chapter.
2. Mr. Kurt chose his pseudonym. All names, for all people and places in this study, are pseudonyms.
3. Mr. Kurt was formerly a teacher education student in a secondary English methods course that I taught at a large Midwestern university. At the time of this study, he was a full-time, first-year teacher; I had known him for two years. I approached Mr. Kurt to participate in my research because he brings a critical and social justice-minded orientation to his work.
4. Due to space constraints, I am unable to include the article in its entirety.
5. In this study, I considered the participants' words and work from a sociocultural perspective (Gee, 2008) and employed Gee's (1991) linguistic approach to discourse to break down interview data into smaller, numbered units for the purposes of clarity.
6. Italicized for emphasis.
7. Field note: Students then share the names of television shows with a focus on black characters and families (e.g., *The Fresh Prince of Bel-Air* and *Family Matters*, popular sitcoms from the

1990s). Important to note is that there is no discussion of how these shows were envisioned under a 'White gaze,' in that the characters, as affluent and influential people of color in high positions of power and authority (e.g., high-powered lawyers and judges able to enroll their children in elite private schools, and a police officer) are deemed "acceptable" to White audiences.

REFERENCES

Bakhtin, M. M. (1981). Discourse and the novel. In *The dialogic imagination*. Austin: University of Texas Press.

Belkhyr, S. (2013). Defining the 'self' and the 'other' in Disney song lyrics. *International Journal of Human Sciences*, *10*(1), 1366–1378.

Berchini, C. (2014). *Teachers constructing and being constructed by prevailing discourses and practices of whiteness in their curriculum, classroom, and school community: A critical inquiry of three first-year English teachers*. Doctoral dissertation. Retrieved from: Proquest, LLC. database. (UMI No. 3630576)

Britzman, D. P. (1991). Decentering discourses in teacher education: Or, the unleashing of unpopular things. *Journal of Education*, *173*(3), 60–80.

Britzman, D. P. (2003). Speculations on qualities of difficult knowledge in teaching and learning: An experiment in psychoanalytic research. *International Journal of Qualitative Studies in Education*, *16*(6), 755–776.

Cheu, J. (Ed.). (2013). *Diversity in Disney films: Critical essays on race, ethnicity, gender, sexuality and disability*. Jefferson, NC: McFarland.

Crowe, C. (2002). *The Mississippi trial, 1955*. New York: Penguin.

Flynn, J., Lensmire, T., & Lewis, C. (2009). A critical pedagogy of race in teacher education: Response and responsibility. In S. L. Groenke & J. A. Hatch (Eds.), *Critical pedagogy and teacher education in the neoliberal era: Small openings* (pp. 85–98). New York: Springer.

Frankenberg, R. (1993). *White women, race matters: The social construction of whiteness*. New York: Routledge.

Gee, J. P. (1991). A linguistic approach to narrative. *Journal of Narrative and Life History/Narrative Inquiry*, *1*, 15–39.

Gee, J. P. (2008). *Social linguistics and literacies: Ideology in discourses*. New York: Routledge.

Giroux, H. A. (1995). Animating youth: The Disnification of children's culture. *Socialist Review*, *24*(3), 23–55.

Giroux, H. A. (1998). Public pedagogy and rodent politics: Cultural studies and the challenge of Disney. *Arizona Journal of Hispanic Cultural Studies*, *2*, 253–266.

Giroux, H. (2014). Critical pedagogy in dark times. *Praxis Educativa*, *17*(2), 27–38.

Giroux, H. A., & Pollock, G. (2010). *The mouse that roared: Disney and the end of innocence*. Lanham, MD: Rowman & Littlefield Publishers.

Haviland, V. S. (2008). "Things get glossed over": Rearticulating the silencing power of whiteness in education. *Journal of Teacher Education*, *59*(1), 40–54.

Heath, S. B., & Street, B. (2008). *On ethnography: Approaches to language and literacy research*. New York: Teachers College Press.

Horn, Jr. R. A. (2003). Developing a critical awareness of the hidden curriculum through media literacy. *The Clearing House*, *76*(6), 298–300.

Hurley, D. L. (2005). Seeing white: Children of color and the Disney fairy tale princess. *The Journal of Negro Education*, 221–232.

King, D. (2006). A cultural studies approach to teaching the sociology of childhood. *Sociation Today*, *4*(1). Available at: http://www.ncsociology.org/sociationtoday/v41/king.htm

Neff, H. (1996). Strange faces in the mirror: The ethics of diversity in children's films. *The Lion and the Unicorn*, *20*(1), 50–65.

Nieto, S. (1999). Foreword. In G. R. Howard, *We can't teach what we don't know: White teachers, multiracial schools* (pp. xiii–xv). New York: Teachers College Press.

Pewewardy, C. (1996). The Pocahontas paradox: A cautionary tale for educators. *Journal of Navajo Education*, *14*(1–2), 20–25.

Picker, M. (Director), Sun, C. F. (Producer). (2001). *Mickey Mouse monopoly: Disney, childhood & corporate power* [Motion picture]. Northampton, MA: Media Education Foundation.

Picower, B. (2009). The unexamined whiteness of teaching: How white teachers maintain and enact dominant racial ideologies. *Race, Ethnicity and Education*, *12*(2), 197–215.

Pitts, Jr., L. (2012, November 24). Don't lower the bar on education standards. *Miami Herald*. Retrieved from: http://www.miamiherald.com/2012/11/24/3111849/dont-lower-the-bar-on-education.html

Shohat, E., & Stam, R. (2014). *Unthinking Eurocentrism: Multiculturalism and the media*. New York: Routledge.

Spradley, J. P. (1979). *The ethnographic interview*. New York: Holt, Rinehart and Winston.

Stake, R. (1995). *The art of case study research*. Thousand Oaks, CA: Sage.

Wright, L. P. (2013). *White royalty: Whitewashing from prince of Persia to Sofia the first*. UMI Thesis.

CHAPTER SEVEN

Disney and the Ethnic Other

A Semiotic Analysis of American Identity

MANISHA SHARMA

While many think of art education as the teaching of studio skills and art history to K-12 students, a contemporary art education paradigm encompasses visual culture and straddles disciplinary striations of cultural and media studies, material culture studies, and (visual) literacy studies (Freedman, 2003; Tavin, 2010). Critical art education focuses on big ideas such as identity, representation, truth/myth, and spectatorship to enable students to become more aware of their own agency in the construction of culture and gain tools to make more informed decisions in their engagements with the ideological positions represented in visual culture (Desai & Darts, 2013; Tavin, 2005). Understanding and unpacking how viewers come to make assumptions about the beliefs and mores of ethnic cultures, using the tools of critical semiotic analyses of Disney, enable learners to examine how stereotypes and misconceptions arise through the uncritical consumption of contemporary visual storytelling. The popularity and status that Disney enjoys in global popular culture translate into teaching opportunities at multiple levels of formal and informal education, including K-12, higher education, and lifelong learning settings.

In this chapter, I describe how Disney emerged as a favored lens to examine the construction of ethnic identity in a general education class on writing about visual culture at a large Midwestern university, even though I had not explicitly asked students to engage with this specific topic. I explore how those students deconstructed American culture and identity—specifically, ethnic identity—through an analysis of Disney films as cultural artifacts. First, I provide an overview of how the consumption of Disney's visual culture is linked to constructions of Americanized cultures and ethnic identity. Next, I contextualize the study of Disney in my teaching of/as critical art education practice. Having set this context, I share my students' deconstructions of Disney, identifying three themes that emerged from their semiotic analyses of how ethnic characters are othered; through their accents, through their portrayal as enacting savage behaviors, and through their representations as lacking visible characteristics that reflect ethnic identity. Finally, I describe how students' ideas about ethnic identity were deeply entwined with ideas of nationality, immigration, and racial identity and discuss how the themes emerging from their analyses led to understandings of American identity as defined through viewing "ethnic" as "other."

DISNEY AND ETHNIC IDENTITY

Disney is a diversified enterprise comprising media networks, parks and resorts, studio entertainment, consumer products, and interactive media. It includes a pantheon of cultural figures and stories that have become embedded in American culture and appropriated elsewhere, leading to pan-Americanized cultures that are "glocal" (Appadurai, 1996; Hall, 1997)—that is, that are concerned with issues and objects that reflect, and are affected by, local and global concerns. Giroux (2004) writes about how Disney fantasy worlds that promote and popularize idealized ways of life become the images "on which America constructs itself" (p. 55). One American ideal constructed through Disney texts is the notion of a "magic kingdom," which is positioned as the happiest place on earth as long as its delightful innocence and moral values remain protected and secure within its borders—a "closed and total category" (p. 54). A number of scholars, including Giroux and Pollock (2010), and Sammond (2005), have problematized and unpacked the influence of Disney on the formation of American society and culture, focusing on how Disney enables children as consumers and commercializes education in public and private spaces (Budd & Kirsch, 2005). Bell, Haas, and Sells (1995), Cheu (2013), and Davis (2014) bring more clarity to how Disney constructs and portrays socio-cultural ideologies of gender, race, and ethnicity. Scholars and artists including Bernardi (2008), Bret (n.d), Brode (2005), and Jhappan and Stasiulis (2005) have highlighted how engagement with Disney culture helps shape self-identity, as participants learn a sense of other, or *not-me*, via specific signifiers within Disney's portrayal of racial and ethnic stereotypes. Adding to this body of work, I ask, who in our culture have we learned, through internalizing Disney's narratives, to position as heroes, villains, sidekicks, and comic relief? How does our engagement with these representations help shape or affect our real-life attitudes and assumptions about ethnicity and nationality?

In this chapter, I address these questions by sharing how university students constructed their own self-identities through a recognition of ethnic identity as "other" as they deconstructed Disney's visual culture. The class in which these analyses took place fulfilled requirements for undergraduate students across many disciplines to hone their academic writing skills, as well as to gain tools to examine and discuss issues of cultural diversity. Students researched and reflected upon their own consumption of culture via visual artifacts in their personal, professional, and cultural lives to build researched personal narrative essays. In doing so, the class critically investigated how personal, national, and global identities of individuals and societies are social constructions inherited through the institutions such as family and education, rather than serendipitous or due to genetics or evolution.

Students conducted this investigation through examining images of their lived worlds as visual text, using semiotic analysis methods such as denotation and connotation and the identification of signs, symbols, and icons. In Charles Peirce's system of semiotic analysis (as described by Hoopes, 1991), denotation refers to the identification of visible aspects of an image, connotation refers to the inferred meanings derived from denotations, and signs, symbols, and icons are categories or types of meaning making. Through semiotic analysis, students examined what they recognized as comprising visual representations of "being American" at a personal, local, national, and global level. Through student writing and in-class discussions, students deconstructed associated aspects of American identity such as race, ethnicity, class, and originary nationalities of America's residents in reference to their own lived experiences; they also reflected on the power dynamics of ethnic identity constructions in America in the context of their personal experiences of engaging with Disney as visual artifacts. In what follows, all quotations are from unpublished student papers and class discussions taught over three years.

ACCENTED OTHERS: LANGUAGE AS A CHARACTER TRAIT

Pinpointing denotations of how they identified central and secondary characters in Disney films, several students noted that main and positive characters typically have noticeably American accents. Sula, for instance, wrote about *Aladdin* (Clements & Musker, 1992) that "It is remarkable that Aladdin and Jasmine, who look white, have American accents, while Jafar, who should be of the same ethnicity, looks darker and has a British accent. This is weird because they are all supposed to be Arab … and should speak the same way. I know it's a fantasy film but that's an odd choice for the filmmakers to have made." Other students reiterated this point, citing the difference between Pocahontas's accent and that of other Native Americans in the film. Discussing Disney films as products of, and fuel for, understanding American culture, students revealed that they were often confused about the differences between *race* and *ethnicity* and thus often used these two terms interchangeably. The tone and language of students' speaking and writing revealed that they very much assumed whiteness to be the norm of being American. Thus whiteness, and an assimilated accent of the sort adopted by national news anchors, was the standard against which otherness was read in terms of recognizing someone's ethnicity.

For example, Jake pointed out in a class discussion that "It seems that the less important or serious the character, the more 'ethnic' and broken, and away from mainstream American the accent gets," while Chelsea noted in her research paper that the sidekicks of the heroes and villains tended to have rather marked accents:

> Reviewing beloved Disney characters from my childhood, I notice with dismay that there is a pattern. The more comical and bumbling characters can always be identified to have a strong accent that is a signifier of race or ethnicity. Clownish Mushu from *Mulan* (Bancroft & Cook, 1998) who should, if anything, sound Chinese, but sounds black; Goofy Sebastian from *Little Mermaid* (Clements & Musker, 1989) is Jamaican, the sly hyenas from *The Jungle Book* (Disney & Reitherman, 1967) and *Lion King* (Disney & Minkoff, 1994) are Hispanic, and fussy Timon, also from *Lion King*, is clearly Jewish. While I appreciate that not everyone sounds white and American, it seems unfair that no Disney hero or heroine has had an ethnic accent, at least as far as I could find. The closest anyone comes to this is Mike Wozowski, the anxious Jewish character from *Monsters Inc.* (Docter, Silverman, & Unkrich, 2001). Although I think he's a sidekick, he's almost a protagonist. Also, I am not sure whether he's actually supposed to represent Jewish ethnicity, or New Yorkers as a tribe!

Kaiya, an international freshman student said that watching the Disney Channel made her cringe because its overt stereotypes of characters in the name of humor seemed racist. She wrote:

> So many characters that are not white are such caricatures. Ravi from *Jessie* (Ryan & List, 2011) has a fake Indian accent which is awful because the actor who plays Ravi doesn't talk like that. Such portrayals make the inclusion of characters like Ravi seem like tokens of multiculturalism, rather than honest representations of American culture. Watching this show, I feel like apologizing to and for both Indians and Americans.

Students like Chelsea, Jake, Kaiya, and Sula effectively used the tools of semiotic analysis to explain their recognition of accented language as a marker of ethnic culture. This enabled them to review and critique problematic representations of multiculturalism and to raise vibrant discussions in classes about the nature of ethnic and racial identity.

Chelsea's remark that "… not everyone sounds white and American," reveals how ethnicity is associated with non-whiteness, as well as with accents that do not follow the linguistic norms of what used to be known as General American (Labov, Ash, & Boberg, 2008); this remark furthermore positions being ethnic as somehow less American. While students who were born and reared in the United

States tended not to see these differences as problematic, students whose families were recent immigrants, acknowledged feeling othered by being perceived as "more ethnic," and were more vocal about the impact of representations such as those described above. Based on these student voices, exaggerated representations in Disney subscribe to and build upon these assumptions, often combining them to reify this into cultural beliefs about how accents signify presence or lack of American identity in terms of ethnicity.

SAVAGERY AS A SIGNIFIER OF ETHNIC AS OTHER

Several students recognized how their engagements with Disney, especially the animated films, led them to identify the good guys and main characters as American or more characteristic of being American. No matter that the story was set in another part of the world, or in a fantasy land with racially diverse characters or even anthropomorphic characters; the heroes of the story–the hopeful, the adventurous, the righteous, the eventually victorious characters–were synonymous with an American ideal. Blake wrote,

> I am amazed by how cleverly Disney switches our perspective as viewers to that of the nice guys. Reflecting on my own gaze as viewer, I realize that I identify the nice guys as American, and from this point of view I notice that in Disney, the nice guys might be characters of any race or ethnicity but if they aren't desirable elements of society, they become significantly more foreign, and ethnic.

In his paper, Blake noted that as a child he always watched *Peter Pan* (Disney et al., 1953) from the perspective of Peter, identifying Peter, as well as himself, as American, while he positioned Wendy, the Native Americans and, the pirates, as foreign. He remarked on his unconscious assumption that Native Americans are non-Americans, explaining that because of the way in which they were portrayed in the film as an "other" culture, they became an ethnic group that was as strange and exotic to him as pirates.

Other students, including two international students, made note of internalizing the hero/heroine as American, even when, as children, they pictured themselves in the roles. Concurrently, they saw savagery and exoticness as a marker of ethnic otherness in the products of Disney studios and entertainment; this dark savagery stands in contrast to the bright "can-do" attitude that is at the center of Disney's American identity. Examples of this dark savagery trope cited by students included vicious Jafar in *Aladdin,* as well as the merchant's song, also in *Aladdin,* that narrates the barbarian nature of the place "where they cut off your nose if you don't like their face"; duplicitous Sher Khan in *The Jungle Book*; and the nefarious villain of *Phineas and Ferb* (Povenmire, 2007), Dr. Heinz Doofenshmirtz, who is from a fictional Eastern European country.

In reflecting upon how he understood which characters depicted American identity in Disney, Blake tried to explain that while early characters like Dumbo and Mickey Mouse are easy to spot as racist because of the contexts of American racial history, more recent ethnic characters portrayed as dark and savage are accepted with little fuss because they are clearly "not us." According to Blake, certain problematic characters are accepted by mainstream viewers because they are so far from any possibility of self-identification as being American or about America, they are easy to dismiss as fantasy or humor. Therefore, in mainstream rhetoric they are not recognized or labeled as racist. He clarifies that, "Disney sets up distinctly non-American characters who will stand out as foreign and alien in every version of good-old-wholesome America. … They have ruthlessly set up ethnic characters who do not confirm to their [Disney's] American ideal as untrustworthy … that's a pretty scary idea to accept as entertainment and good fun."

This reading is evidence of Disney's success in promoting the rhetoric of American-ness as a land of the free and home of the brave—a narrative recognizable in fantasy settings, and internalized by both Americans and those who are not American—to create a glocal cultural instinct that perceives goodness, rightness, and being on the winning side as American, and everything else as foreign. That Disney leads us to conflate this subconscious idea with overt ethnic characteristics of physicality (color, facial features, accents, and clothing), confirms the need to continue teaching criticality using Disney.

"I HAVE NO ETHNIC IDENTITY"

The previous two themes contain indications that many students conflate whiteness with a lack of ethnicity. "I'm just white," they insist. "I'm not ethnic." They most commonly support this claim by demonstrating their lack of an accent (even though I insisted that everyone has an accent) and by stating that neither they nor their families observe ancestral rituals. Through further discussion and genealogical research, students would investigate and reveal their ethnic heritages, and Caucasian students were often struck by the idea that they too might be understood as "being ethnic." The class then investigated how rhetoric in popular culture supports the idea that whiteness equals a lack of ethnicity. Reflecting on their personal lives, students mused that the lack of a dominant culture's rituals led them to assume that they did not have an ethnic affiliation. Normalized Christian rituals were understood as mainstream and hence not interpreted as ethnic. Based on their descriptions, whiteness, a "normal" American accent, lack of overt ritualistic religious practice, and normative Western dress signified the absence of ethnicity, which was equated with Americanness. Students observed that Disney consistently contributes to the idea that ethnicity, skin color, and linguistic accents are directly linked. They argued that a majority of positive protagonists had no ethnicity and claimed that these characters were "just more American" even if they obviously *weren't* American, as in the case of John Smith of *Pocahontas* (Disney, Gabriel, & Goldberg, 1995) who was supposed to be English, or the protagonists, Dory and Marlin, from *Finding Nemo* (Stanton & Unkrich, 2003), which is set in Australia.

During class discussions on their own ethnic identities, students repeatedly voiced the idea that unless they had inherited hyphenated identities such as Italian-American, Chinese-American, African-American, Indian-American, or American-Indian, they did not identify as "being ethnic." In a discussion on hyphenated national identity, I asked students to visually portray such hyphenated identities, and then just American identity. Assured of a safe space, students portrayed hyphenated identities with ethnic signifiers such as food, dress, and physical characteristics. However, when asked to portray "American," they portrayed non-ethnic symbols like McDonald's and the American flag. It appeared that most students thought that an unhyphenated American identity was not ethnic and (usually) white. In one particularly heated discussion, a student declared, "I know I'm going to sound racist, but basically white people are not ethnic," to which another rebutted, "Irish-Americans are white and they're ethnic." To this, the first speaker promptly replied, "Only if you're a leprechaun and in *Luck of the Irish*."

In follow-up discussions about ethnically hyphenated identity in America, students explored what it means to conflate whiteness with non-ethnicity, and as a corollary, what it means to "other" people even in the presence of difference. For example, they discussed how Aladdin growing whiter through the duration of the Disney film might signify his receding ethnicity as he develops from a rather rascally vagabond into a hero who we can admire and trust and explored whether stereotypical "hick" characters like Mater in *Cars* (Disney, Lasseter, & Ranft, 2006) become less lovable for their drollery when they are read as portraying Appalachian culture as an ethnic type. Finally, one student ruminated that after the blatant racism of Si and Am in *Lady and the Tramp* (Disney et al., 1955), Disney has never featured any other overtly Thai characters; rather, such ethnic specificities have dwindled into general Asian racial types or become altogether absent. This student mused about whether this is a step forward or backward in globalized visual culture, questioning whether the incorporation of overt ethnic and racial types to accommodate multiculturalism is necessarily a good thing. The student further wondered if the removal of such stereotypes means that Americans have truly gone beyond caricatured misrepresentations of non-normative cultures and asked whether it is productive or unproductive to portray characters in ways that lead us to think about constructions of "us" and "them" in our visual cultures.

AMERICAN IDENTITY AND IMPLICATIONS OF IDENTIFYING "ETHNIC" AS "OTHER"

These investigations into Disney's representations of ethnicity reveal, first, that to these students, the "ethnic" is easily recognizable as a culture of "otherness," where otherness is understood in terms of being non-white, or overtly foreign in appearance, accent, or behavior. While stereotypes in early Disney productions such as the crows in *Dumbo* (Disney et al., 1941), or the Siamese cats in *Lady and the Tramp* are easily recognizable as troublesome by being overtly distasteful caricatures that call to mind America's racist past, more recent depictions, as in *Aladdin*, *Lion King*, *Jessie*, or *Pocahontas* need closer scrutiny because they set up ideas of generic feel-good protagonists who must bear, battle, or be amused by less powerful, or just lesser characters, just as the superpower America must battle, support, tolerate, or mentor the rest of the world. In Disney, acting as the representation of a noble, "magic kingdom" America, the ethnic others can be funny, silly, well-meaning, dangerous, untrustworthy, or just plain awkward, but they rarely fit the mold of the central character—the easily recognizable "American" protagonist. The exceptions reported by students included Lilo and her sister, who are read as "ethnic Hawaiian," in *Lilo and Stitch* (DeBlois & Sanders, 2002), and Russell, who is Asian American, from Pixar's *Up* (Docter & Peterson, 2009).

For these students, it appears that the issue is not only that ethnic minorities are stereotyped, but also that only certain ethnicities are visible or represented at all. This is an important issue given that The Walt Disney Company is so vast and holds such sway over how American culture is imagined at home and throughout the world. As my student, Hussain, wrote, "Disney needs to realize that America and the world is a lot more than black, white, and pan-Asian. Pixar has helped with *Up*, while *Brave* (Andrews, Chapman, & Purcell, 2012) and *Ratatouille* (Bird & Pinkava, 2007) are clearly about non-American contexts, which is a more honest and promising direction to go toward." In order to be truly global and respectful of its influence and embrace an inclusive American culture, Disney will need to stop rendering cultures invisible or in any way lesser.

Also emerging from student discourse addressing Disney's use of accents, clothing, and other signifiers of identity, is the suggestion that in order to be recognized as truly American, one needs to give up identification with aspects of a hyphenated ethnic identity. For instance, according to several students, one cannot be fully American as long as one continues to identify with an "other" culture that connotes loyalty to another nation's culture–such as Asian-American or Indian-American, or African-American. While this reads as somewhat absurd and casually racist, since the same students did not necessarily feel this way about Italian-Americans, Irish-Americans, or indeed, any European hyphenations, their views were supported by illustrations from representations in Disney. Validating existing research (Crum, 2010; Jhappan & Stasiulis, 2005) students provided examples of Disney where villains, crafty characters, and buffoons tend to have British, Islamic, and Latino/Hispanic characteristics, exotic characters tend to be Eastern European or Romani, and haughtiness is conveyed as French or British. They illustrated that a sense of belonging, as seen in shows on Disney XD, is conveyed by distinctly "American" accents, clothing, and behaviors. On shows like the *Suite Life of Zack and Cody* (Cross & Hoge, 2010) *Lab Rats* (Kallis, 2005), and *Pair of Kings* (Moore & Peterson, 2012), the racial and ethnic diversities of main characters are dissolved into a fun- and adventure-filled melting pot where no harm ever comes from what would, in real life, be generally considered pretty bad behavior on the part of a child. For example, Yung explained on a class discussion board that "These shows make you think (that) you can be Asian-American, or American. Whether or not you are a brat or urban princess, or a science nerd like in *Lab Rats,* it can be less awkward if you see yourself in there, as *just American* (emphasis added); it's less painful for a kid if there is not the added stereotype of identifying as—oh yes, that's me, the Asian-American." To this, another student, Jared, responded that Disney XD was getting it right—that to be American, people needed to give up their obsessions with the past. "You don't see a lot of white people hanging on to their German or English ancestry—like, I don't hyphenate as German or English though my family has both. Get over it, and show you're proud to be American." While Jared displays white privilege, Yung's writing indicates that visual culture giants like Disney could do a better job in conveying the dilemmas of American youth without reducing them to a fantasy-driven common denominator of all American-ness.

Finally, student analyses of the cuteness of obviously ethnic or foreign characters revealed that they find such representations othering—that is, those representations can be embarrassing, alienating, or condescending. While students found the acquisition of Pixar and Marvel to have brought more balance to Disney's portrayals of diversity (as in *Up*, *Brave*, *Wall-E* [Stanton, 2008], and the *The Avengers* [Whedon, 2012]), Disney Channels such as XD have a long way to go in producing critical shows that depict ethnic characters in unbiased ways or portray them as falling within the normative collection of character templates. As Jared shared in his culminating paper for the class, "It seems that Disney movies are examined a lot in classes like this, but no one seems to be looking at Disney TV, which is what kids nowadays are watching." Considering the popularity of Disney Channel shows among children and pre-teens, we might further examine how the ideologies of identity and ethnicity expressed through those texts have shaped the perceptions of older students.

DISNEY AND CRITICAL ART EDUCATION

In an era of globalization, the power of nation-states as controlling social imaginaries is on the decline. In retaliation, these nation-states regress to a "defensive and highly dangerous form of national identity (Hall, 1997, p. 178)," which may develop in two directions—global and local. As they impact each other reciprocally, these two directions become glocal (Appadurai, 1996; Hall, 1997). The danger in selling a mythical, singular national identity presented as a unified vision is that this singular identity diffuses difference and ignores the impacts of difference felt by those who are deemed non-normative or non-mainstream. In other words, fostering such singular identities leads to false articulations of the sociocultural and historical experiences of those who are identified as inside or outside of a mainstream culture but who inhabit and are affected by the politics and policies of nation-states. Such singular articulations of national identity, when translated into understandings of self and other, can result in the creation and maintenance of imbalances of power among peoples in the form of discrimination, invisibility, misunderstanding, and dis-identification or alienation. The reflections presented above, which revealed how ethnic otherness can be read in Disney's construction of a singular, normative American identity, are examples of how othering happens in visual culture.

In all their variation, the discussions examined here reflect a microcosm of the slipperiness and struggles of defining racial and ethnic identity in the United States, and of the global pervasiveness of American visual culture that Disney creates in and perpetuates through kinder-culture and beyond. Students' reflections on ethnicity as part of American identity point to national and global questions of social justice. Their discussions and writings addressed difference and raised queries about how representative images affect people in real ways as they process and communicate ideas about personal and national identity. As Tavin and Anderson (2003) note, "as critical art educators, we should investigate how corporations produce knowledge about the world, distribute and regulate information, help construct identity, and promote consumption in visual culture" (p. 34). Because Disney is so beloved, familiar, and globally recognized, it can be difficult to engage students in questioning their comfortable and unproblematized engagements with their own values and belief systems and to encourage them to consider points of view other than their own in order to understand and challenge their own problematic constructions of identity. Yet, because the ethnic fantasies constructed by Disney continue to perpetuate harmful stereotypes and cultural misconceptions, they must "be interrogated for the futures they envision, the values they promote, and the forms of identification they offer" (Giroux & Pollock, 2010, p. 7).

DISCUSSION QUESTIONS

1. How do current shows on the Disney XD channel construct normative representations of a generic American-ness, through their depictions of ethnic characters?
2. What is your understanding of what, or who, can claim an ethnic identity? Explain, using as an example, one or more of Disney's visual culture artifacts.
3. If you were to redesign a key Disney character to look, talk, or behave as a different ethnicity without losing their defining characteristics, how would you represent them differently? How might these changes affect the character's status and recognizability as an American cultural artifact?

REFERENCES

Appadurai, A. (1996). *Modernity at large: Cultural dimensions of globalization*. Minneapolis: University of Minnesota Press.

Bancroft, T. & Cook, B. (Producers), Bancroft, T., & Cook, B. (Directors). (1998). *Mulan* [Motion Picture]. United States: Walt Disney Pictures.

Bell, E., Haas, L., & Sells, L. (Eds.). (1995). *From mouse to mermaid: The politics of film, gender, and culture*. Bloomington: Indiana University Press.

Bernardi, D. (2008). *The persistence of whiteness: Race and contemporary Hollywood cinema*. New York: Routledge.

Bret, T. (n.d.). Racebent Disney. Retrieved from: http://lettherebedoodles.tumblr.com/post/102741589289/heres-a-compilation-of-my-racebent-series-with

Brode, D. (2005). *Multiculturalism and the mouse: Race and sex in Disney entertainment*. Austin: University of Texas Press.

Budd, M., & Kirsch, M. H. (Eds.). (2005). *Rethinking Disney: Private control, public dimensions*. Middletown, CT: Wesleyan University Press.

Cheu, J. (2013). *Diversity in Disney films: Critical essays on race, ethnicity, gender, sexuality and disability*. Jefferson, NC: McFarland.

Clements, R., & Musker, J. (Producer), Clements, R., & Musker, J. (Directors). (1989). *The little mermaid* [Motion Picture]. United States: Walt Disney Pictures.

Clements, R., & Musker, J. (Producer), Clements, R., & Musker, J. (Directors). (1992). *Aladdin* [Motion Picture]. United States: Walt Disney Pictures.

Cross, D., & Hoge, D. (2010, October 10). *Pair of kings* [TV Broadcast]. USA: Disney Channel.

Crum, M. R. (2010). *The creation of black character formulas: A critical examination of stereotypical anthropomorphic depictions and their role in maintaining whiteness*. M.A. Thesis. The Ohio State University. Retrieved from: https://etd.ohiolink.edu/ap:10:0::NO:10:P10_ETD_SUBID:71035

Davis, A. M. (2014). *Handsome heroes and vile villains: Masculinity in Disney's feature films*. Bloomington, IN: John Libbey Publishing.

Desai, D., & Darts, D. (2013). Critical art education: The art of social (ex)change. In K. Tavin & C. B. Morris (Eds.), *Stand(ing) up, for a change: Voices of arts educators* (pp. 20–27). Reston, VA: National Art Education Association.

Disney, W. (Producer), Allers, R., & Minkoff, R. (Directors). (1994). *The lion king* [Motion Picture]. United States: Walt Disney Pictures.

Disney, W. (Producer), Armstrong, S., Ferguson, N., Jackson, W., Kinney, J., Roberts, B., Sharpsteen, B., & Elliotte, J. (Directors). (1941). *Dumbo*. [Motion Picture]. United States: Walt Disney Pictures.

Disney, W. (Producer), Gabriel, M., & Goldberg, E. (Directors). (1995). *Pocahontas* [Motion Picture]. United States: Walt Disney Pictures.

Disney, W. (Producer), Geronimi, C., Jackson, W., Luske, H., & Kinney, J. (Directors). (1953). *Peter Pan* [Motion Picture]. United States: Walt Disney Pictures.

Disney, W. (Producer), Geronimi, C., Jackson, W., & Luske, H. (Directors). (1955). *Lady and the tramp* [Motion Picture]. United States: Walt Disney Pictures.

Disney, W. (Producer), Lasseter, J., & Ranft, J. (Directors). (2006). *Cars* [Motion Picture]. United States: Walt Disney Pictures.

Disney, W. (Producer), Reitherman, W. (Director). (1967). *The jungle book* [Motion Picture]. United States: Walt Disney Pictures.

Freedman, K. (2003). *Teaching visual culture: Curriculum, aesthetics, and the social life of art*. New York: Teachers College Press.

Giroux, H. A. (2004). Are Disney movies good for your kids? In S. R. Steinberg & J. Kincheloe (Eds.), *Kinderculture: The corporate construction of childhood.* 2nd ed. (pp. 53–67). Boulder, CO: Westview Press.

Giroux, H. A., & Pollock, G. (2010). *The mouse that roared: Disney and the end of innocence*. Lanham, MD: Rowman & Littlefield.

Hall, S. (1997). The local and global: Globalization and ethnicity. In A. McClintock & Social Text Collective (Eds.), *Dangerous liaisons: Gender, nation, and postcolonial perspectives* (pp. 173–187). Minneapolis: University of Minnesota Press.

Hoopes, J. (Ed.). (1991). *Peirce on signs: Writings on semiotics by Charles Sanders Peirce.* 1st ed. Chapel Hill: The University of North Carolina Press.

Jhappan, R., & Stasiulis, D. (2005). Anglophilia and the discrete charm of the English voice in Disney's *Pocahontas* films. In M. Budd & M. H. Kirsch (Eds.), *Rethinking Disney: Private control, public dimensions* (pp. 151–180). Middletown, CT: Wesleyan University Press.

Kallis, D. (2005, March 18). *The suite life of Zack and Cody* [TV Broadcast]. United States: Disney Channel.

Labov, W., Ash, S., & Boberg, C. (2008). *Atlas of North American English: Phonetics, phonology and sound change* (pp. 187–208). New York: Mouton de Gruyter.

Moore, B., & Peterson, C. (2012). *Lab rats* [TV Broadcast]. United States: Disney Channel.

Povenmire, D. (2007, August 17). *Phineas and Ferb* [TV Show]. United States: Disney Channel.

Ryan, D., & List, P. (2011, September 30). *Jessie* [TV Broadcast]. United States: Disney Channel.

Sammond, N. (2005). *Babes in yomorrowland: Walt Disney and the making of the American child, 1930–1960*. Durham, NC: Duke University Press.

Tavin, K. M. (2005). Opening e-marks: Critical antecedents of visual culture in art education. *Studies in Art Education*, *47*(1), 5–22. http://doi.org/10.2307/25475769

Tavin, K. M. (2010). Art education as culture jamming: Public pedagogy in visual culture. In J. A. Sandlin, B. D. Schultz, & J. Burdick (Eds.), *Handbook of public pedagogy: Education and learning beyond schooling* (pp. 434–443). New York: Routledge.

Tavin, K. M., & Anderson, D. (2003). Teaching (popular) visual culture: Deconstructing Disney in the elementary art classroom. *Art Education*, *56*(3), 21.

Walt Disney Pictures Morris, J. (Producer), Stanton, A. (Director). (2008). *WALL·E*. [Motion Picture]. United States: Walt Disney Pictures.

Walt Disney Pictures (Producer), Stanton, A., & Unkrich, L. (Directors). (2003). *Finding Nemo* [Motion Picture]. United States: Walt Disney Pictures.

Walt Disney Pictures (Producer), Whedon, J. (Director). (2012). *The avengers*. [Motion Picture]. United States: Walt Disney Pictures.

Walt Disney Pictures, & Pixar (Producers), Andrews, M., Chapman, B., & Purcell, S. (Directors). (2012). *Brave* [Motion Picture]. United States: Walt Disney Pictures.

Walt Disney Pictures, & Pixar (Producers), Bird, B., & Pinkava, J. (Directors). (2007). *Ratatouille*. [Motion Picture]. United States: Walt Disney Pictures.

Walt Disney Pictures (Producer). DeBlois, D., & Sanders, C. (Directors). (2002). *Lilo & Stitch* [Motion Picture]. United States: Walt Disney Pictures.

Walt Disney Pictures, & Pixar (Producers), Docter, P., & Peterson, B. (Directors). (2009). *Up* [Motion Picture]. United States:: Walt Disney Pictures.

Walt Disney Pictures, & Pixar (Producers), Docter, P., Silverman, D., & Unkrich, L. (Directors). (2001). *Monsters, inc.* [Motion Picture]. United States: Walt Disney Pictures.

PART THREE

Teaching Consumers

CHAPTER EIGHT

Teaching Disney Critically in the Age of Perpetual Consumption

WILLIAM M. REYNOLDS

Yes, I will admit it. I was a proud member of the Mickey Mouse Club. I had a Mickey Mouse Membership pin, Mouseketeer ears, and a Mouseketeer Member t-shirt. I was, indeed, a card-carrying member. The Mickey Mouse Club was on television weekdays from 1955–1959 and then in syndication from 1962–1968. I was happy to belong to the club. Bauman (2000) comments on this feeling of wanting to belong that is so often tied to consuming:

> Inside their temples the shoppers/consumers may find moreover, what they zealously, yet in vain, seek outside: the comforting feeling of belonging—the reassuring feeling of being part of a community. (p. 99)

The original series featured a memorable all-white cast. Jimmy Dodd, who wrote the theme song (Dodd, 1955), was the host and head Mouseketeer. He spoke words of inspiration and morality to eager young viewers. Big Roy, whom Walt Disney apparently picked for the show because he was big and funny looking, was the adult Mouseketeer. Among the most memorable Mouseketeers were Annette Funicello, who went on to become a beach icon in films with Frankie Avalon, Cubby O'Brien, who became a drummer for the Carpenters, and Bobbie Burgess, who later danced his way to fame on the *Lawrence Welk Show*. Most of the profits from the *Mickey Mouse Club* went into funding the development of Disneyland. In the 1950s, Disney also produced the television program, *Disneyland*, which had the divisions, *Frontier Land*, *Tomorrow Land*, *Adventure Land*, and *Fantasy Land*, and which included famous segments such as *Zorro* and *Davy Crockett*. The show and spin-off consumer items were profitable; for example, sales of Davy Crockett raccoon skin caps in the 1950s reached "$300 million ($2.6 billion in 2014 dollars)" (Crockett, 2014, p. 1). Yes, I had one of those, too.

I include this stroll down Mickey Mouse memory lane as a reminder that, while we may shake our heads and wonder why youth are so infatuated, enamored, and unwaveringly loyal to Disney, some of us were just as taken not so long ago. These fond childhood memories also provide an important example of the allure of nostalgia and the important role that corporations can have in shaping our early lives. In an advanced capitalist society where media conglomerates like Disney are ever present, no one stands outside the enticements of the "consuming life" (Bauman, 2007), whether lured by a Lexus or by a raccoon skin cap. America is, as Bauman (2007) observes, a "society of consumers" in which the choice to consume is promoted, encouraged, and enforced above "all alternative cultural options" (p. 53). In other words, we live in "a society in which adapting to the precepts of consumer culture and following them strictly is, to all practical intents and purposes, the sole unquestionably approved choice" (Bauman, 2007, p. 53). Considering the inevitability of this consumer consciousness, I argue that teaching critically through Disney, as I attempt to do with my undergraduate students in education, requires an understanding of the ways in which youth are invested in consumption. I advance such an understanding in this chapter first by positioning Disney within the context of the politics of the culture of consumption. Then, I examine the process of critically teaching Disney within that context in order to explore current attitudes of youth toward Disney. Finally, I examine Disney loyalty as an example of the ideologies produced by neoliberal educational policies and free market practices within a culture of perpetual, disposable consumption, and explore possibilities for resisting those ideologies.

DISNEY AND THE CULTURE OF CONSUMPTION

The Walt Disney Company, as one of the largest corporations within what Bauman (2007) terms a "society of consumers," has a ubiquitous cultural presence. Disney owns Touchstone Pictures, Marvel Entertainment, Lucas Film, Walt Disney Pictures, and The Muppets Studio. The Walt Disney Company also owns radio stations across the globe, publishing companies, theme parks and resorts around the world, ESPN, Baby Einstein, and Disney retail stores (Columbia Journalism Review, 2013). As one of the major entertainment corporations, its influence on popular culture is significant. One of its most notable influences is its fostering of perpetual consumerism; that is, Disney, through its consumer products, processes, and experiences, facilitates consumer longing. This consumer longing, in turn, produces particular types of human beings. As Bauman (2011) observes, this schooling in consumerism is never-ending, fueled by a consumer logic that teaches us to always aspire for "new and improved" commodities:

> Today's tokens of 'being ahead' have to be acquired quickly, while those of yesterday must be just as swiftly confined to the scrapheap. The injunction to keep an eye on 'what has already gone out of fashion' must be observed as consciously as the obligation to keep on top of what is (at this moment) new and up to date. (p. 22)

Here, Bauman (2011) uses fashion as one example of this kind of perpetual consumerism in which we dispose of "outdated" commodities for "updated" ones, but this longing can be applied to any realm of consumption or consumer product, including those produced by Disney.

Children desire cultural artifacts, and oftentimes these desires are directed specifically towards Disney products, and, like fashion, there are always new products coming onto the market and old ones falling out of favor. Because of the desire to keep up with new trends, children anxiously await the newest Disney film or theme park ride. Children have a feverish desire to follow Disney's pathways to buying, which occur not by happenstance, but through marketing practices such as synergy. A typical pattern to this consumption begins with children, their excitement at high levels, being taken to see a Disney film. Next, children see advertisements for goods depicting the films' characters and then desire to be taken to Walmart, Kmart, Target, or to the closest Disney store to buy some of the hundreds of choices in toys, posters, clothes, furniture, or bedding items. On the way home from the store, with their newly acquired Disney items, children might desire to go to McDonald's or Burger King. While they might like the food in their Happy Meals or want to play on the playground, they also might want the toy in the Happy Meal that is linked to the Disney film they just saw. Through this cycle Disney becomes part of their McChildhood (Horan, 2013). In addition to the longing for each individual item or toy, children also often wish to own the entire collection. It is even possible to acquire those toys via sites like eBay to, perhaps, nostalgically complete a collection. The desire to acquire these items is as intense as having just the right piece of fashion from the acceptable designer.

Then, just as with clothing, when a particular Disney-branded product goes out of fashion, the old products are tossed into the scrapheap and new products are purchased. An interesting factor in the more recent consumer mentality is that the length of time between in style and out of style has become increasingly shorter. The same is true for childhood desire for consumer items. Many Disney, Hasbro, and Mattel toys now sit in boxes in attics or basements of childhood homes, relegated to obscurity for millennials. When young adults do think of those discarded toys, it is to wonder whether they could sell some of the old toys as collector items and make money to buy the latest piece of technology or some other consumer item. Nothing lasts very long in the consumer society agenda whether it is Disney items or smart phones. Those items are as quickly disposed of as they are acquired.

The ability to dispose of "outdated" commodities for "updated" products requires a certain degree of economic privilege and thus constructs the extent to which one belongs to the consumer society. Consuming just the right Disney items and having them displayed in a child's room provides, in our consumer society, a sense of belonging. We all have the same hip stuf and feel the strong need to keep doing so. As Bauman (2007) observes:

> The reference to '*staying* ahead' intuits a reliable precaution against the danger of overlooking the moment when the current emblems of 'belonging' go out of circulation, having been replaced by fresh ones, and when their inattentive bearers risk falling by the wayside—which, in the case of the market-mediated bid for membership, translates as the sentiment of being rejected, excluded, abandoned and lonely, and ultimately rebounds in the searing pain of personal inadequacy. (p. 83, italics in original)

Thus, the stuff we have is intimately connected to our identities and to our feelings and experiences of being included or left out. Disney is particularly adept at capitalizing on our need for belonging by constantly producing new products and experiences that constitute the Disney experience. A recent ad campaign that asserts, "We All Have a Disney Side," even goes so far as to suggest that we "all" belong to the Disneyverse in some way. The discourses of belonging, both to Disney and to consumer society writ large, perpetuate the cycles of consumption.

TEACHING DISNEY CRITICALLY

Is there a way to demystify the lure of consuming Disney? To be sure, meaningfully engaging students in critically analyzing Disney is a complex enterprise. However, guiding students in understanding Disney's role in the consumer society is a step in that direction. My personal attempts at teaching Disney critically within the context of the kind of society described above demonstrate that difficulty and raise questions about the ties millennial youth have to Disney. My experiences, some of which I describe here, also illustrate how crucial it is to neither demonize Disney nor impose our own views on Disney onto students. Rather than telling my students what Disney "means," I take the "different approach" to the study of Disney described by Giroux (1999), which "highlights the pedagogical and the contextual by raising questions about Disney itself (p. 10). Following Giroux's model, I engage my undergraduate pre-service teachers in exploring the role that Disney plays in "(1) in shaping public memory, national identity, gender roles, and childhood values; (2) in suggesting who qualifies as an American; and (3) in determining the role of consumerism in American life" (p. 10).

I have used this approach every semester for the past decade or so, and each time I discuss Disney with the undergraduate pre-service teachers in my classes, they get angry with me. One student wrote in an anonymous evaluation that he or she thought I was pretty cool until I started criticizing Disney. This student also indicated that I was making the entire class angry. I believe this ire arises because when we critique Disney, we are also calling into question students' strongly held beliefs. The hegemony of Disney is deeply embedded in their subjectivities, and by challenging their beliefs, I am, in the students' words, pushing it too far. Initially, I was shocked by the anger and resistance to the critical discussion of Disney and surprised by the fierce loyalty my students, 20-something millennials, demonstrated for Disney. Clearly, I was treading on sacred ground for these young adults, who were strongly invested in the idea that Disney is not so much a form of education but merely "harmless entertainment." However, as Giroux (1999) explains, "Education is never innocent, because it always presupposes a particular view of citizenship, culture, and society. And yet it is the very appeal to innocence, bleached of any semblance of politics that has become a defining feature of Disney culture and pedagogy" (p. 31). As Giroux and Pollock (2010b) explain, The Walt Disney Company has long capitalized on its reputation of innocence:

> Indeed, Walt Disney quickly saw the advantages to linking childhood innocence with home entertainment, which became the pedagogical vehicle to promote a set of values and practices that associate the safeguarding of childhood with a strong investment in the nuclear family, middle class Protestant values, and the market as a sphere of consumption. (p. 18)

Disrupting that ideology of innocence can be a difficult task because it is tied to the nostalgia for childhood. Thus, when we begin to critically discuss Disney films, shows, theme parks, suburban communities, cruises, vacations, and consumer items, we are questioning not only Disney, but also the heartfelt nostalgia of a particular generation.

The millennial generation might appear to be unattached from anything other than their smartphones, but my experiences teaching them have shown me that they are also fiercely attached to their past (Rodriguez, 2014). As Boym (2001) explains, nostalgia may be a response to the fast-paced, fragmented society in which these students have come of age:

> In counterpoint to our fascination with cyberspace and the virtual global village, there is no less global epidemic of nostalgia, an affective yearning for a community with a collective memory, a longing for continuity in a fragmented world. Nostalgia inevitably reappears as defense mechanism in a time of accelerated rhythms of life and historical upheavals. (p. xiv)

I have seen nostalgia as a counterpoint to virtual existence expressed in discussions with students. Although my students are extremely attached to technology, they engage with critiques of that technology in ways that are vastly different than with critiques of Disney. For example, they do not take offense when we criticize smart phones; they find it humorous when we discuss how attached they are to technology from smart phones to big screen televisions. But when the critique is centered on Disney, an iconic and beloved element of their past, the tone is very different. For example, when I show *Mickey Mouse Monopoly* (Sun & Picker, 2001), a documentary that critically examines the stories that Disney films tell about race, gender, and class, my students become defensive. Some claim that films made in the 1940s and 1950s are old and outdated and argue that films have "improved" since then, in spite of the fact that more recent films can also be read for their regressive ethnic, racial, and gender stereotypes. Perhaps their reluctance to critique Disney may be because these students are the "zero generation relegated to zones of social and economic abandonment and marked by zero jobs, zero future, zero hope" (Giroux, 2013, p. 1). When faced with the realistic possibility that they will encounter huge student loan debts and teaching jobs that pay very low wages and are not guaranteed for the long term, the Disney-constructed vision of the world seems very desirable. Students also want to preserve that romanticized vision for their future children. A critique of Disney is thus viewed as an assault, an attack on their nostalgic sense of stability or continuity, a longing for a time of stability that never existed. Such nostalgic sentiments are reflected in a quote from a Disney fan of the same generation:

> "There's something about Disney," said Megan Eisenberg, a second-year exercise science major from Roswell. "There's something about what you saw when you were younger and are now like 'Let's watch it again, even though we're all 20 years old and shouldn't be watching' [*The Lion King* (1994)] but it was fun when we were five, so it should be fun when we're 20." (Abercrombie, 2014, p. 1)

In a time of uncertainty for these millennials, the nostalgia of Disney allows them some comfort.

The powerful nostalgia that students have constructed around Disney is inevitably linked to their experiences as consumers of Disney products. Disney films and consumer items were a large part of their childhoods. Most of the students can sing along to every song from Disney films. They had many of the consumer products that Disney produced and sold in Disney stores and in Walmart as well as the items that were provided as prizes in McDonald's Happy Meals. Their bedrooms were decorated with *Lion King* sheets, pillowcases, and wall posters. The women in my classes fondly recall dressing up like Disney Princesses and collecting Princess memorabilia. They had Disney backpacks and clothing featuring licensed characters.

Yet, while they are quick to describe themselves as enthusiastic consumers of Disney products, students have difficulty deconstructing the strong connection between their desire to consume those products and the impact Disney has had on their thinking. However, my discussions with students have revealed that their nostalgic longing is closely connected to their consumption both of Disney films themselves and of the corresponding merchandise. Disney thus becomes part of how they see and construct both themselves and their childhoods.

When Disney is approached through critical pedagogical lenses, then, educators should understand that students have emotional and nostalgic ties to Disney that are connected to their very identities. Thus, critical analysis of Disney should not consist of the imposition of critical notions, which can be read by students as just another form of oppression. The critique of consumerism alone is already a huge first step for these millennials, who often ask me—"What is wrong with buying things?" With regard to Disney, student comments frequently center on the notion that critics are reading too much into Disney texts, whether the analysis centers on race, gender, class, or consumption. Students also often ask me, "Don't you have anything better to do?" These questions and subsequent class discussions suggest that students are rarely asked their opinion and are not comfortable disagreeing with the professor. And, although they have been told in many classes that it is acceptable to disagree with the professor, they have found that it is not true in other contexts. Furthermore, professors seldom actually listen to student opinions even if they share them—this is a major impediment that must be dealt with before Disney dialogue enters the class.

Instructors must also ensure that the critical pedagogies students encounter are not totalizing critiques of Disney as evil (Burdick, Sandlin, & O'Malley, 2013, p. 85). Discussing Henry Giroux's critique of Disney, Savage (2013) writes:

> Popular public pedagogies, therefore, are reduced to little more than mechanisms for exercising ideological domination over children. The core problem here is similar to that of political publics, insofar as these readings veer into totalizing visions of public pedagogy, which gloss over the disparate and often contradictory ways cultural texts and discourses are translated into cultural meanings. (pp. 85–86)

Instead of demonizing Disney, critical pedagogical analysis in pre-service teacher classrooms can be, rather, an attempt to teach Disney within a framework of radical listening, open dialogue, and radical love. Radically listening to student points of view and trying to establish a community of understanding with students are an important part of the pedagogical process. Freire (1998) explains the importance of mutual listening to forming critical dialogues within communities of critical teaching and learning:

> True listening does not diminish in me the exercise of my right to disagree, to oppose, to take a position. On the contrary, it is in knowing how to listen well that I better prepare myself to speak or to situate myself vis-à-vis the ideas being discussed as a subject capable

> of presence, of listening "connectedly" and without prejudices to what the other is saying. (p. 107)

Engaging in open, honest dialogue about Disney can open a pathway for other critical discussions because students can discuss popular culture and do so willingly. Freire (2006) also discusses the role that radical love plays in fostering critical dialogue:

> Dialogue cannot exist, however, in the absence of a profound love for the world and for people. The naming of the world, which is an act of creation and recreation, is not possible if it is not infused with love. Love is at the same time the foundation of dialogue and dialogue itself. (p. 89)

For me, radical love in a classroom is possible when instructors care about students enough to not only share and discuss knowledge but also to allow critique and the development of critical consciousness.

Teaching Disney critically is not about positioning the teacher as the expert possessing the ideologically correct point of view on Disney as the Darth Vader of popular culture. In this situation, the teacher becomes just as reprehensible as those who enjoy banking useless information into students for test taking. But, a dialogical classroom is about mutually discussing and attempting to understand a cultural phenomenon/corporation that has influenced us all and made us good consumers starting in childhood. None of us stands outside the consumer imperative. Critical pedagogy is about developing classrooms where we, as a community, try to acknowledge the power of corporate capitalism to create our way of being in the world and try through dialogue to understand how this hegemony systemically operates. How does the critical teaching of Disney assist in the deconstruction and demystification of the present milieu? How does placing Disney within a critical pedagogical context resist the onslaught of the corporatization of the university and public education? I turn to these questions next.

THE PRECARIOUS FUTURE OF DISNEY MILLENNIALS

Contemporary educational reform policies reflect the neoliberal, social Darwinist, consumerist, and free-market discourses that have replaced pragmatic progressivism over the last six decades. These policies, such as the No Child Left Behind Act and the Common Core State Standards Initiative, have further ensconced children in the same market-oriented ideologies that drive Disney loyalty. School thus becomes part of the same educative process through which children learn consumer habits and are purposely directed toward consumption. Schooling, like Disney, "promotes cultural homogeneity and political conformity, waging a battle against individuals and groups who believe that central to democratic public life is the necessity of democratizing cultural institutions" (Giroux, 2009, p. 250). Millennial consumers are directed toward becoming not active citizens who engage in the process of democracy and social justice but insatiable buyers who want the latest products. As Giroux and Pollock (2010a) observe, "If Disney had its way kids' culture would become not merely a new market for accumulation of capital, but a petri dish for producing new commodified subjects" (p. 11). Similarly, schooling, with its test-driven, factory model ideology, turns our children into compliant purchasers who wait impatiently for the next new thing to buy. The free market depends on them. Disney depends on them. Apple depends on them. Vera Bradley depends on them.

While Disney provides an ideal lens through which to explore the power of corporate media conglomerates to shape consumer ideologies, we have to remember that Disney is just one Lego in the consumerist building, but it is a big Lego that has been around for a long time. As I have described here, students are strongly attached to Disney, which poses a challenge for meaningful critical analysis. Furthermore, their embeddedness in the global, corporate capitalist agenda of consumerism places them in an interesting dilemma. Can the seductive discourses of neoliberalism be resisted? And, if they resist free-market ideologies, what are their other choices? Every aspect of education and living in general is a target for privatization, corporatization, and global capitalism, processes which have helped to create what Standing (2011) has called the *precariat*, a term derived from the two words *precarious* and *proletariat*. *Precarious* is a term that reminds us of the dangerous, risky, and unstable. The proletariat refers to the working class who we still think of as industrial workers. Standing further explains that those in the precariat

> have lives dominated by insecurity, uncertainty, debt and humiliation. They are becoming denizens rather than citizens, losing cultural, civil, social, political and economic rights built up over generations. The precariat is also the first class in history expected to endure labor and work at a lower level than the schooling it typically acquires. In an ever more unequal society, its relative deprivation is severe. (p. 1)

My students, as potential members of this precariat, will be hired for jobs for which they are overqualified and that offer little financial security. They are being trained to be public school teachers at a time when even the continuation of public schools is risky and unstable. What I prefer to call not teacher education but, rather, the "training of teachers," is now being privatized by companies like Pearson, a corporate giant in its own right:

> If you haven't heard of Pearson, perhaps you have heard of one of the publishers they own, like Adobe, Scott Foresman, Penguin, Longman, Wharton, Harcourt, Puffin, Prentice Hall, or Allyn & Bacon (among others). If you haven't heard of Pearson, perhaps

> you have heard of one of their tests, like the National Assessment of Educational Progress, the Stanford Achievement Test, the Millar Analogy Test, or the G.E.D. Or their data systems, like PowerSchool and SASI. (Job, 2012, p. 1)

Considering Pearson's growing ubiquity as a purveyor of educational commodities, it is easy to envision the actual content of teacher education courses being determined by corporations. Any opportunity for pre-service teachers to engage in critical ideas and questions fades into the merciless onslaught of megacorporations like Pearson, as students training to be teachers are increasingly becoming part of Standing's (2011) precariat. They will have the education to qualify them to become teachers but may very likely have to settle for jobs that have little or no security, no healthcare, and little intellectual satisfaction. The type of education that a Pearson teacher-training program would provide would be the type that will allow certification only if the potential candidate can spew forth the Pearson-produced codes. This is not what either critical educators or teacher education students want. A Pearson-infused training of teachers will certainly not have in its curriculum outlines a place for a unit on the dialogue about consumer consciousness and Disney, and thus the future of critical pedagogy in teacher education is precariously at risk.

Considering the prevalence of perpetual consumption, moving toward education for critical consciousness, complicated conversations, and social justice is a daunting task. However, there are glimmers of hope in the resistance on the part of teachers who refuse to give standardized tests, students who refuse to take them, and parents who support both those teachers and students. These initial resistances to market-oriented educational policies are the beginnings of more resistance and real change in the public schools and in the neoliberal society in which they exist (Reynolds, 2014). Perhaps, teaching Disney in ways that raise questions about our connections to consumer life and our nostalgic visions of the past littered with various consumer products can play a part in promoting resistance to the ever-growing importance of things. Indeed, the importance and elevation of things over human beings is one of the central questions for critical pedagogues in the 21st century.

DISCUSSION QUESTIONS

1. What are some of your fondest childhood memories? How did those memories contribute to the formation of your identity? What role did corporations like The Walt Disney Company play in producing these pleasurable childhood experiences?
2. Reflecting on your own educational experiences, in what ways were you encouraged toward cultural homogeneity and political conformity? What are

the benefits and disadvantages of contemporary educational reform policies that reflect the neoliberal, consumerist, and free-market discourses?

3. Teaching Disney critically is one small way to challenge our nostalgic visions of the past and our investments in consumer culture. What other possibilities are there for resisting the ideology of perpetual consumption?

REFERENCES

Abercrombie, C. (2014). Generation nostalgia: Millennials choose '90s entertainment over newer material. *The Red & Black.* Retrieved from: http://www.redandblack.com/variety/generation-nostalgia-millennials-chooseentertainment-over-newer-material/article_38307bdc-c5fd-11e3-992b-0017a43b2370.html

Bauman, Z. (2000). *Liquid modernity.* Malden, MA: Polity Press.

Bauman, Z. (2007). *Consuming life.* Malden, MA: Polity Press.

Bauman, Z. (2011). *Culture in a liquid modern world.* Malden, MA: Polity Press.

Boym, S. (2001). *The future of nostalgia.* New York: Basic Books.

Burdick, J., Sandlin, J. A., & O'Malley, M. (Eds.). (2013). *Problematizing public pedagogy.* New York: Routledge.

Columbia Journalism Review. (2013, February 14). *Who owns what.* Retrieved from: http://www.cjr.org/resources/?c=disney

Crockett, Z. (2014 October, 13). When coonskin caps were cool. *Priceonomincs.* Retrieved from: http://priceonomics.com/when-coonskin-caps-were-cool/

Dodd, J. (1955). The Mickey Mouse Club March. On *Official Mickey Mouse club record* [Vinyl]. Burbank, CA: Buena Vista Distribution Company.

Freire, P. (1998). *Pedagogy of freedom: Ethics, democracy and civic courage.* Lanham, MD: Rowman & Littlefield.

Freire, P. (2006). *Pedagogy of the oppressed.* 30th Anniversary ed. New York: Continuum.

Giroux, H. A. (1999). *The mouse that roared: Disney and the end of innocence.* Lanham, MD: Rowman & Littlefield.

Giroux, H. A. (2009). Turning America into a toy store. In J. A. Sandlin & P. McLaren (Eds.), *Critical pedagogies of consumption: Living and learning in the shadow of the "shopocalypse"* (pp. 249–259). New York: Routledge.

Giroux, H. A. (2013, February 27). The politics of disimagination and the pathologies of power. *Truthout.* Retrieved from: http://www.truth-out.org/news/item/14814-the-politics-of-disimagination-and-the-pathologies-ofpower#xiv

Giroux, H. A., & Pollock, G. (2010a, August 21). How Disney magic and the corporate media shape youth identity in the digital age. *Truthout.* Retrieved from: http://www.truth-out.org/opinion/item/2808: howdisney-magic-and-the-corporate-media-shape-youth-identity-in-the-digital-age

Giroux, H. A., & Pollock, G. (2010b). *The mouse that roared: Disney and the end of innocence.* Lanham, MD: Rowman & Littlefield.

Horan, M. (2013, November 8). 15 Happy Meal toys that made your McChildhood. Mashable.com. Retrieved from: http://mashable.com/2013/11/08/mcdonalds-toys/

Job, J. (2012). *On the rise of Pearson (oh, and following the money).* Retrieved from: http://teacherblog.typepad.com/newteacher/2012/11/on-the-rise-of-pearson-oh-and-following-themoney.html

Reynolds, W. M. (2014). Reforming the schooling of neoliberal, perpetual zombie desire. In P. L. Thomas, B. Porfilio, J. Gorlewski, & P. R. Carr (Eds.), *Social context reform: A pedagogy of equity and opportunity* (pp. 33–49). New York: Routledge.

Rodriguez, M. (2014, June 25). *The millennial generation clings to its childhood.* Tempe, AZ: The State Press. Retrieved from: http://www.statepress.com/article/2014/06/the-millennial-generation-clings-to-its-childhood/

Savage, G. (2013). Chasing the phantoms of public pedagogy: Political, popular and concrete politics. In J. Burdick, J. A. Sandlin, & M. P. O'Malley (Eds.), *Problematizing public pedagogy* (pp. 79–91). New York: Routledge.

Standing, G. (2011). *The new precariat: The new dangerous class.* New York: Bloomsbury.

Sun, C. F. (Producer), Picker, M. (Director). (2001). *Mickey Mouse monopoly: Disney, childhood and corporate power* [DVD]. United States: Art Media Production.

CHAPTER NINE

"How many do you have?"

Disney English (as a) Language (of) American Acquisition

LAURA RYCHLY AND STACIE K. PETTIT

"Disney English." No, it's not a place to sharpen your skills naming princesses or to learn Disney terms like *bippidy*, *boppidy*, *boo* and *supercalifragilisticexpialidocious*, but after reading this chapter, one might wish it were that simple. Disney English is a language-learning program that uses videos featuring Disney characters to teach English to Chinese children ages 2 to 12, who attend classes once a week. Disney English is one of the five areas of revenue for Disney Publishing Worldwide (DPW), the publishing group controlled by The Walt Disney Company that includes print books, magazines, and digital books and is considered DPW's language-learning business (Disney Consumer Products, 2014). By 2015, Disney plans to have 148 English language-training centers in China, teaching 150,000 children (D'Altorio, 2010). The classrooms, called "Magic Theatres," are movie themed and feature an interactive whiteboard, projection wall, and wireless technology (Disney English, 2014).

In examining the implications of Disney English, we accept Giroux's (2004) charge to hold Disney accountable by "challeng[ing] and disrupt[ing] the images, representations, and values offered by Disney's teaching machine" (p. 180). In this chapter, we use critical discourse analysis to examine the ways in which Disney English is teaching "Disney" as a paradigm of Westernism and to explore the implications of Disney English as a global cultural force. In the following sections, we provide a brief overview of the program and explain the theoretical perspectives we bring to an examination of this relatively new approach that Disney is taking to reach children around the world. Then, we explore two themes that emerged as we learned what Disney English is and what it does. The first theme shows how Disney constructs "Americanness" through English language instruction. The second theme depicts a cycle of commodified language and the vocabulary of consumption. Together, these themes illustrate the ways Disney English operates to teach Chinese children into a particular understanding of Americanness centered on acquisition.

SCALING THE GREAT WALL: LANGUAGE LEARNING AS DISNEY'S ENTRANCE INTO THE CHINA MARKET

China, the fastest-growing private English education sector worth over $2 billion annually (D'Altorio, 2010), was primed for and receptive to its first learning center opened by Disney in Shanghai, in 2008. Selling English education is a convenient way to bring Disney to a country that historically has not officially allowed all of Disney's products into its borders. China has strict publishing rules and a history of keeping Disney films out of the country; however, piracy is rampant with Disney films in China. Disney films such as *Kundun*, which glorified the Dalai Lama, and *Mulan* (Cook et al., 2004) were particularly controversial in China. In 2009, a Hong Kong director even made a new live-action movie about Hua Mulan as a way to counteract the glorification of Mulan from Disney's blockbuster. Because of China's limits on foreign media, Disney has not been able to start a television channel or to distribute all of its movies in China, so teaching English has become an important way for Disney to gain access to the Chinese market. China has such strict policies on allowing foreign films in the country that the World Trade Organization even ruled in 2009 that China had violated international trade rules by its restrictions of foreign media. In 2012, China eased restrictions by adding 14 more foreign films to the current quota of about 20 and by increasing the amount of revenue that studios could receive from ticket sales from 13% to 25% (Verrier, 2012). *The Avengers* (2015) was allowed to release in China and accounted for 95% of all box office sales in China, indicating that the Chinese market is hungry for what Disney has to offer (Tartaglione, 2015).

Through Disney English, Disney seems to have found a way around China's entertainment roadblocks by positioning Disney products as educational tools. As Areddy and Sanders (2009) posit, "classroom and homework exercises introduce the kind of Disney books, TV shows, and movies that China's government otherwise restricts" (p. 2). The timing of Disney English's establishment in China coincides well with the upcoming opening of Disneyland Shanghai in 2016. Since opening in 2005, Disneyland Hong Kong has seen fewer than the projected numbers of visitors, but in 2012, the park finally achieved an annual profit, bringing in $14 million (Einhorn, 2013). Clearly, Disney has cleverly found ways around the television programming limitations by infiltrating the Chinese culture through the theme parks as well as through Disney English centers.

"LET'S SHARE!"—VIDEOS AS SOURCES OF DATA

Our Internet searches for Disney English led us to online job application portals such as "Disney English Home/Jobs and Careers," and to blogs and review boards such as "Glassdoor," where current and former employees post descriptions of their experiences. The reviews posted about Disney English are both positive and negative. Negative experiences include both working for the company itself and working with the specific curriculum used at Disney English. Complaints include inadequate training, discrepancies between promises made during recruitment and on-the-ground realities such as cost of living versus compensation and time demands, and a scripted curriculum. Obtaining actual materials used in the Disney English classrooms proved impossible; we did find what were described as "textbooks" on eBay and ordered two, but they never arrived. The difficulty of obtaining curricular materials leads us to believe that there might be an agenda of concealment at work here.

We were, however, able to find some helpful materials to analyze, including one video advertisement, one video excerpt from a Disney teaching video, and a document titled, "Disney English Fact Sheet" (DEFS, 2011), which served as our primary sources of data. The first video, titled, "The David and Yuki Story/Disney English" (Fly Eye Media, 2012), is a 3:15-minute official (i.e., Disney-approved/sponsored) advertisement for Disney English. David and Yuki are five-year-old children who attend the learning center. At the beginning of the promotional video, Yuki's mother is heard describing her first visit to Disney English for the "demo class" and comparing it to the "black and white texts" that she used to learn English as a child (Fly Eye Media, 2012). Yuki's mother speaks Chinese in the video and her words are translated into English subtitles. David is introduced next, while a Disney English employee explains that children are excited to attend Disney English classes because "every lesson is a new experience (Fly Eye Media, 2012). In the final minute of the promotional video, children are heard talking to the characters they see on the interactive screens and engaging in activities with each other and with teachers. At the end, David and Yuki share their "passports" with one another and count how many stickers they have earned.

The second video is a 14:58-minute excerpt from a Disney English-teaching video titled, "Disney English DVD Feature—Play" that we found on YouTube (Disney English, 2014). After a short introductory song' the first lesson, "Let's Share!" begins. Six children take turns introducing themselves and acting out scenarios, such as jumping rope, counting various items such as pencils and stuffed animals, and showing each other their toys, all while describing their items and actions in English. Musical numbers that give repetitive practice with the language presented are interspersed among these exchanges between the children.

The "Disney English Fact Sheet" is a three-page document that summarizes the program. The document lists various benefits of learning English with Disney, such as the "authentic and unique … language experience," and the "joy and fun" that are unique to Disney's classrooms (DEFS, 2011, p. 1). Other information provided includes the fact that the curriculum was shaped by principles from influential educational theorists such as Howard Gardner and John Dewey, and that "Only Disney has the ability to leverage our rich stories to make English language learning fun and accessible" (p. 2).

CRITICAL DISCOURSE ANALYSIS: LANGUAGE, POWER, AND IDENTITY

This chapter was approached from a critical theory perspective with the ultimate goal of raising critical consciousness and exposing the power relations that exist in Disney English classrooms. Our purpose has not been to merely describe, as in an interpretivist perspective but to critique and change (Patton, 2002). For our analysis of data, we applied principles of critical discourse analysis (CDA), which is the study of how language is used in texts, while taking context into account. CDA is a method that examines how social and power relations, identities, and knowledge are constructed through texts and through the contexts of their production and consumption (Lewis, 2006). What makes our analysis critical, and therefore aligns our particular investigation with other scholarship in critical theory, is that we believe there are troubling consequences that could result from the power that Disney has, and wields, over Chinese children and their families as it takes advantage of a strong desire for children to develop competence with the English language, and not only with English but with skills deemed necessary for navigating the future as "global citizens."

Andrew Sugerman, the executive vice president of Disney Publishing Worldwide, said, "We took a look at the ways in which kids learn language—traditional ways, using books, whiteboards, teacher interaction—and the view was that Disney really could bring a lot more magic to what has been a pretty traditional industry" (Pescatore, 2009, p. 83). His words make clear Disney's intention to earn a profit from its English language learning centers. A dynamic such as this, driven by a "for-profit" view of language learning, puts Disney in a position of power over its Chinese students learning English. Scholars such as Coulter (2012) use the metaphor of colonization to expose the imbalance of power that exists between corporations and consumers, specifically children-as-consumers: "categories of young people such as the toddler, the teen and the tween are rendered 'knowable,' made 'visible,' and produced as 'unified' by the vast discursive frames of market research available to companies such as Disney in their quest to colonize young people as new markets" (p. 152). Critical discourse analysis, "which seeks to understand how contemporary capitalism ... enables ... [and] limits human well-being and flourishing, with a view to overcoming or mitigating these obstacles and limits" (Fairclough, 2010, p. 11), is a fitting methodology for our analysis.

In addition to critical theory and CDA methodology, we have approached our data from a sociolinguistic perspective informed by scholarship that examines the notion of the self as being always under construction and shaped by culture (Hall & Du Gay, 1996), and that informs us of the role of language in identity formation (Bucholtz & Hall, 2004). Language is closely associated with culture and with ethnicity, which are components of one's self-identity. Language always consists of social identities, social relations, and systems of knowledge and belief (Fairclough, 2010), and language is the most pervasive of the cultural productions of identity (Bucholtz & Hall, 2004); therefore, language learning will inevitably have an effect on identity development.

THE SOUNDS OF DISNEY ENGLISH: AMERICANIZATION AND CONSUMPTION

The evidence we found through our critical analysis can be categorized into two themes related to the identity development of children enrolled in Disney English. The first theme is that Disney is exploiting, for profit, a desire shared by Chinese families for their children to learn "American" language and culture in order to be well positioned for the future. The second theme is a cycle of commodification: first, the English language is commodified by Disney and sold to families in China for profit, and then, the language these families are buying is ultimately language for acquisition and consumption. In the following sections we will explore and problematize these themes.

Becoming Americanized Chinese

Yuki's mother, in "The David and Yuki Story," begins her explanation of why the Disney English center was the right choice for Yuki by explaining that "learning English will be so important for her future" (Fly Eye Media, 2012). Scholars such as Cameron (2012), Heller (2012), and McKay (2010) have documented how English functions as a requirement for social and economic mobility and stability in an ever-changing and globalized world. One specific way that English grants speakers this power is through a perception of "added value"; if one can speak English well, he or she is more likely to find employment and is therefore more valuable than a non-English speaker seeking work (Heller, 2012). Unequal power relations thus exist in "imagined communities" (Anderson, 1983, p. 6) through which people see themselves belonging to a privileged group. This imaginary sense of participation in a community of fellow English speakers is powerful enough to convince people that "if they invest in English learning, they will reap the benefits of social and intellectual mobility" (McKay, 2010, p. 96). Reasons such as these legitimize the desire Chinese families have to help their children acquire proficiency in English. Additionally, we found evidence of a desire for American-ness that goes deeper than the language layer. Hua Lan, a mother featured in another advertisement video for Disney English, says, "Actually, what I really like about Disney English is its development of a culture. What is behind the teaching of English here is the original culture of America" (Disney Takes English to the Chinese, 2010). The significance of "culture" here may be a perception that if Chinese children learn how to mimic American children in other ways, perhaps in their ability to recognize symbols of American popular culture (i.e., Disney characters), then they will be able to navigate other characteristics of what Gee (as cited in McKay, 2010) defines as "big D" Discourse: "multiple ways of acting-interacting-speaking-writing-listening-reading-thinking-believing-valuing-feeling with others at the 'right' times and in the 'right' places" (p. 100). Cultural competencies such as these would enhance children's English language skills, and ideally, prepare them to be even stronger participants in "imagined communities."

The Disney English materials we reviewed provide evidence that Disney is more than happy to attempt to Americanize the Chinese children enrolled in Disney English through how they look, speak, and learn. The first example comes from the Disney English Mission statement: "We aim to inspire children to confidently communicate with the world in their own voice." This desire to inspire confidence is echoed in the advertisement video as well, when the voice-over explains that children learn "soft skills including confidence, teamwork, and creativity" (Fly Eye Media, 2012). However, later in the fact sheet is the claim, that they "Focus on pronunciation practice of English sounds that tend to be difficult for Chinese children to master" (DEFS, 2011, par. 13). One of these sounds is the English/l/ sound because there is no equivalent sound in their native Chinese language, and language acquisition theory explains that the ability to produce sounds which are not heard and produced by age 11 will fall away (Hagège, 1999). As if to highlight this "strength" of the program, Yuki is heard saying "hello," six times in the three-minute video clip, each time with very clearly annunciated/l/sounds (Fly Eye Media, 2012).

Such a focus on perfecting the sounds made by native Chinese speakers learning to speak English raises concerns about what these children internalize about themselves as English speakers. While we never observed anyone correcting a mispronunciation in the videos, and the Fact Sheet does not say *how* the curriculum will focus on pronunciation practice, this emphasis nevertheless has potentially negative consequences regarding identity development. In the United States, scholarship on the experiences of African American children who speak Standard English presents the challenges they encounter when engaging in the process of language assimilation, including receiving criticism from family members and peers for abandoning their home language and "talking white" (Delpit, 2006; Ferguson, 2001). Their challenge to identify with either group may be mirrored in the Chinese children who go out into their communities fresh from attending Disney English class with their perfectly pronounced 'l's.' Contrary to what Disney presents, diversity should be recognized and accepted as part of language development and used in second language learners and users as it is with first language users (Karra, 2006).

The second example comes in the form of the images that Disney English relies on in order to build its instructional materials. An article published in the fall 2009 *Alumni Magazine* for the College of William and Mary, which summarizes an interview with Andrew Sugerman (vice president of Disney Publishing Worldwide) provides some insight into these teaching materials. In one unit "in which the English words relating to hair are taught … Disney English teachers show *The Little Mermaid* [1989] clip where Ariel combs her hair with a fork. Subsequent activities feature Ariel and other characters from the movie" (Pescatore, 2009, p. 1). The scene in which Ariel actually does this is well into the film, after she has given her voice to Ursula in exchange for turning her mermaid tail into legs. (The irony here is not lost: Ariel is voice-less in a scene used to silence Chinese children's voices about their own hair, and in the silence, children learn words to describe Ariel's hair.) Another set of images is in the second video clip we described, the 14-minute excerpt from an instructional video. There are six children featured in the video, none of whom shares physical features with the Chinese children in the Disney English classrooms (Disney English, 2014). The problem with this imagery is its potential for conveying a Western ethnocentrism, which would serve to "implicitly [proclaim] the triumphalism of white culture" (Giroux & Pollock, 2010, p. 41). Children should be presented with positive images that show people of all ethnicities, particularly their own (Ramsey, 2003). Furthermore, Chinese is not allowed to be spoken in Disney English classrooms. As language and culture are undeniably linked, this "English only" environment perpetuates the idea that English and American culture are what are valued.

The third example of Disney's attempt to Americanize the Chinese students is the mismatch between Disney's teaching methods and the traditional approach to education in China. The evidence comes from both video clips we analyzed, as well as from the job description on the "Disney Careers" webpage itself. As Ma

(2014) posits, education methods in one country might not benefit students coming from a different culture to the same degree. Specifically, Ma, who is a teacher-educator with experience teaching in both China and in the United States, discusses the prevalent ideology of Chinese collectivism in contrast to the individualist ideology of Westerners. In Chinese collectivism, which is influenced by Confucianism, individuality is subordinate to other virtues such as moral conduct and social duty (Ma, 2014). The creators of Disney English should be reminded that "ideology and cultural differences have a significant impact on learning and teaching" (p. 12). In other words, what works with one culture might not be the most beneficial in another context, and China and the United States can have very different methods concerning education and learning.

Furthermore, the "foreign trainer"—the title Disney gives to its English language teachers—is "responsible for ensuring measurable academic results in a fun and lively learning environment, delivering an outstanding service experience to learners and parents" (Disney Careers, 2015, p. 1). Disney does not seem to consider the fact that pedagogy is context dependent, and while the traditional Chinese rote-learning method is not preferred in the West, it has produced positive results with Chinese learners (Ma, 2014). According to Ma (2014), Chinese students regard learning as something that requires them to endure hardship and to go through with diligence. Therefore, there may be a cultural mismatch with Disney ideals, which is the third example of Disney's attempt to Americanize the Chinese students enrolled in Disney English.

These three examples of ways Disney seems to be overwriting inherent ways of being Chinese (speaking, looking, and teaching/learning) call forth the notion of *cultural invasion* as described by Paulo Freire (1993): "The invaders penetrate the cultural context of another group, in disrespect of the latter's potentialities: they impose their own view of the world upon those they invade and inhibit the creativity of the invaded by curbing their expression" (p. 152). We see this "invasion" as a threat to the identities that young Chinese students bring with them into the Disney English classrooms. Their inherent ways of speaking, looking, and learning, are displaced in these classrooms where Disney charges in with its own notions of what is "right" regarding these characteristics. Willinsky (1998) calls displacement such as this "the kidnapping of identity" (p. 95).

Consuming the Language of Consumption

We found a cycle of consumption when we listened closely to the words used both by Disney when it describes its English language centers, and also by the children themselves as they practice their new language. The first part of the cycle is the way Disney has captured, packaged, and sold a version of English that is marketed in China as being desirable. Families enroll their children in Disney English and pay large sums of money for this fashionable style of English. Evidence of it being "desirable" and "fashionable" can be found in the Sugerman interview that appears in the College of William and Mary's alumni magazine, in which focus groups are said to reveal a view that "no one speaks the language of children and connects with kids better than Disney" (Pescatore, 2009, p. 1). China is consuming a commodified brand of English, and this raises questions about what it means to package a static, objective version of language that is, by its nature, a dynamic and subjective practice. The next part of the cycle happens when children, as they ingest this fashionable, branded form of English, begin practicing the actual words and phrases they will share with other English speakers. In the two videos we studied, words and phrases are presented in exchanges between actors who are discussing and showing off objects they have purchased or wish to own. In this section, we explore this cycle and its potential consequences for the identity development of the children in Disney English.

The mother of a child enrolled in Disney English who was quoted in a recent *Wall Street Journal* article said that she is willing to pay over $1,000 a year for the classes because she wants her daughter to be "international" and explained that Disney is a "familiar and trustworthy brand" (Areddy & Sanders, 2009, p. 2). The mother's characterization of the Walt Disney brand reinforces profit-making as the company's primary role in language teaching as Andrew Sugerman's use of the word "industry" in a quote we discussed above reveals. Viewing language learning as "an industry," a site for production and consumption, positions the teachers and students as workers tasked with earning a profit, which in turn places them as cogs in the Disney teaching machine.

Alongside an industrial, business-model view of what it means to learn language is a question about what it means to package and sell language in the first place. Consequences of language that becomes commodified are explored by scholars in the context of globalization, as described above, such as the ways English adds value to people seeking employment and is perceived as giving people everywhere the ability to participate powerfully in the world (Cameron, 2012; Heller, 2012). Once language has been packaged and branded, problems arise over who has the power to decide what kinds of usage make the language a *correct* version; we thus see "struggles over legitimacy, that is, over who has the legitimate right to define what counts as competence, as authenticity, as excellence, and over who has the right to produce and distribute the resources of language and identity" (Heller, 2003, p. 474). In the case of Disney English, Disney has claimed this "legitimate right" over what kind of language will be considered correct. Before we examine further why we find this disturbing, it is necessary to explain the second part of the cycle, the actual version of English that is being taught and learned.

In the roughly 20 minutes of video we studied to understand what goes on in these language centers, we found countless instances of language that one would use to acquire things, or to engage in acts of consumption. For example, the second complete sentence spoken by a child in the excerpted instructional video is, "Hi Lauren, I like your doll. Is it new?" (Disney English, 2014). At 2:20 minutes the six children all say together, "We love toys!" (Disney English, 2014). The video includes songs, which are presumably examples of the research-based, learner-centered pedagogy that was "specifically designed for Chinese children" and is meant to be responsive to the many ways in which people learn (DEFS, 2011, par. 13). The first song is 2 minutes long, and this time the lyric, "Let's have fun; let's play with our toys… your jump rope and my video game. …" is repeated three times (Disney English, 2014). All of the images are of toys from Disney's *Toy Story* (1995), Wall-*E*, and *Cars* movies. In the shorter advertisement video the students are shown practicing the phrase, "How much?" together and counting play American money aloud. At the very end of the clip, David and Yuki sit down to compare how many stickers each has in their Disney Passports. Each child asks of the other, "How many do you have?" (Fly Eye Media, 2012).

If these clips are indeed a representative sample of the language children learn through Disney English, then Disney English centers are teaching a version of English for which the primary function seems to be shopping. Because, as was explained above, Disney has commodified English and is powerful over what constitutes a standard version of the language, we argue that the particular standardized version of English that children in these centers are being subjected to may be uniquely detrimental due to its insistence on consumption. Disney standardizes English for consumption and makes it "the norm," then sends children into the world who are best able to communicate about things they want to have (McKay, 2010). We see this as detrimental because of the way language influences identity formation. Holland and Lachicotte Jr. (2007) explain that people "develop a higher order psychological function—an identity—which personalizes a set of collectively developed discourses about a type and cultivates, in interaction with others, a set of embodied practices that signify the person" (p. 134). If children internalize a language mostly purposeful for the acquisition of things, then their identities become shaped by this purpose, and they view their worth and validity in terms of their possessions.

Further justification for calling this language "detrimental" comes from scholarship on the effects of consumer culture on children and on the consequences of children developing a sense-of-self aligning too closely with consumption. In addition to Coulter's (2012) metaphor of colonization, where corporations view children as sites for exploitation and for profit, there are other concerns that focus on outcomes affecting individual children, the general health of societies, and the planet. Regarding the children themselves, evidence exists that shows "immersing children in a message that material goods are essential to self-fulfillment promotes the acquisition of materialistic values, which have been linked to depression and low self-esteem" (Linn, 2010, p. 64). Pressure to engage in the world through acts of buying and acquiring goods can "diminish citizenship to a largely privatized affair in which civic responsibilities are reduced to the act of consuming" (Giroux, 2000, p. 114). Individuals retreat from a collective body that might otherwise fulfill purposes that would benefit the greater good. These concerns come together in a discussion of language and identity because as individuals they "organize and narrate themselves in practice in the name of an identity [they], thus achieve a modest form of agency" (Holland & Lachicotte Jr., 2007, p. 134). The form of agency that develops when children internalize a language for consumption is one that prompts them to act in and on the world as acquirers. This form of agency serves to strengthen a corporate hold on citizens and acts against the kind of agency geared towards acting in and on the world in ways that fulfill our potential to affect positive change (Giroux, 2000; Linn, 2010).

CONCLUSION: HELPING DISNEY SEE THE WORLD AS NOT-SO-SMALL

Our examination only scratches the surface of issues surrounding Disney's language teaching practices. A critical analysis of the materials we were able to examine revealed the two themes presented here: first, that Disney's English schools seek to "Americanize" their Chinese learners, and second, that language in the Disney English schools is a commodified form of English and seems to teach language for the purpose of consumption. We are concerned about an English language program that seems to rely on overwriting more natural ways of coming to know oneself as a cultural and linguistic participant in his or her community. This concern is especially valid given the company's plans to expand to other countries, such as Brazil. We also find problematic a language that seems to primarily teach children to label items they would like to have and compare quantities of things they have with each other because of the potential implications for children who come to understand the world through a language of consumption. To this end, we acknowledge that such consumption-oriented language is likely present in American classrooms too, when teachers and students engage in language and literacy activities. Any time our focus drifts to noticing types and quantities of things children in stories have, or want, and we make this the emphasis of our discussions, then the troubling outcomes described here apply to our own students as well. Perhaps this look at teaching practices in a foreign country can help shed light on our own practices, too.

We find other troubling ideas within Disney English. As we noted, the form of U.S. culture it presents, is being accepted as the "original" culture of America. However, as American parents, we can speak to the simultaneously undesirable influence of Disney on our children, and to know that Disney is relying on a false notion of its relationship with our children as being unquestionably "safe, fun, and nurturing," to sell itself overseas is frustrating (DEFS, 2011, par. 9). Also, we wonder how Disney perceives its responsibility and its opportunity in countries with different political, social, and cultural structures than the ones it encounters in the United States. This is important both for Disney, as it continues on its mission to spread English around the globe, as well as for those who continue to critique the program. For example, positions such as Giroux's (2000), which examine the ways corporate interference in education reduces learners' agency as democratic citizens, work for American democratic and capitalist structures but may not be applicable in other realms. As non-Chinese citizens, our perceptions and perspectives are necessarily limited to our own lived experiences, and we accept that more comprehensive, contextualized examinations are needed to fully understand the troubling phenomenon that is Disney English, but we offer here what we hope is just the beginning of a global conversation about the impact of Disney's brand of English language learning.

ACKNOWLEDGMENT

The authors would like to thank Christopher Baxter, a graduate assistant at Georgia Regents University, for his invaluable technical assistance with this chapter.

DISCUSSION QUESTIONS

1. In what other ways (past and present) has language been commodified and/or commercialized? What are the consequences of these examples? How do they compare with what we have found about Disney English?
2. As the relationship between China and the United States continues to evolve, and as Disney English reaches other countries, what positive and negative outcomes could there be as a result of such "Americanized" English teaching? How might this position native and non-native English speakers in relation to one other?
3. In "The David and Yuki Story" video, Yuki's mother says that the way Disney teaches English is more engaging than the "black and white" way that she was taught English. How does this support, or not support, our point about a possible cultural mismatch between the teaching and learning methods in China and Disney English? What other implications might there be of a comparison between "modern" and "traditional" methods?

REFERENCES

Anderson, B. (1983). *Imagined communities.* New York: Verso.

Areddy, J. T., & Sanders, P. (2009, April 20). Chinese learn English the Disney way. *Wall Street Journal.* Available at: http://online.wsj.com/news/articles/SB124017964526732863?tesla=y&mg=reno64-wsj

Bucholtz, M., & Hall, K. (2004). Language and identity. *A Companion to Linguistic Anthropology, 1,* 369–394.

Cameron, D. (2012). The commodification of language: English as a global commodity. In T. Nevalainen & E. C. Traugott (Eds.), *The Oxford handbook of the history of English* (pp. 352–361). New York: Oxford University Press.

Cook, B., Bancroft, T., Coats, P., Hsiao, R., Sanders, C., LaZebnik, P., & Singer, R. Buena Vista Home Entertainment (Firm). (2004). *Mulan.* United States: Walt Disney Home Entertainment.

Coulter, N. (2012). From toddlers to teens: The colonization of childhood the Disney way. *Jeunesse: Young people, texts, cultures, 4*(1), 146–158.

D'Altorio, Tony. (2010, July 12). Disney works its magic on China ... No wishing on a star required. *Investment U.* Retrieved from: http://www.investmentu.com/article/detail/14971/disney-works-its-magic-on-china#.VJHIwZgo7cs

Delpit, L. (2006). *Other people's children: Cultural conflict in the classroom.* New York: The New Press.

Disney Careers. (2015). *Disney English.* Retrieved from: http://disneyenglish.disneycareers.com/en/default/

Disney Consumer Products. (2014, September 7). *About us.* Retrieved from: https://www.disneyconsumerproducts.com/Home/display.jsp?contentId=dcp_home_ourbusinesses_company_overview_us&forPrint=false&language=en&preview=false&imageShow=0&pressRoom=US&translationOf=null®ion=0&ccPK=null

Disney English. (2014, January 14). *Disney English DVD feature—PLAY.* Retrieved from: https://www.youtube.com/watch?v=sy5sWCfirHk

Disney English Fact Sheet (DEFS) (2011, September 7). Retrieved from: https://enterpriseportal.disney.com/gopublish/sitemedia/dcp/Home/Our%20Businesses/dpw_lob_disney_english_fact_sheet_021012.pdf

Disney takes English to the Chinese (2010, August 3). Retrieved from: https://www.youtube.com/watch?v=t6U29dSm7FA

Einhorn, B. (2013, February 19). Disney's Hong Kong theme park finally turns a profit. [Web log post]. Retrieved June 16, 2015, from: http://www.bloomberg.com

Fairclough, N. (2010). *Critical discourse analysis: The critical study of language.* New York: Longman.

Ferguson, A. A. (2001). *Bad boys: Public schools in the making of black masculinity.* Ann Arbor: University of Michigan Press.

Fly Eye Media. (2012, December 31). *The David & Yuki story.* Retrieved from: https://vimeo.com/56545493

Freire, P. (1993). *Pedagogy of the oppressed.* New York: Continuum.

Giroux, H. (2000). *Stealing innocence: Corporate culture's war on children.* New York: Palgrave.

Giroux, H. (2004). Cultural studies, public pedagogy, and the responsibility of intellectuals. *Communication and Critical/Cultural Studies, 1*(1), 59–79.

Giroux, H., & Pollock, G. (2010). *The mouse that roared: Disney and the end of innocence.* Lanham, MD: Rowman & Littlefield Publishers.

Hagège, C. (1999). "L'enfant aux deux langues" (The child between two languages), Greek translation. Polis editions, Athens. (Original publication: Editions Odile Jacob, 1996).

Hall, S., & Du Gay, P. (1996). *Questions of cultural identity*. London: Sage.

Heller, M. (2003). Globalization, the new economy, and the commodification of language and identity. *Journal of Sociolinguistics, 7*(4), 473–492.

Heller, M. (2012). The commodification of language. *Annual Review of Anthropology, 39,* 101–114. doi: 10.1146/annurev.anthro.012809.104951.

Holland, D., & Lachicotte Jr. W. (2007). Vygotsky, Mead, and the new sociocultural studies of identity. In H. Daniels, M. Cole, & J. V. Wertsch (Eds.), *The Cambridge companion to Vygotsky* (pp. 101–135). New York: Cambridge University Press.

Karra, M. (2006). Second language acquisition: Learners' errors and error correction in language teaching. *Translator Education*. Retrieved from: http://www.proz.com/translation-articles/articles/633/

Lewis, C. (2006). "What's discourse got to do with it?" A meditation on critical discourse analysis in literacy research. *Research in the Teaching of English, 40,* 373–379.

Linn, S. (2010). Commercialism in children's lives. *State of the World 2010*. Retrieved from: http://www.commercialfreechildhood.org/sites/default/files/linn_commercialisminchildrenslives.pdf

Ma, W. (2014). *East meets west in teacher preparation: Crossing Chinese and American borders*. New York: Teachers College Press.

McKay, S. L. (2010). English as an international language. In N. H. Hornberger & S. L. McKay (Eds.), *Sociolinguistics and language education* (pp. 89–115). Bristol, UK: Multilingual Matters.

Patton, M. Q. (2002). *Qualitative research and evaluation methods*. 3rd ed. Thousand Oaks, CA: Sage.

Pescatore, B. (2009). Sugerman '93: Bringing magic to English language learning. *William & Mary Alumni Magazine, 75*(1), p. 83. Retrieved from: http://wmalumnimagazine.com/wp-content/uploads/2014/05/vol_75_no_1_WMAlumMag_fall2009.pdf

Ramsey, P. (2003). Growing up with the contradictions of race and class. In C. Copple (Ed.), *A world of difference: Readings on teaching young children in a diverse society* (pp. 24–28). Washington, DC: National Association for the Education of Young Children.

Tartaglione, N. (2015, May 13). 'Avengers: Age of ultron' has top Disney/Marvel China opening day ever. [Web log post]. Retrieved June 16, 2015, from: http://www.deadline.com

Verrier, R. (2012, February 17). U.S. and China reach deal to allow more movies into China. *The Los Angeles Times*. Retrieved from: http://latimesblogs.latimes.com

Willinsky, J. (1998). *Learning to divide the world: Education at empire's end*. Minneapolis: University of Minnesota Press.

CHAPTER TEN

Images of Teachers

Disney Channel Sitcoms and Teachers as Spectacle

DENNIS ATTICK

The Kaiser Family Foundation (2010) recently reported that over 80% of young people between the ages of 8 and 18 watch more than four hours of television programming each day. The same study revealed that the average young person in the United States grows up in a house with four television sets. More recently, a television industry report from 2013, revealed that television viewership among youth between birth and 10 years of age was at an all-time high during the 2013 television season (Viacom, 2013). Despite the fact that we live in an increasingly media-saturated world, television continues to play an important role in the lives of young people, as it has over the past fifty years. While a study of youth television programming may seem anachronistic in the early 21st century, recent research reveals that while young viewers are spending less time watching programming on a traditional television set, they are increasing their television viewing on other platforms such as laptops, smartphones, and personal tablets (Viacom, 2013).

Using the continued growth of youth television viewing habits as impetus, this study explores the ways in which two live-action sitcoms on the Disney Channel portray teachers. There exists a history of cultural studies examining the portrayal of teachers on television that stretches back to the early days of the medium (Gerbner,1963; see also Dalton & Linder, 1998; Delony & Delony, 2013). More recently, there is growing research around the role that specific kids' television networks like the Disney Channel play in shaping young people's notions of race in a post-racial America (Turner, 2014). And while there is no shortage of studies regarding the Walt Disney Company, there is little exploration today of the depiction of teachers on popular Disney Channel programming.

I undergird this work with George Gerbner's (1998) cultivation theory, which posits that television teaches young people early lessons about the world. Cultivation theory holds that media messages shape young people's first notions of the world outside their own homes. It is my contention that Disney Channel sitcoms have the potential to influence the notions that children and young adults develop regarding teachers. In this chapter I trace historical research into how mass media have portrayed teachers before looking at specific portrayals of teachers in two popular Disney Channel sitcoms. I situate the portrayals of teachers around the theme of teachers as apathetic and pathetic adults, a theme that has roots in historical portrayals of teachers in popular media. I then explore how these portrayals contribute to trivialized notions of teachers and students today, as well as how these portrayals support and maintain the notion of education as spectacle today.

TELEVISION AS TEACHER: CULTIVATION THEORY

Throughout the past century, television has become a central means by which children are exposed to ideas, values, and cultures that exist in the world outside their own homes. George Gerbner (1969) was an early proponent of a cultivation analysis model of effects research that studied the effect that television programming had on society's understanding of itself. Gerbner was extending the work of Frankfurt School scholars, Adorno and Horkheimer (Adorno, 1991), who argued that television was a communication technology designed to serve the interests of the ruling class by inculcating and distracting the general public through a system they named the culture industry (Bronner & Kellner, 1989). Gerbner's (1998) cultivation analysis model was born of his cultural indicators project that attempted to extend effects research by concentrating on the long-term effects of living with television. Gerbner's research revealed that television viewing caused behavioral and emotional changes in individuals who were regular viewers of the medium. For example, the cultural indicators project found that exposure to violence on television cultivates in the viewer a belief that the world is a mean and dangerous place, a condition that Gerbner and his colleagues referred to as "mean world syndrome" (Signorelli, Gerbner, & Morgan, 1995, p. 121). In Gerbner's model, television acts as teacher, shaping an individual's understanding of his or her reality to such a degree that the television viewers understand their world as similar to the world presented on television.

Carlos Cortes' (2000) work is instructive here as well, especially his argument in *The Children Are Watching: How the Media Teach about Diversity*. Cortes argues that television is one of our "societal curricula where young people learn language, acquire culture, develop beliefs, hone perceptions, internalize attitudes and observe patterns of behavior" (p. 18). For Cortes, media, like television, function as a type of textbook, teaching students about the world around them. The idea of television as teacher, grounded in Gerbner's work, was also forwarded by Potter and Chang (1990) who found that television has a profound impact on how middle school students construct reality and develop attitudes and beliefs about their world. Television teaches viewers, especially young viewers, what to desire, what to believe, and how to behave.

IMAGES OF TEACHERS, SCHOOLS, AND SCHOOL CULTURE ON TELEVISION

Gerbner (1963) was one of the first scholars to study the portrayal of teachers, students, and schools in popular media. In his analysis of more than one hundred portrayals of teachers on early television sitcoms, Gerbner found that teachers were often depicted as outsiders, existing on the fringes of the communities in which they taught. Often the teachers lacked agency, and many were characterized as suffering mental anguish wrought by the financial difficulties of living on a teacher's salary. In general, Gerbner found that television programs, even in their earliest iterations, were not very successful in accurately portraying teachers, students, or schools. One theory as to why television has not been very successful in creating compelling, accurate portrayals of teachers is that teaching and learning are complex processes, not easily reducible to the narrow scope of a television sitcom format (Maeroff, 1998). To this end, television portrayals of teachers have tended to fall into simple binary categories of good and bad, which allow for non-critical consumption by viewers. Ayers (2001) has argued that popular media portrayals of teachers often reduce teachers to "saints" or "slugs" (p. 201). More often than not, teachers in films have been portrayed more positively than teachers on television; in fact, teachers are often portrayed as capable, and even heroic in Hollywood films (Dalton & Linder, 1998; Wells & Serman, 1998).

As mentioned earlier, Gerbner highlighted early negative portrayals of teachers on television. Considering that school is not a positive experience for many people, it is possible that the public finds it easier to consume media programming that is derisive of teachers and schools. On the other hand, Weber and Mitchell (1995) have found that television portrayals of teachers throughout the latter part of the 20th century have promoted a rather simplistic idea of a teacher. What is often missing in these portrayals of teachers are the everyday struggles, the highs and lows associated with the profession, and the complex relationships that mark the real work of teaching.

In their critical study of the history of teachers on television, Dalton and Linder (1998) argue that there are "many factors that determine our attitudes toward education, but the portrayal of teachers and schools on television is an often-neglected piece of the puzzle" (p. 21). Most of us, in fact, will encounter more fictional teachers over time in mediated classrooms than actual teachers in real classrooms. As Weber and Mitchell (1995) illustrate, images from films and television influence the ways that children and adults come to develop beliefs about teachers and students that persist over time. These ideas permeate society's general notion of schools over time, leading, as Stacy Otto (2005) argues, to our ideal of "a shiny classroom where equally shiny-clean boys and girls face forward in rapt attention of their beloved [quietly homey, homely] teacher" (p. 12). This is a notion that stems from a nostalgic idea of schools often perpetuated by television and films throughout the 20th century.

APATHETIC TEACHERS ON THE DISNEY CHANNEL

The Disney Channel debuted in 1993, as a commercial-free cable network available by paid subscription to cable customers. By the late 1990s, the Disney Channel had become a twenty-four hour, basic cable network. Between 1996 and 2008, the Disney Channel's exposure in American homes soared from 14 million homes in 1996, to over 100 million by 2008 (Disney, 2014). From 2012–2014, the Disney Channel's primetime programming was ranked number one among children between the ages of 5 and 14, with the Disney Channel having three of the top five shows in the pre-teen and teen demographic for 40 consecutive weeks (Disney, 2014). The ratings mark the Disney Channel's 14th consecutive quarter at number one among kids between the ages of 6 and 11, and the 22nd consecutive quarter at number one among tweens between the ages of 9 and 14 (Disney, 2014). The Disney Channel's shows have such large viewership that several shows are consistently rated in the top ten for all television viewership.

Considering the strong hold that the Disney Channel has on the youth television viewing market, in what follows, I examine the portrayal of teachers on two of the Disney Channel's most popular live-action television shows, *Girl Meets World* (Jacobs, 2013) and *Jessie* (O'Connell, 2011). Each of these shows consistently places in the top five of most-watched shows in the 5-to-14-year-old demographic, with *Girl Meets World* being the number one show in that demographic throughout the fall of 2014. As both *Jessie* and *Girl Meets World* focus on the lives of teen and preteen characters, much of the action of the shows takes place in fictional schools, with teachers and school administrators featured in recurring roles in each of the shows.

The fictional teachers in both *Jessie* and *Girl Meets World* are mostly infantilized, portrayed as pathetic adults, leading joyless lives and left to be spectators of the students' dynamic, playful, and capricious activities. As Gerbner (1963) has shown, the characterization of teachers as apathetic, disenfranchised outsiders is not new. More recently, Juliet Schor (2005) points out that teachers are often depicted in youth television programming as nerdy, boring people living in a world that is repressive and marked by missed opportunities and hopelessness. Schor's research resonates with the work of Weber and Mitchell (1995), and Glanz (1997), who found that teachers and school administrators are often depicted in youth televisual media as absent-minded, apathetic, and naïve about what is really happening in their classrooms, schools, and students' lives.

A central theme that emerges in the portrayal of teachers on both *Jessie* and *Girl Meets World* is that teachers are equally pathetic and apathetic. The teachers portrayed on both shows often show indifference towards and contempt for their students, as well as a disregard for academic achievement in general. In season 1, episode 1 of *Jessie,* "New York, New Nanny" (O'Connell & Koherr, 2011), we are introduced to a science teacher, who after judging a science fair type competition boasts to a class of students, "Well, students, you are all a disgrace, and the reason this country is 28th in the world in science!" As with many of the derogatory remarks from teachers and students about their lives and work, this insult produces laughter from many of the students in the class, as well as rolling laughter for the viewer which is provided by the canned laugh track that is part of the televised production.

The trope of the apathetic teacher is something that is seen in multiple episodes of *Jessie* and *Girl Meets World.* In season 2, episode 3 of *Jessie*, "Make New Friends, but Hide the Old" (Lapiduss, Dunlap, & Lewis, 2012), we encounter an art teacher who regularly disparages her job as a teacher, while also belittling the achievements of her students. Early in the episode, she enters the art classroom and mockingly exclaims, "I look at all of your enthusiastic faces and think to myself how much I hate my life. If only my art career had taken off." This longing for another career, and apathy about being trapped in the seemingly joyless life of a teacher is a recurring theme in both *Jessie* and *Girls Meets World.* The teachers often bemoan their poor life choices that led them to become teachers, while reflecting on how much better life could have been had they been successful in finding other more important or rewarding careers.

Later in the same episode, the art teacher returns to the classroom at the start of a new school day and upon seeing her students says with exasperation, "Oh, you all showed up. Uh, in that case, you should all keep working on your projects." She says this while shaking her head in disgust and speaking of her regret that her art career never took off. Throughout the class period, the teacher mocks the assignment she gives to the students, which she jokingly asserts is to "paint your essence." While one could possibly find a redeeming quality in such an assignment, the activity simply fills a void for the art teacher, who presents the assignment in a derisive manner, simultaneously denigrating art as an act of expression, and setting up the assignment for ridicule from the class and laughter for the television viewer. Later, when one of her students paints a skull and crossbones that was supposed to represent the student's rejection of capitalism and corporate greed, the art teacher mocks the student's attempt at an anti-consumerist message, while again reinforcing the notion that any attempt to engage in critical scholarship is a waste of time. When several of her students flee the room in frustration over the teacher's apathy and absurdity, the art teacher screams out, "Wait! Take me with you!" as if she is desperate to be liberated from her students and teaching responsibilities. Before she leaves the room, she tells the few students remaining in the room to "Do your homework, if you feel like it," which is met with big laughs from the audience.

In both *Jessie* and *Girl Meets World*, frequent displays of teacher apathy and longing for a different career are coupled with ongoing concerns about financial burdens. In season 2, episode 9 of *Jessie*, "Teacher's Pest" (Lapiduss, Dunlap, & Flynn, 2013), viewers are introduced to a history teacher who is presented as a frantic, delusional adult, obsessed with teenage role-playing science fiction games. At one point in the episode, the teacher is ridiculed for her lack of fashion sense, which is attributed to her financial burdens. When one of the students in the class sarcastically compliments the teacher's clothing, the teacher replies, "Thank you, I got my pantsuit when I submitted the winning bid on a storage locker." Viewers are led to believe that the teacher cannot afford to buy clothing but must wear clothes she finds in abandoned storage lockers and auctions. Again, the situation is presented as comic relief, the teacher's misfortune cause for ridicule and laughter.

The character of the poorly compensated and mistreated teacher holds with the trope Gerbner first identified fifty years ago in television's portrayal of teachers as living with the financial burdens wrought by a low-paying career in education. Further illustration can be found in Adorno's (1991) argument that the television character of the underpaid schoolteacher is an attempt to reconcile society's contempt for intellectualism, with the traditional sense of respect one is expected to provide to teachers. Adorno argues, "The script is a shrewd method of promoting adjustment to humiliating conditions by presenting them as objectively comical and by giving a picture of a person who experiences even her own inadequate position as an object of fun apparently free of any resentment" (p. 167). The teacher, despite her training and presumed intellectual ability, is reduced to self-loathing that is open to ridicule and laughter.

The underpaid and underappreciated teacher character is also seen in *Girl Meets World*, where the middle school history teacher frequently demonstrates apathy toward both his career as well as his students' academic pursuits. In season 1, episode 7 of *Girl Meets World*, "Girl Meets Maya's Mother" (Nelson & Whitesell, 2014), the same history teacher leads his class through a discussion of careers. When his wife, a lawyer, visits the class on career day, the teacher deflects students' questions away from his career as a teacher saying that his wife is "a lot smarter than I am." When he jokingly asks his wife on a date after school, he tells her, "I get off of work at 3:15 each day, except on Tuesday when I have playground duty," which he says while sheepishly hanging his head as if he's embarrassed that he's been reduced to being a provider of care for children. Again, the teacher's comments produce laughs, his situation in life something to be mocked and derided.

In season 1, episode 3 of *Girl Meets World*, "Girl Meets Flaws" (Blutman & Zwick, 2014), the history teacher and his students make a mockery of both Gandhi and Jackie Robinson while attempting to discuss historical leaders. Responding to questions from the teacher about who the great people pictured in photos on the wall are, one student jokingly asserts that Gandhi freed Ireland. The only African American male student in the classroom then responds that Jackie Robinson was "The first Irish guy to play in the major leagues after Gandhi freed him." Both comments produce roaring laughs from the students and rolling laughter from the canned audience laugh track. The teacher, after hearing the students' answers, smirks, shakes his head, and jokingly asserts, "I quit." What is lacking is for all involved is any discussion of who Gandhi and Jackie Robinson were, and why a student might actually want to learn about the important contributions of each of those individuals. In keeping with the recurrent theme of teachers and schools as spaces to be mocked and ridiculed, these interactions produce big laughs for the students in the class as well as for the television audience.

TEACHERS AND SCHOOLS AS SPECTACLE

While this chapter explores the characterization of teachers in two of the most popular shows currently airing on the Disney Channel, there are numerous other Disney Channel shows like *Austin & Ally* (Kopelow & Seifert, 2011), and *Shake It Up* (Thompson & Lotterstein, 2010), which present similar portrayals of teachers as generally apathetic and incompetent adults. The portrayal of teachers in what is mostly a negative light is problematic considering that The Walt Disney Company has, since its inception, championed itself as a promoter and as a supporter of civic responsibility and traditional family values. The company has also positioned itself as a supporter of American education throughout the 20th century. Consider, for example, the Disney Teacher of the Year program, now in its 25th year, that recognizes the country's best teachers according to Disney's criteria. Disney also sponsors numerous scholarship programs such as Dare to Dream, which offers college scholarships to high school students.

Despite these seemingly altruistic efforts to promote education, Disney Channel sitcoms characterize the teaching profession as something to be denigrated and ridiculed, while also portraying schools as spaces that are absent of individuals engaging in critical thought and action. I am not arguing, however, that kids' television programs should be expected to always accurately depict real life. One of the main functions of televisual entertainment is that it provides an escape from the real world. One could argue that the Disney Channel sitcoms cited in this chapter are nothing more than entertainment, an opportunity for kids to laugh at school situations with which they are familiar. That being said, the negative portrayal of teachers on Disney Channel programming can be seen as another means by which to reduce education to spectacle, while also forwarding the idea that teaching is a pathetic career that does not involve critical thinking or action.

The idea of society as spectacle was forwarded by Guy Debord (1967/1983) in *Society of the Spectacle*, where he furthers Hegelian and Marxist arguments for a new understanding of how modern capitalist societies create and sustain alienation among the population. Debord posited that human beings are not just alienated from their labor in a capitalist economy as Marx argued; rather, Debord offers that advanced capitalist societies ultimately come to depend on the economy alone for survival. In turn, and over time, sustaining the capitalist economy requires that members of society become primarily consumers of commodity spectacles. Ultimately, under such conditions, human beings become alienated from real experiences and from each other. Debord writes, "In societies where modern conditions of production prevail, all of life presents itself as an immense accumulation of spectacles. Everything that was directly lived has moved away into a representation" (p. 1). For Debord, the visual spectacle is not simply a series of images, but rather, the spectacle mediates human relationships via an incessant barrage of images. In the end, real experiences, real relationships, become less valuable than the accumulation of spectacle. The appearance of the thing itself provides validation for the consumer that what is seen is good and therefore worthy of consumption. It is here where the capitalist economy thrives, in the consumption of the spectacle.

Using Debord's model, we can understand society's notions of education today as being dominated by the consumption of the education spectacle without much real understanding of the complexities of teaching, learning, and actual school life. When the education spectacle is understood as a problem, it allows for the creation of solutions that often only contribute to the problem. When lack of school efficacy becomes understood as a widespread problem, the spectacle of failing schools can begin to reinforce the problem. Edelman (1988) asserts that the construction of social or political problems often has a far-reaching effect: it helps perpetuate and intensify the conditions that are defined as the problem. Over time, the public stops asking what the real problem is and instead turns to get answers from the politicians or experts who may have helped to construct the problem in the first place.

In a Debordian sense, Disney Channel programs create spectacles for consumption by young viewers. I argue that the specific depiction of teachers as apathetic and worthy of ridicule could be read as a forwarding of the narrative that says that schools are failing due in large part to inadequate teachers. Holding with cultivation theory's construct that mass media shape young people's understanding of the world, one must question why Disney Channel sitcoms create a spectacle that presents negative portrayals of teachers. Furthermore, recalling Adorno (1991), one could argue that the content provided by the Disney Channel does what the corporate culture industries do; it distracts young viewers from asking critical questions about teachers, schools, and education by getting them first to laugh at those ideas.

Today, information reaches children and adolescents through an ever-increasing barrage of digital sounds and images. It is important for anyone today, but especially young people, to develop the ability to think critically about the multiple media to which they are exposed. As clinical and scholarly research has shown, children are more susceptible than adults to the messages provided by television programming (Crane & Chen 2003; see also Signorelli, Gerbner, & Morgan, 1995). To counter the Disney Channel spectacle, young people need to develop the tools to critique visual culture and think critically about its impact on their lives. Furthermore, teachers and teacher educators can play an important role in questioning the portrayals of teachers in mass media. As Soetaert, Mottart, and Verdoodt (2004) argue, one way to do this is to allow teacher education students to confront and to deconstruct the portrayals of teachers in television, films, and popular literature. Too often, an examination of the intersection of education, mass media, and popular culture is missing from teacher education programs.

The portrayal of teachers on Disney Channel sitcoms is evidence of a larger issue in how teachers and the teaching profession are viewed negatively in most aspects of modern media. Young people receive normative messages through television media like the Disney Channel about how to act, behave, and dress, and about which experiences are valued and whose experiences are less important. Stated differently, modern communication media like the Disney Channel influence the development of young people's norms and values. In a media-saturated world, the socialization and education of children must include teaching them to be critical observers of media like the Disney Channel and its influence on their ideas of power, democracy, and agency. In our media-saturated visual culture, images help us make meaning now more than ever. A problem arises when these images begin to shape not only young viewers' notions of teaching and learning; the images can have even greater consequences when they sustain a distorted understanding of the complexities of teachers, schools, and education today.

DISCUSSION QUESTIONS

1. This chapter argues that the negative portrayal of teachers on Disney Channel sitcoms is evidence of the larger issue of how teachers and the teaching

profession are viewed negatively in most aspects of modern media. Why do you think teacher incompetency has become one of the primary focal points of educational critique? Where else do you see this reflected in modern media?

2. How might teacher education programs benefit from a closer study of the intersection of education, mass media, popular culture, and technology, including negative portrayals of teachers in popular culture?
3. What questions might we need to ask young viewers/students about the portrayals cited in this chapter to get an understanding of how they view the portrayal of teachers on the Disney Channel and in other popular media? How can teachers help students become more critical of mass media?

REFERENCES

Adorno, T. (1991). *The culture industry*. New York: Routledge.

Ayers, W. (2001). A teacher ain't nothin' but a hero: Teachers and teaching in film. In P. B. Joseph & G. E. Burnaford (Eds.), *Images of schoolteachers in America* (pp. 201–210). Mahwah, NJ: Lawrence Erlbaum Associates.

Blutman, M. (Writer), & Zwick, J. (Director). (2014). Girl meets flaws [Television series episode]. In M. Jacobs (Producer), *Girl Meets World*. Burbank, CA: The Walt Disney Company.

Bronner, S. E., & Kellner, D. M. (1989). Theodor Adorno, the culture industry revisited. In S. E. Bronner & D. M. Kellner, D. (Eds.), *Critical theory and society: A reader* (pp. 128–135). New York: Routledge.

Cortes, C. (2000). *The children are watching: How the media teach about diversity*. New York: Teachers College Press.

Crane, V., & Chen, M. (2003). Content development of children's media. In E. L. Palmer and B. M. Young (Eds.), *The faces of televisual media: Teaching, violence, selling to children* (pp. 55–81). Mahwah, NJ: Lawrence Erlbaum Associates.

Dalton, M., & Linder, L. (1998). *Teacher tv: Sixty years of teachers on television*. New York: Peter Lang.

Debord, G. (1983). *Society of the spectacle*. Detroit: Black & white. (Original work published in 1967).

Delony, M., & Delony, S. (2013). Professional paradox: Teachers in film and television. In E. Janak & D. F. Blum (Eds.), *The pedagogy of pop* (pp. 101–120). Lanham, MD: Lexington Books.

Disney (2014). Disney channel ratings highlights for October 2014. Disney Channel industry report. Available at: http://www.disneychannelmedianet.com/DNR/2014/DC_DJ_OCT14.pdf

Edelman, M. (1988). *Constructing the political spectacle*. Chicago: University of Chicago Press.

Gerbner, G. (1963). Smaller than life: Teachers and schools in the mass media. *Phi Delta Kappan 44*, 202–205.

Gerbner, G. (1969). Toward cultural indicators: The analysis of mass mediated message systems. *AV Communications Review, 17*(1), 137–148.

Gerbner, G. (1998). Cultivation analysis: An overview. *Mass Communication & Society, J*, 175–194.

Glanz, J. (1997). Images of principals on television and in the movies. *The Clearing House, 70*(6), 295–297.

Jacobs, M. (Producer). 2014. Girl Meets World. Burbank, CA: The Walt Disney Company.

Kaiser Family Foundation (2010). *Generation M2: Media in the lives of 8–18 year olds.* New York: Kaiser Family Foundation. Available at: http://kff.org/other/event/generation-m2-media-in-the-lives-of/

Kopelow, K., & Seifert, H. (Executive Producers). (2011). *Austin & Ally* [Television Series]. Burbank, CA: The Walt Disney Company.

Lapiduss, S., Dunlap. E. (Writers), & Lewis, P. (Director). (2012). Make new friends, but hide the old [Television Series Episode]. In P. O'Connell (Producer), *Jessie.* Burbank, CA: The Walt Disney Company.

Lapiduss, S., Dunlap. E. (Writers), & Flynn, S. P. (Director). (2013). Teacher's pest [Television Series Episode]. In P. O'Connell (Producer), *Jessie.* Burbank, CA: The Walt Disney Company.

Maeroff, G. (1998). *Imaging education: The media and schools in America.* New York: Teachers College Press.

Nelson, M. (Writer), & Whitesell, J. (Director). (2014). Girl meets Maya's mother [Television Series Episode]. In M. Jacobs (Producer), *Girl Meets World.* Burbank, CA: The Walt Disney Company.

O'Connell, P. (Writer), & Koherr, B. (Director). (2011). New York, New nanny [Television Series Episode]. In P. O'Connell (Producer), *Jessie.* Burbank, CA: The Walt Disney Company.

Otto, S. (2005). Nostalgic for what? The epidemic of images of the mid-20th century classroom in American media culture and what it means. *Discourse: Studies in the Cultural Politics of Education, 26,* 459–475.

Potter, W. J., & Chang, I. C. (1990). Television exposure measures and the cultivation hypothesis. *Journal of Broadcasting and Electronic Media, 34,* 313–333.

Schor, J. (2005). *Born to buy: The commercialized child and the new consumer culture.* New York: Scribner.

Signorelli, N., Gerbner, G., & Morgan, M. (1995). Violence on television: The cultural indicators project. *Journal of Broadcasting & Electronic Media, 39,* 278–283.

Soetaert, R., Mottart, A., & Verdoodt, I. (2004). Culture and pedagogy in teacher education. *The Review of Education, Pedagogy & Cultural Studies, 26*(2–33), 155–174.

Thompson, C, & Lotterstein, H. (Executive Producers). (2010). *Shake It Up* [Television Series]. Burbank, CA: The Walt Disney Company.

Turner, S. E. (2014). BBFFs: Interracial friendships in a post-racial world. In S. Nielsen & S. E. Turner (Eds.), *The colorblind screen: Television in post-racial America* (pp. 237–257). New York: NYU Press.

Viacom (2013). The story of me. *Viacom, nc.* Available at: http://www.4-traders.com/VIACOM-INC-9548248/news/Viacom-Inc--Nickelodeon-Introduces-The-Story-of-Me-Research-Study-Providing-Inside-Look-At-Tod-17481902/

Weber, S., & Mitchell, C. (1995). *That's funny, you don't look like a teacher: Interrogating images and identity in popular culture.* London: The Falmer Press.

Wells, A. S., & Serman, T. W. (1998). Education against all odds: What films teach us about schools. In G. Maeroff (Ed.), *Imaging education: The media and schools in America* (pp. 101–119). New York: Teachers College Press.

CHAPTER ELEVEN

Gaia Taking Back Disneyland

Regenerative Education for Creative Rewilding

MARNA HAUK

I grew up in Southern California, and from third grade to high school graduation, lived within a few miles of Disneyland in a tract called, "Suburbia Park." During that time, I probably visited Disneyland two dozen times. It was a place of great personal innocent delight for my child-self. In fact, ironically, I credit my visit to Disneyland's Tom Sawyer Island as my first wilderness (like) experience. Years later, I left my job because the technology company for which I worked was to be acquired by Disney, and the CEO's vision of cultural colonialism was unacceptable to me. Cultural colonialism, evidenced by the omnipresence of multi-media conglomerates in the spread of global capitalism, marks the age of the Anthropocene, the epoch in which the activities of human beings have significantly impacted Earth's ecosystems.

Contemporary media discourses enforce tropes, troupes, and troops that cultivate a culture of petroleum dependency, consumption, colonized creativity, and domesticated dependence. In the distortions and twists of cultural colonialism, imperial consciousness is a mythical vacation destination, as Disney has ascended to a mega-religion. The pilgrimage to Disneyland overshoots travel to Mecca annually by a factor of five: 16.2 million visitors went to Disneyland in 2013 (Themed Entertainment Association, 2014), compared to 3.2 million pilgrims to Mecca in 2012 (Hafiz, 2013). More people visit Disneyland than attend high school in a given year (14.7 million in 2014, according to the National Center for Educational Statistics, 2014). Disney theme parks generate $2.2 billion in profit annually (Niles, 2013), stirring more energy and engagement than elementary school, and the Disney entertainment empire continues to grow as profits rise.

All of this touristic consumption of, and at, Disneyland (and at the other Disney parks) comes at a grave price. As Shiva (2008) noted, "Our consumption and production systems are devouring the planet. This entropic degradation is putting our very existence at risk" (p. 137). Indeed, The Walt Disney Company is not merely a harmless purveyor of entertainment; its teachings are harmful and harm-causing. The imperial gloss of collaborative creativity generates shiny, fun entertainment while the dismal reality of colonized creativity spawns technologized, anti-nature and oppressive discourses that shunt creative impulses into consumption and internalized conquest. However, alternative cultural trajectories that are earth-honoring and life-enhancing of the vital planetary processes and biocultural co-evolution in particular place-cultures are possible through transformative sustainability education, which "integrate[s] transdisciplinary study (head); practical skill sharing and development (hands); and translation of passion and values into behavior (heart)" offering a transdisciplinary, place-based, unified framework (Sipos, Battisti, & Grimm, 2008, p. 68). The "frontiers" of sustainability education (Selby & Kagawa, 2009) include critical and transformative voices to "interrogate root drivers of the crisis of unsustainability" (p. 277), to challenge underlying assumptions, and to mobilize for action; and include "belittled or overlooked" sources, drawing from critical, creative, and imaginative entanglement (p. 278) in trans-disciplinary learning deeply immersed in nature, leaving behind formal settings and systems as needed (p. 279).

Such learning requires theoretical and pedagogical approaches that are synthesizing and oriented to confluence, congruence, and celebration. Keating (2013) advocates for radically interconnective and non-oppositional pedagogies of invitation inspired by a desire to create an alternative to critical pedagogy. Post-oppositional pedagogies of invitation "employ relational, connectionist thinking… shifting from critique to invitation…to establish a…climate of generosity and respect" (p. 182). Congruent with Keating's (2013) interdependent and intersubjective pedagogies of invitation are Gaian methods, which embrace ecological and connected knowing, connected dialogue (Clinchy, 1996), connected ecological consciousness (Sterling, 2009), and what Ettinger (2006) has characterized as trans-subjective or matrixial consciousness. Gaian methods share lineages with the Gaia hypothesis/Gaia Theory (Margulis, 2004), deep ecology (Mathews, 2008), and emergent notions of place-based and ecocentric agency (Barrett, 2009), congruent with indigenous and traditional ecological knowledge systems understandings (Berkes, 1999; Cajete, 2008).

A type of Gaian method, terrapsychology is a set of research methods for exploring "our largely unconscious (because disregarded) connections to and interdependencies with the multi-leveled presence of our living Earth, including specific places, creatures, and materials" (Chalquist, 2010, p. 6). Terrapsychology imagines places as archetypally alive and explores the significance and possibilities within the embedded archetypes. It also engages, re-imagines, and can work to heal distortions places are evidencing (echoed in the human experience with/in them), and it imagines the possibilities of places and materialisms. In place of the space cleared by terrapsychological perception, visionary futurecasting generates an alternative future, a cultural imaginary. Cultural imaginaries are the deep stories or narratives undergirding and driving cultural momentum and can catalyze "the urgent task of restorying the ways we live on this earth" (McKenzie et al., 2009, p. 1). McKenzie et al. describe working with cultural imaginaries as encouragement to engage in "disruptive daydreams" to sense "when embeddedness in particular understandings and practices ... may call for attempts at unsticking, for disruption" (p. 2).

This chapter aims to unstick domination narratives about imagination and creativity embedded in Disneyland as embodied curriculum by using creative imagination and futurecast cultural imaginaries in which the earth system reinhabits agentic powers. I seek to open up alternative understandings of non-dominated, regenerative creativities in order to begin to heal the colonized imagination of Disneyland and the educational cultures of colonization it otherwise proliferates. I explore the underbelly of the pervading land of creativity to reclaim the roots of magic, animistic co-affiliation, trans-species collaborative creativity, and matrixial embedment within the generative living systems of the planetary. Focusing on the actual, physical genesis place of Disney, the Disneyland theme park in Anaheim, California, I consider, through three disruptions, what is possible in a future imaginary. The first disruption involves upending consumerism, including green consumerism, and instead forwarding ecoliteracy and ecological intelligences towards a return to radical ecocentrism. The second disruption explores how turning the outdoors into a domesticated interior invites regenerative rewilding. The third disruption proposes that the creativity suppressed by the conquest-disordered authoritarianism, that in Disneyland positions humans at the center of the act of creation yoked to the purpose of purchase, can be unleashed for justice and liberation. Here, Gaia breaks through Disneyland, and the imagination of the earth liberates the curriculum of consumption and the domestication of magic toward an education that is creative, collaborative, and connective, in which Gaia takes back Disneyland, from animation to animism.

DISRUPTION ONE: RE-AIMING CONSUMERISM TO ECOCENTRISM—FROM GREEN CONSUMERISM TO ECOLITERACY AND ECOLOGICAL INTELLIGENCE FOR THE BIOCULTURAL COMMONS

Ecological intelligence is theorized as holistic, critical, appreciative, inclusive, systemic, creative, and ethical, integrating "experiential, inquiring, experimental, participative, iterative, real-world, and action-oriented, invoking 'learning-as-change'" (Sterling, 2009, p. 82). Bowers (2006, 2012) described how Goleman's (2009) initial work on ecological intelligence was limited to green consumerism. Goleman's framing has since expanded to educating for ecological intelligence for deep ecoliteracy (Goleman, Bennett, & Barlow, 2012). Not just greenwashing consumerism, Bowers (2012) imagined a "life sustaining ecological intelligence" (p. 112) in which educational reformers "escape from the linguistic colonization of the present by the past" (p. 118) to surface and reframe the cultural language and metaphors that further the enclosure of the commons and to revitalize the local cultural commons. Through the concept of ecological intelligence, Bowers conveyed (1) that the scale of intelligence is not the individual but the culture; (2) that the scale of intelligence is not just the cultural but the biocultural honoring of long-standing indigenous knowledge systems and intergenerational knowledge of cultures-in-place; (3) that the biocultural commons is the context for ecological intelligence; (4) that reframed ecological intelligence includes a connectionist attention to context, purpose, meaning, tacit understandings, and histories of relationship; (5) that print and computer-based abstractions are dangerously decontextualizing; and that (6) embodied experiential engagement with the local cultural commons offers a "life sustaining" alternative to industrial production and "consumer dependent" lifestyles that can support even the most exploited and vulnerable in industrial money economies towards a postindustrial, low-carbon flourishing (pp. 119–120). There is an echo here of what Heinberg, Sachs, and Shiva (2008) call a post-carbon culture of moderation, what the transition movement calls energy descent for a soft landing to a post-carbon future (Transition Network, 2013), what climate change educational theorist Selby (2010) proposed as cultures of contraction and moderation that favor connection over consumption. Selby advocated for anti-consumption education as a requisite for carbon descent: "Anti-consumerism education ... protects the ecosphere and the ethnosphere" (p. 7).

Shiva (2008) clarified that one of the three paradigm shifts needed as a solution to climate chaos is "[f]rom a consumerist definition of being human to one that recognizes us as conservers of the earth's finite resources and co-creators of wealth with nature" (p. 43). Upending the Disney curriculum does not just mean, therefore, "buying green"—it means refraining from purchasing. It means shifting to a paradigm of conservation, moderation, and wealth understood as shining from the biocultural commons and economies of generosity and sharing. Ecological intelligence and learning for the biocultural commons, informed by a critical pedagogy of place, can hearken a shift from consumerism resonant with sustainability education approaches such as garden-based learning and nature immersive educational praxis, which will be explored below as "regenerative rewilding."

DISRUPTION TWO: REGENERATIVE REWILDING AND RELOCALIZING

We can imagine regenerative rewilding as a massive depaving project similar to the move in permaculture in which certain seed trees can be planted in the cracks of cement and crumble the cement to liberate the earth beneath (Depave, 2015; Williams & Brown, 2012). Decolonizing Disneyland curriculum involves depaving the human heart as well. The scale must deflate from the "reactionary gigantism" (Chalquist, 2009, p. 75) of Southern California and Disneyland's uncanny valley of mega-mice and plastic princesses. This deflation grounds us soundly in the local, experiential, and in a state of power-from-within.

Efforts of relocalization, local food movements and food justice, intercultural and intergenerational school gardens (Williams & Brown, 2012), and localized transition projects for energy descent for a gentle landing to a post-carbon future (Hopkins, 2008) are all movements towards cultural imaginaries that are local in scale, organic in approach, and rewilding for learners. Chalquist (2009) emphasized that shifting from mega-scale to small-scale helped surface a multitude of examples of groundswelling empowerment, inviting visitors to Southern California to "look beyond the blaring surfaces of reactionary giantism and see the numerous experiments blossoming here and elsewhere" (p. 75).

Sustainability scholar Shiva (2008) affirmed how refocusing on building small-scale, local food systems can spark creative alternatives. Shiva saw small-scale and sustainable approaches as a form of "renewable energy of ecology and sharing, of solidarity and compassion, that we need to generate and multiply to counter the destructive energy of greed that is creating scarcity at every level" (p. 144). These forms of local, ecosocial renewable energy offer generative and generous alternatives to scarcity and dependence and can hallmark a shift from addiction to empires of consumption to liberation within localized rewilding and undomestication. Critical pedagogies of place support education for both re-inhabitation and decolonization (Gruenewald, 2003). As Williams and Brown (2012) affirmed, sustainability education nourishes these movements towards and with earthly abundance and economies and ecologies of solidarity. These connect ecological rewilding with ecologies of creativity, the decolonization of our creativity, and reclamation of the imagination.

DISRUPTION THREE: CREATIVITY UNLEASHED—RECLAIMING CULTURE CREATIVES AND ECOLOGIES OF CREATIVITY

The hidden Disney curriculum works through animatronic technology and animation, marking the erasures, absences, and distortions of terrestrial and cultural colonization. "Magic" is coopted into animating these absences and breathing false life into the erasure. There is a displacement of creativity, universe, evolution, deity, or nature as maker. At Disneyland, the animation-makers, the hidden creatives, have become deity, setting their clockwork minions in motion to perpetuate a more than fifty-year empire in the domain of creativity. Disney marks the pinnacle of the clockwork fantasy of the Cartesian split, human dominion writ large and reductionism's finest hour. Life can be replaced with the semblance of dynamism motivating and reinforcing a larger stasis: life can be replaced with moving dolls.

The rules regarding the conduct and appearances of Disney theme park employees are extreme and also reinforce dominion mentality and the near doll-like normativity of the workers-as-actors, who are referred to as crew members. Workers are fully colonized and commoditized. It takes tremendous work to maintain these Disney fantasies of enclosure and dominion. Workers have to endure great heat, especially in summer months, to perform in elaborate costumes. The totalistic obsession with appearance-making and fantasy-maintenance continues as humans thus are subsumed inside the culture-making machinery. The workers themselves are domesticated and "play an important role as representatives of the Disney brand" (Disney, n.d., par 2). There are very specific rules and prohibitions to achieve the "friendly classic appearance" (par. 1) "clean, natural, polished, and professional" (par. 2). These highly normative and controlling rules include strict personal grooming guidelines and the erasure of any personally specific or unique signifiers. The "crew members" themselves become breathing animatronics, with specified haircuts and styles and prohibitions and rules on personal conduct and grooming.

Resisting the curriculum of Disneyland involves dismantling the animatronic clockworks, including those we may have internalized. Jardine (1998) suggested that phenomenological deepening could help us "awaken from Descartes's nightmare" (p. 21). The work of unhinging the Disney curriculum involves phenomenological noticings and understandings. Chalquist's (2010) call for terrapsychology echoed Jardine's suggestions regarding ecological imagination. Chalquist described how "the modernist moaning about the separateness, randomness, and 'thrownness' of life fades out" with the terrapsychological realization of "how we belong to this lively world and the glittering cosmos all around it" (p. 8). Chalquist's words resonate with Jardine's (1998) language about "winning back the surging, delicate life … that slips between the cracks, frustrating the desire for stasis, foreclosure, and clarity" (p. 21).

Walt Disney positioned himself as engineering the imagination, via "imagineers." One could argue that Disney colonized creativity itself. Thus the work of reclaiming culture at Disneyland also becomes the work of reclaiming the creative process, which has been (1) coopted to dominator ends, including generating cultural reinforcements for domination; (2) twisted into selling consumer goods and proliferating consumption cultures; (3) stymied, so people have a lack of self and self-connection, causing an internal hunger that can be pseudo-sated through consumption; and (4) stunted, so people are confused about who they are. When people do not know who they are, if they are culturally and/or physically deracinated, they will tend to internalize oppressions and turn to consumption to allay their hopelessness and despair, and their existential angst at feeling cut from the earthly ties and what the ecoeducator Clinebell (2013), termed *earthy groundedness.* Macy and Johnstone (2012) emphasized the importance of cultivating a connected sense of self, embedded in larger circles of connection, resilience, and support, to address the vulnerable-making inner deficiencies associated with consumption and affluenza (p. 91).

Creativity can be a force of liberation. This is why creativity is critically controlled, subsumed, and colonized in cultures of domination. Creativity, when not twisted by dominion culture, is a connective force supporting life-giving cultures and liberatory movement. Creativity is emergent and has emergent properties (Hauk, 2014). It is part of regenerative and life-giving cultures and part of sustainability education. I have elsewhere (Hauk, 2013) posited that sustainable and regenerative education can connect learners with ecologically sourced patterns in what Gerofsky (2013) called "geometries of liberation." I have further shown that emergent collaborative creativities inspired by ecological and biocultural relating, which might be termed *ecosocial* and *biocultural creativities*, or *complex earth regenerative creativities*, are regenerative in nature and produce ethical thinking in learners and learning collectives (Hauk, 2014; Hauk & Bloomfield, 2016).

As I have argued, Disneyland offers an indexical case of a culture of petroleum dependency, consumption, colonized creativity, and domesticated dependence, all of which are pushing the earth to the brink. As Shiva (2008) observed, "we can either let the processes of destruction, disintegration, and extermination continue unchallenged or we can unleash our creative energies to make systemic change and reclaim our future as a species, as part of the earth family" (p. 144). Unleashing creative energies is part of the process of the disruptions I have performed, above. That is, I seek not only to clear space through terrapsychological perception, but also to enact visionary futurecasting to generate an alternative narrative of the future of living on, and with, the earth. In what follows, I present my "disruptive daydream" (McKenzie et al., 2009, p. 2) of Gaia breaking through and reclaiming Disneyland, as the Earth in all of its creative power disrupts Disney's imagination and builds a collaborative and connective new curriculum.

FUTURE IMAGINARY: GAIA

The giantism of Disneyland has let out a clarion call, and the Earth jumps up from herself and births giant daughters of compassion to claim magic and to liberate

Disneyland. Gaia comes back down to Earth. She lands—whallumph—on the solid-seeming veneer of Disneyland, and her "feet" go down twenty feet into the Earth. It's like she's churning up the soil, piercing through, coming across. Who are the Earth goddesses of Sustainability who appear, breaking out of the imperial Disney gloss? Daughters of Earth, including Annapurna (Hindu), Aje (African), Erda (Norse), Fjörgynn (Scandinavian), Gaia/Ge (Greek), Mou-Njami (Siberian), Ponniyamman (Southeast Asian), Tellus (Roman), Terra (Roman), and Zemyna (Slavic) (Monaghan, 2010), along with Earth and mountain goddesses of many other cultures. Goddess of Santa Ana River, rising and unfurling. Goddess Pacifica coming from the ocean westward to the former sacred groves. Goddess of Oranges, mighty daughter of Oestara arrives, thrummeling the Earth, with orchards arising where her feet have passed. We hear the Earth pummel-thrummeling, "the primordial power of creation, the self-organizing, self-generative, and self-renewing creative force of the universe in feminine form" (Shiva, 2008, p. 136).

At first, Disneyland visitors think it is an earthquake. There is a thuddering shudder, then a pause. Thunder. Pause. Thunder. Pause. The California theme park is near the San Andreas Fault. On a sunny day, fifty thousand people are receiving their edutainment, hurrying and flittering about. The rides shriek to a stop. First, she is spotted near Bear Country Jamboree, where people in line for the "Thunder Mountain Railroad" ride realize two large trees are moving towards them. They then realize that they are not actually trees. Each leg is a different bark. Her left leg is a conifer bark, rough redwooded, calf the diameter of a ballfield. Her right leg thunders down next, the white of a willow, sweetly curved and massive. After a long time, she has risen. Summoned by the long-slumbering Earth. She is not the last of her kind, but the first of a new generation. While some humans, ecofeminists, environmentalists, and surfers (of these three, there are more of the latter in Orange County; the other two are almost extinct) see her as savior, rescuer, Earth goddess; she is not that exactly. She is compassionate and fierce combined (Macy & Johnstone, 2012). She splits into five and then recombines. Each aspect is a fractal dimension of her generative and regenerative wholeness. Matrixial, Recombining, Connective, Alive. What does animation have on animism? She has risen to where she lifts the roof off of Space Mountain to show the actual constellations. Her sisters sluice living waters into the carefully orchestrated swill that has been perking in the Jungle Cruise.

She is not a human, though we see her as humaniform. Mists swirl around her body. She is countermythic, counterhegemonic. But humans are like ants to her; she is sympathetic, but she will not be stopped. She is a countervailing force of peace. Saviors are the mythos of victimization—we move into the hands, heads, heart, the senses, and what is emergent.

We have moved beyond Eden. Earthvox (Hauk, 2014) pervades the hearing range. Dominion has become so huge, so overinflated, even a mouse is humaniform and large. Earthvox is not a voice, discernible in sound. She whispers, speaking into the part of her that is us. She is moving from The Matrix to the matrixial. The air contains the new ideas; the waters roll up from the ocean in a tsunami. There is a wrenching grief, a wailing keening that starts for what has been lost, the balloons, the fantasy of domination, the loss of the spoils of extraction, and the devastating knowledge and witness of the subjugation and enslavement. The Earth shimmies in a move of obversity (Grahn, 2007), a form of metacognitive compassionate engagement with cultural conditioning and internalized oppression. The wails and shrieks are not towards anything or running away from something. That is the modern/old way. The way of subjugation, victim/oppressor/savior. The older way unfolds, before the rupture and unraveling. This way honors life; it is in our blood and bones. This is the way of embedment of mutuality and belonging (Flinders, 2002). This is the way of sustainable contraction with its cultures of moderation (Selby, 2010).

Humans at the park that day put down their cotton candy and their bubble gum balls, their latest wares, and lay their weary heads down on the shimmering Earth. Earth rises up through a kind of squiggle jiggling and depaves itself. Cement gives way to dirt and verdure. There is a shimmering rainbow glittering airswirl around each person. Each child regains what had been drained through the colonization of their creativity. The vacuous sucking whole of scarcity, of earth hunger, closes. The lack that consumption was consuming ebbs. The wholeness that was always there reasserts itself. The goddesses shrink down now; Gaia ebbs from a uniform largeness and emerges instead into the wholeness of each being, leaf, gnat, human, fungal mat. The humans, who had been lying on the ground to regain their center in the shaking chaos, now feel a part of Gaia seep and stir within their sinews and bones. They rise up in the groundswelling wholeness, and we hear patriarchal domination's last gasp of stealing making and creation from nature. Animatronics become a kind of modern Frankenstein depositing the natural resilience (and governance) of nature and biocultural symbiosis for anthrodominion, an ineluctable doom that anthropocentric posthumanism's dreams of singularity and long-lived tech-extension has completely ignored.

There are new romances, more ecological and matrixial: A princess who is an affiliative symbiont falls in love with a fungal cluster. Tom Sawyer's Island offers educational programs in appropriate technology and energy descent to post-carbon possibilities. The haunted mansion has become the House of Guidance with rituals of summoning, celebrating, and listening to Wise Ancestors. This includes the more than human with representatives from extinct species. This new Earthland fosters localized spin-offs, as we re-open our senses to the immediate opportunities for living mythos for cultures of energy descent and moderation, opportunities for biocultural flourishing in every place, the place we find ourselves, without high-carbon pilgrimages to grimacing giantism. Instead, we realize the deepest magic, welcoming the living Earth in our own location, the possibilities for reconciliation and regeneration rife within five feet of our apartment window or nearby park.

DISCUSSION QUESTIONS

1. As an act of cultural reclamation, how might you take one dimension, narrative, or character in Disney's pantheon and untwist it to reclaim a strength?
2. In your home place and cultural context, what is an asset, characteristic, or strength of the land or place? Are there myths, histories, landforms, or intuitions you can draw from to generate a new mythology?
3. In consumer culture, we are trained to feel insufficient, dependent, and needy, and that others and technology are the source of meaning, entertainment, and fulfillment. Cultivate ecological intelligence through expanding your sense of self. What would it be like to perceive and think as the planet?
4. What are strengths we can cultivate in an age of climate crisis and ecological unraveling, in a time inviting the cultivation of active hope?
5. Inspired by an exercise from *Active Hope: How to Face the Mess We're in Without Going Crazy* (Macy & Johnstone, 2012), write a letter to yourself from a being two hundred years in the future. This being knows exactly the kinds of actions and flows of events that brought about a world in which they are able to thrive. What do they have to say, in thanks for your courageous actions and creativity?

REFERENCES

Barrett, M. J. (2009). *Beyond human-nature-spirit boundaries: Researching with animate earth.* Doctoral dissertation. Published online at http://www.porosity.ca

Berkes, F. (1999). *Sacred ecology: Traditional ecological knowledge and resource management.* Philadelphia: Taylor & Francis.

Bowers, C. A. (2006). *Revitalizing the commons: Cultural and educational sites of resistance and affirmation.* Lanham, MD: Lexington Books.

Bowers, C. A. (2012). The challenge facing educational reformers: Making the transition from individual to ecological intelligence in an era of climate change. In D. Ambrose & R. Sternberg (Eds.), *How dogmatic beliefs harm creativity and higher-level thinking* (pp. 112–122). New York: Routledge.

Cajete, G. (2008). Seven orientations for the development of indigenous science education. In N. K. Denzin, Y. S. Lincoln, & L. Tuhiwai Smith (Eds.), *Handbook of critical and indigenous methodologies* (pp. 487–496). Thousand Oaks, CA: Sage.

Chalquist, C. (2009). *The tears of Llorona: A California odyssey of place, myth, and homecoming.* Walnut Creek, CA: World Soul Books.

Chalquist, C. (2010). *RebEarths: Conversations with a world ensouled.* Walnut Creek, CA: World Soul Books.

Clinchy, B. M. (1996). Connected and separate knowing: Toward a marriage of two minds. In N. Goldberger, J. Tarule, B. Clinchy, & M. Belenky (Eds.), *Knowledge, difference, and power: Essays inspired by women's ways of knowing* (pp. 205–247). New York: Basic Books.

Clinebell, H. (2013). *Ecotherapy: Healing ourselves, healing the earth.* Hoboken, NJ: Taylor & Francis.

Depave. (2015). Depave: From parking lots to paradise. Retrieved from: Depave.org.

Disney (n.d.). The Disney look [Web page]. Disneyland Careers [Website]. Retrieved from: http://dlr.disneycareers.com/en/working-here/the-disney-look/

Ettinger, B. L. (2006). *The matrixial borderspace. Theory out of bounds, 28.* Minneapolis: University of Minnesota Press.

Flinders, C. (2002). *The values of belonging: Rediscovering balance, mutuality, intuition, and wholeness in a competitive world.* San Francisco, CA: Harper.

Gerofsky, S. (2013, April). Always an abundance: Non-linear teacher education in the orchard garden with the urban weavers. In S. Gerofsky (Chair), The geometries of liberation: The hidden wealth of patterns and materials outside the grid. Interactive symposium conducted at the American Educational Research Association Conference, San Francisco.

Goleman, D. (2009). *Ecological intelligence: How knowing the hidden impacts of what we buy can change everything.* New York: Broadway Books.

Goleman, D., Bennett, L., & Barlow, Z. (2012). *Ecoliterate: How educators are cultivating emotional, social, and ecological intelligence.* San Francisco: Jossey-Bass and the Center for Ecoliteracy.

Grahn, J. (2007). Cultural obversity. *Metaformia: A Journal of Menstruation and Culture.* Retrieved from: http://www.metaformia.org/articles/cultural-obversity/

Gruenewald [Greenwood], D. (2003). Best of both worlds: Critical pedagogy of place. *Educational Researcher, 32* (4), 3–12.

Hafiz, Y. (2013, October 11). Hajj 2013, Islam's pilgrimage to Mecca: Facts, history and dates of the Muslim holiday. Huffington Post. Retrieved from: http://www.huffingtonpost.com/2013/10/11/hajj-2013_n_4064513.html

Hauk, M. (2013). Geometries of liberation paper. Paper presented at the American Educational Research Association. San Francisco.

Hauk, M. (2014). *Gaia e/mergent: Earth regenerative education catalyzing empathy, creativity, and wisdom.* Dissertation. Prescott, AZ: Prescott College. UMI 3630295. Retrieved from: http://pqdtopen.proquest.com/pqdtopen/doc/1563382491.html?FMT=ABS

Hauk, M., & Bloomfield, V. (2016). Blanking out [ ] (whiteness): Decolonizing systems of domination, connecting with ancestral place-cultures for reinhabitation. In V. Stead (Ed.), *RIP Jim Crow: Fighting racism through higher education policy, curriculum, and cultural intervention.* New York: Peter Lang.

Heinberg, R., Sachs, W., & Shiva, V. (2008, January/February). Transition strategies. *Resurgence Magazine, 246.* Retrieved from: http://www.resurgence.org/

Hopkins, R. (2008). *The transition handbook.* Totnes, Devon, UK: Green Books.

Jardine, D. W. (1998). *To dwell with a boundless heart: Essays in curriculum theory, hermeneutics, and the ecological imagination.* New York: Peter Lang.

Keating, A. (2013). *Transformation now!: Toward a post-oppositional politics of change.* Urbana: University of Illinois Press.

Macy, J., & Johnstone, C. (2012). *Active hope: How to face the mess we're in without going crazy.* Novato, CA: New World Library.

Margulis, L. (2004). Gaia by any other name. In S. H. Schneider, J. R. Miller, E. Crist, & P. J. Boston (Eds.), *Scientists debate Gaia: The next century* (pp. 7–12). Cambridge, MA: MIT.

Mathews, F. (2008). Thinking from within the calyx of nature. *Environmental Values, 17*(1), 41–65.

McKenzie, M., Hart, P., Bai, H., & Jickling, B. (2009). Educational fields and cultural imaginaries. In McKenzie, M., Hart, P., Bai, H., & Jickling, B. (Eds.), *Fields of green: Restorying culture, environment, and education* (pp. 1–10). Cresskill, NJ: Hampton Press.

Monaghan, P. (2010). *Encyclopedia of goddesses and heroines* (Vol. I). Santa Barbara, CA: Greenwood.

National Center for Educational Statistics. (2014). Public high school graduation rates [Online data and table]. Retrieved from: http://nces.ed.gov/programs/coe/indicator_coi.asp

Niles, R. (2013, November 7). Disney keeps raking it in: $2.2 billion in theme park profits for the year. *Theme Park Insider*. Retrieved from: http://www.themeparkinsider.com/flume/201311/3763/

Selby, D. (2010). 'Go, go, go, said the bird': Sustainability-related education in interesting times. In F. Kagawa & D. Selby (Eds.), *Education and climate change living and learning in interesting times* (pp. 35–52). New York: Routledge.

Selby, D., & Kagawa, F. (Eds.). (2009). *Education and climate change: Living and learning in interesting times*. Florence, KY: Routledge.

Shiva, V. (2008). *Soil not oil: Environmental justice in an age of climate crisis*. New York: Zed.

Sipos, Y., Battisti, B., & Grimm, K. (2008). Achieving transformative sustainability learning: Engaging head, hands and heart. *International Journal of Sustainability in Higher Education, 9*(1), 68–86.

Sterling, S. (2009). Riding the storm: Towards a connective cultural consciousness. In E. J. Wals (Ed.), *Social learning towards a sustainable world* (pp. 63–82). The Netherlands: Wageningen.

Themed Entertainment Association. (2014, June 17). TEA & AECOM publish global theme park and museum attendance numbers for 2013. Retrieved from: http://tea-connect.blogspot.com/2014/06/tea-and-aecom-publish-global-theme-park.html

Transition Network. (2013). Energy descent action plans [Web site]. Retrieved from: https://www.transitionnetwork.org/ingredients/building/energy-descent-action-plans

Williams, D., & Brown, J. (2012). *Learning gardens and sustainability education: Bringing life to schools and schools to life*. New York: Routledge.

PART FOUR

Teaching Ourselves

CHAPTER TWELVE

"But He Was Your Prince Charming!"

Accounting for the End of "Ever After" with a Divorce Fairytale

SHANNON DAHMES PUECHNER

Marriage is a story we explicitly tell *together*: the transfiguration of girl into bride cannot be accomplished alone but requires the actions of magical others. When vows are spoken, it is a promise made not only to one's spouse, but also to everyone who bears witness. It is a promise to step into certain cultural narratives and to uphold and live out the categories that help us understand each other. I had not fully realized the ways that others were bound up in the story of my marriage until happily ever after proved to be false. I soon discovered that my divorce wasn't just about me; the problem of my unwritten identity also created profound anxiety for others.

I had expected that it would be difficult for me to share the news with everyone I knew. I was grieving and I was ashamed. But I had not anticipated the anxieties my dissolution would produce in others. My mother was merely the first of many to implore, "What happened? He was your prince charming. …" The assertion of the fairytale-ness of my marriage was almost always followed by the same litany of questions: "Did he cheat? Did he beat you? Did he gamble? Did he drink?" While these interrogations did not position me directly as the false/failed/fallen princess, the wicked queen, and as the ruiner of happy endings, they put me in jeopardy of these positions. I attempted to evade this entire line of questioning, asserting that there were no villains, that the details were private, and that it was complicated. However, these evasions proved to be insufficient; they did not address the anxieties being expressed.

All of this remained frustrating and mysterious to me until some years later when I read Bronwyn Davies's *Shards of Glass: Children Reading and Writing Beyond*

Gendered Identities (2003), which gave me some insight as to why my divorce created such anxiety and why fairytales became such a central part of these concerns. Drawing on poststructural conceptions of identity formation, Davies asserts that we do not possess a "real," "inner," or pre-existing "self," but rather, our sense of self, and the meanings others make of us are constituted through discourse. Put another way, we all *speak and write ourselves into existence* (p. 1). However, the task of self-creation cannot be accomplished alone. In order to be recognized by others, we must tell *legible* stories by drawing on recognizable cultural discourses. Because we are all constructing ourselves through these shared narratives, others become invested in how we perform our roles. As Davies explains, we "must learn to be coherent members of others' narratives" (p. 18).

In *Shards of Glass*, Davies is particularly concerned with the ways children write themselves into existence through fairytales, particularly stories of the victimized, helpless, rescued princess. She is interested not only in how these stories constrain the kinds of futures they can imagine for themselves but also how the construction of new fairytales might provide opportunities to open up new possibilities. While Disney is not the only purveyor of princess stories, it is certainly the most dominant (Do Rozario, 2004; Whelan, 2012). And while Disney films are loosely based on the classic tales, particularly as told by the Grimm Brothers, Disney simplifies, sanitizes, and Americanizes the tales (Giroux & Pollock, 2010; O'Brien, 1996; Zipes, 1995), drawing sharp lines between good and evil (Wasko, 2001). Hoerrner (1996) conducted a quantitative coding of prosocial and antisocial behaviors in Disney's animated films, finding that Disney characters tend to be almost entirely good or entirely evil. In fact, Snow White and Cinderella exhibited *only* prosocial behaviors, whereas the Disney villains exhibited almost none. Furthermore, in the Disney versions, Snow White, Cinderella, and Sleeping Beauty lost any cleverness and agency they may have possessed in the traditional tales. As a result, while the Grimms' heroines are relatively uninspiring, "those of Walt Disney seem barely alive. In fact, two of them hardly manage to stay awake" (Stone, 1975, p. 44).

In this chapter, I also concern myself with the project of self-construction through fairytales, but not through the experiences of children. Instead, I will examine a surprisingly literal example of my own experience of constructing myself through fairytales as an adult woman, specifically a fairytale I wrote on March 25, 2009, in response to the chorus of questions about my "prince charming." Drawing on an intuitive assemblage of techniques borrowed from collective memory work (Haug, 2008), literary analysis, and discourse analysis, I examine my tale through the lens of Davies's work in *Shards of Glass*, asking the following questions: Why was I, so explicitly and with such anxiety, called upon to account for the violation of the "happily ever after" fairytale story? How did these anxieties position me and limit the ways I could construct a new identity for myself as a divorced woman? And finally, how was I able to construct a more desirable position for myself through the appropriation of Disney princess tropes?

BECOMING AND UNBECOMING THE PRINCESS WIFE

The Little Mermaid (Clements & Musker, 1989) came out in theaters when I was thirteen years old, an age when I began constructing myself as an adult woman. I remember feeling a kinship with Ariel's curiosity, rebelliousness, and desire for independence. She felt so different from the old classic, helpless, beautiful but boring princesses. However, in the end, seemingly more agentic princesses like Ariel and Belle eventually surrendered their independent dreams to become a princess wife (Whelan, 2012). As Henke, Umble, and Smith (1996) put it, these princesses all "inevitably [succumb] to the dominant heterosexual, patriarchal notion that, in the final analysis, satisfaction is defined not by self-knowledge, being or accomplishments, but by a role prescribed through marriage" (p. 247).

Looking back, I see that my own life took a similar course. Before I married, it had been possible for me to draw upon feminist counter-stories when constructing myself. There were plenty of cultural resources for constructing such a story, including those of Ariel and Belle. As a single woman it was easy to persuade others to read me according to these narratives. However, after graduating from college, I found myself depressed, unemployed, and entirely unsure of what to make of my future, and, as a result, I became readable less as an independent feminist and more as a damsel in distress. When I subsequently fell in love with a charming, handsome, and upwardly mobile man, who on our very first date told me I was "the one," it became nearly impossible to avoid reading him as my rescuer and prince charming.

So, despite my attempts at resistance, the shoe fit, and I found myself taking up the story of the princess as my own: planning an elaborate wedding, assembling a court of attendants, donning a gown and crown, and dragging a magnificent train as I walked in procession to the altar. I tried to encode small symbols of resistance—my dress was not white but "mocha"; I was not "given away" and I certainly did not promise to obey—but in the end, the magic words were spoken and I was transformed from a mere woman to the princess wife. Seven years later, the story of happily-ever-after had come undone. This magic, so easily spoken into existence, was written asunder by lawyers—a new magical incantation that wrote our marriage, and, consequently, my princess identity, out of existence. It was an inversion and perversion of the fairy godmother moment—when the wave of a wand dissolves the servant girl into a glittering whirl before she is reconstituted into a proper princess. No longer wife, not yet something else, I hung suspended, swirling in that moment of transformation, made of nothing but fairy dust.

WRITING MYSELF INTO EXISTENCE

It is terrifying to disappear. As a result, I found myself writing more than I have ever written in my life, five to ten typed pages a day in journals, essays, emails to self, and blogs. I see now that I was desperately trying to write myself back into existence. The vast majority of my writing had nothing to do with fairytales; in fact, they rejected or ignored heteronormative expectations entirely. These new constructions of self were accepted enthusiastically by most of the people I spent time with in my new queer, feminist, and scholar spaces; however, in heteronormative spaces, where others had a stake in the ways I had composed myself as a married woman, these new stories proved insufficient.

Davies (2003) explains that if others cannot, or will not, read us the way we have written ourselves, we run the risk of becoming *illegible*, creating anxiety in others who have produced themselves through, and are therefore bound up in, our stories. This anxiety can lead to what Davies calls *category maintenance*, which is the process through which members of a community "assert the obviousness" of meaningful categories of group membership by "signaling the unacceptability of activities that disrupt the obvious meaning of the categories" (p. 20). This process of category maintenance is essential for keeping recognizable categories stable. "Otherwise the signs have no meaning" and the taboos that organize our lives fall apart (p. 23). Importantly, "Those category memberships are most often conceptually and practically elements of an oppositional binary pair" (p. 19), such as girl/boy, child/adult, or single/married. So when my mother said, "but he was your prince charming …" she was not so much asking about the prince himself, but more so calling into question my claim to the category of princess. Through divorce, and through the refusal of prince charming, I was violating the category of princess.

INNOCENT PRINCESS OR EVIL QUEEN

To understand how I was being positioned, we need to consider what constitutes the category of princess. Davies (2003) asserts that the princess is characterized by her "virtue" and "her passivity" (p. 5). This is particularly true of the princesses of the first three Disney princess films, *Snow White and the Seven Dwarfs* (Cottrell et al., 1938), *Sleeping Beauty* (Geronimi, 1959), and *Cinderella* (Geronimi, Jackson, & Luske, 1950), which were produced under the direct creative control of Walt Disney himself. In these films, the princess possesses child-like innocence. She is sweet and kind even under oppressive conditions, and her greatest happiness seems to be in her service to others (Henke, Umble, & Smith, 1996; Hoerrner, 1996; O'Brien, 1996; Wasko, 2001; Whelan, 2012; Zipes, 1995). But it is not enough for the princess to be "good"; she must also be a victim—a passive, helpless victim at that. Her very lack of wits, strength, and even desire for freedom, become criteria for proper princesshood. Henke, Umble, and Smith (1996) explain, "She never disobeys an order, never defends her rights, and never challenges their authority over her" (p. 235). Altogether, these characteristics represent an ideal performance of femininity so perfectly executed that the prince falls in love with her at first sight.

This construction of the princess puts girls, and the women they become, in a bit of a double bind. Of course we want to be "good" and "worthy" of true love, but as Davies (2003) explains:

> The attraction of the heroic male to the heroine, his desire to save her, depends entirely on her absolute virtue and on her passivity. And in Snow White's case this is passivity approximating death. The relevant desire for any reader positioning herself as Snow White would therefore be to be sufficiently virtuous and passive that she might be saved by a prince who would give her security in an otherwise dangerous world. (p. 5)

Of course, I wanted to resist being positioned as the helpless dependent princess. Unfortunately, Disney versions of the princess tales narrow the possible categories available for women. Despite the claims to family values, wives and mothers generally do not exist in the Disney films. They are silent, absent, dead—their purpose of marrying the prince having been fulfilled (Bell, 1995; Wasko, 2001). The good fairies and godmothers of the Disney films are nearly as vacuous as the princesses. Henke, Umble, and Smith (1996) further explain that, "While Fairies and Godmothers are females who use their powers for good, they are also limited in strength, bumbling, inept, and absentminded" (p. 244). Furthermore they are de-sexualized, "postmenopausal" with "bodies [that] are nonthreatening, unavailable, and harmless" (Bell, 1995, p. 119). In this way, Disney has left only two viable alternatives for a legible womanhood, thus strengthening the binary of princess and the queen.

The evil queen stands in stark contrast to the princess, representing everything that the princess is not, everything she *cannot* be. The queen is anything but passive: desiring, clever, and of course magical. According to Zipes (1995), "The witches are not only agents of evil but represent erotic and subversive forces that are more appealing both for the artists who drew them and the audience" (p. 37). They possess a queer sexuality, erotic and seductive (Bell, 1995; Henke, Umble, & Smith, 1996), yet entirely without desire for men. Disney's evil women emasculate, evade, and even eliminate the king, representing "the patriarchal view that strong women are evil and are detrimental to the proper upbringing of children" (O'Brien, 1996, p. 162). While the queen is appealing, we know her to be "wild ... selfish, and greedy" (Murphy, 1995, p. 128). Thus, the princess is rewarded for her pleasantness and for her servitude with everlasting happiness via heterosexual union with the prince, and the queen is punished, often by death.

IMAGINING NEW POSSIBILITIES WITH FEMINIST FAIRYTALES

Even though the binary of princess/queen is strong, I was not entirely trapped within this binary. To a certain degree, we must respond from within the discourses in which we are positioned; however, we do not simply repeat the stories we are told. We improvise, imbricating other available discourses to strategically construct a self in relation to others. Davies (2003) explains that "as a speaking subject, [we], can also invent, invert and break old structures and patterns and discourses and thus speak/write into existence other ways of being" (p. xx). So while we cannot write entirely new stories, we can put together the stories already available to us in new ways.

Davies (2003) draws on the work of Barthes to explain what it takes for such "new" stories to work. She explains that, according to Barthes, new meaning can be achieved through the construction of disruptive texts that work by *cutting*. These texts have two edges, "an obedient, conformist, plagiarizing edge," that Barthes calls the "pleasure" edge, and "another edge, mobile, blank ..." (quoted in Davies, 2003, p. 191), with the potential to cut a new space for what is now unimaginable. Therefore, Davies explains,

> All feminist stories we write [must] necessarily contain the familiar, known, pleasure edge ... if it is to be comprehensible, if it is to be pleasurable enough to capture the reader's imagination. ... One cannot live entirely on the other disruptive edge (p. 192).

Without the benefit of all this theorizing, it seems that I took up just this sort of project in an attempt to reconstruct a legible self. Several months into that messy year of transformation between the decision to end a marriage and its formal dissolution, I wrote the following in my journal:

> *My mother said that our marriage was like a fairytale. That he was my prince charming. And that was the truth. This is the story:*
>
> *Once upon a time there was a woman. She lived in a shack in the wilderness. She had once been wise, and wild and strong, but now was broken. Almost too weak and tired to care for herself. She was dirty, and sad, and alone; she survived. She waited.*
>
> *And then one day, along came a prince. The woman was not waiting for a prince. In fact, she was so alarmed at his arrival that when he came knocking, she thanked him kindly, shut the door, and left him in the yard.*
>
> *But he was strong ... and handsome ... and he saw in her the embers of a fire that had once been. He came again and again to her door and despite herself, she grew to love him. And when at last she allowed it, he swept her up onto his big, strong horse and brought her to his beautiful castle, a world filled with friends, family, festivals, and feasts. The prince held her and loved her and made things right. Bit by bit, in his care, she grew stronger and stronger. She learned to dress like a lady,*

and talk like a lady, and do all the things that ladies did. And he was happy and she was happy and it seemed they would live happily ever after.

But really, she never wanted to be a lady. She never was very fond of jousting, or feasting, or courtly manners. She was a wise woman, shaman, a wild woman of the woods. She missed the fairies and the magic and the open air. And she found that she would spend the day with her eyes cast down because to see the sky and the horizon was too bittersweet. And he saw that she was sad.

He wanted her to be happy, so he told her to let down her hair, walk about the castle without her shoes on, and plant herbs with the roses. So she did, and she started to take long walks in the woods. One day as he watched her coming in from out of doors he saw that the color had come back to her cheeks and her eyes were glittering with that spark the prince had envisioned those many years ago.

But his heart was heavy for he knew he saw this fire only when she was leaving the walls of the castle, or like this before the fairydust had yet been shaken from her travel clothes. And so he went out to meet her and took both hands into his own and smiled a little crooked smile. "My love," he said, "it is time for you to go home to the woods where your heart sings and your spirit is strong. I cannot bear to be the one who keeps you from your joy."

The woman was grieved, and ached and thought to return to her castle ways. But once the words were spoken she could think of nothing else. And so they gathered together the things she'd need to begin a new life in the wilderness. They rode a ways together, right up to the edge of the kingdom and made their goodbyes, promising to hold a piece of their love in their hearts forever.

APPROPRIATING DISNEY: THE PLEASURE EDGE

Davies (2003) says that it is difficult to examine the ways in which self-construction takes place, but "it surfaces through dreams, in tranquil meditative moments, in poetry and other forms of creative writing" (p. 120). So in order to "[catch] texts in the act of shaping them" (p. 66), she gathered with other female scholars to collectively analyze their written memories, utilizing the methodologies set forth by Frigga Haug (2008). Following her lead, I met with three colleagues to engage in similar analyses of my tale as a moment of self-construction. In addition to this collective work, I examined my text independently, engaging in literary analysis and using tables and figures to analyze language choices more systematically.

Before meeting with the collective memory group, I hadn't given much thought to the words that preceded "Once upon a time." The collective, however, drew my attention to the prologue, where I wrote, "That is the truth. This is the story." With these words I set up an expectation for a remixed tale, one that would establish a plagiarizing, familiar, pleasurable edge (the truth) while introducing something new and disruptive (the story). The first consequence of this is that, no matter what twists and turns I weave into my story; it will first and foremost, be recognizable as a fairytale. In this way I am signaling my contingent acceptance of the narratives into which I was positioned, even as I challenged my position within them. In other words, to establish this pleasure edge, my story had to "feel" like Disney. Members of the collective said that the rhythm of the language in the story felt familiar and reminded them of the safe and predictable feeling of being read to as a child. They were also very interested in two linguistic peculiarities: an abundance of "be" verbs signaling a sense of naturalness, and the heavy use of "but" and "and," which propels the story forward with a sort of obviousness that doesn't require the logic of cause and effect. In these ways, I had inadvertently taken advantage of one of the most fundamental characteristics of Disney storytelling, what Giroux and Pollock (2010) call Disney's "pedagogy of innocence," by which moral lessons are pleasurably conveyed through a sense of familiarity, naturalness, and inevitability.

When I examined my story independently, I coded the language of the text and produced tables. The most productive of these involved dividing the text of the story into two columns:

1. *On-Script*: Language in this column can be linked directly to one of the early Disney princess films, enabling me to examine the plagiarizing, familiar, pleasure edge of my story (e.g., … *he swept her up onto his big strong horse and brought her to his beautiful castle.*).
2. *Off-Script*: Language in this column does not fit within the Disney princess tales, enabling me to consider how I was trying to expand beyond the constraints of the narrative into which I was positioned (e.g., *She was a wise woman, shaman, a wild woman of the woods.*).

By sheer volume, the quantity of text recognizably drawn from Disney fairytales significantly outweighs text that exceeds these language practices. When I looked at my completed table, I could see a rhythm of language shifting back and forth between columns, braiding in complications and desires that I did not feel I could express directly without the risk of being positioned as the villain.

As I started to analyze the table, I found it necessary to add a third column, *Improvisations*, to account for language that was clearly recognizable from the Disney films but had been repurposed to represent something entirely different. For example, consider the moment when "color had come back to her cheeks and her eyes were glittering." This aptly describes the Disney moment when the prince brings the princess back to life and claims her as his own through the magic of true love's kiss. In my tale, conversely, this language marks the inversion of this moment, when the prince realizes that for the princess to come alive, he must relinquish his hold on her. With moves like these I was able to layer certain Disney meanings onto realities that did not easily fit into Disney expectations. In this example, I intermingled the "goodness" of the prince's rescue, not with impending marriage but with impending divorce.

BREAKING DOWN THE BINARY—THE BLISS EDGE

With this table I also created a main character that makes ambiguous claims to be both princess and queen. On the one hand, the woman's apparent inability to either express or act on her own desires allows her to retain the "innocence" of the princess. On the other hand, while the story going on around her clearly calls for a princess, the woman in the story never actually *is* one. She is a "woman," a "wise woman," a "shaman," and a "wild woman of the woods." And while she begins a kind of transformation when she is rescued by the prince, this transformation is never completed. In fact, there is never a wedding! The best she can manage is to be "like" a lady.

So if I was not the princess, how could I avoid being cast as the evil queen? I took up the identity of the "wise woman," the "wild woman." While this figure alludes to the sorcerer, the witch, the bad fairy that is Disney's evil queen, the specific language draws upon feminist appropriations of the archetype of the witch, the wise woman, and the midwife (Eigler & Kord, 1997). These women exist outside the masculine sensibilities of proper civilization where they hold illicit, yet *valuable* knowledge and power. In this way, I construct the woman as possessing *dormant* agency and power, which is both illicit and good. Furthermore, as a wise woman, her desire to leave the castle can be seen, not so much as a violation of the fairytale, but as a fulfillment of it—she is going *home* to the woods.

These woods, and the fairies within them, are familiar in the Disney tales, constituting the margins of the kingdom, the margins of reason and order. But, in traditional fairytales, fairies are double coded as tricksters and troublemakers. Furthermore, fairies, along with rainbows and unicorns, have been taken up as mascots and symbols of queerness. Glittered with fairy dust, dancing in the night, they revel in an eternal unmarried otherworld, laughing at grounded, earthly, heteronormative expectations. By encoding the woods with these desires, I am able to draw upon recognizable, if marginalized, tropes from the Disney narrative, opening up the possibility of a queer subjectivity, potentially legible even from within the Disney paradigm.

TELLING NEW TALES

In *Shards of Glass,* Davies suggests that we are written into existence, in part, through fairytales, and that we live these fictions even if we think we "know better." She invites students to write new feminist fairytales in order to imagine themselves into new ways of being. It is easy and dangerous to imagine that the fairytales into which we are positioned overdetermine the stories we can tell about ourselves. It is also too easy, and Davies says, insufficient, to imagine that we can simply negate these stories and turn away. My story shows that even as an adult woman, I was literally called upon to account for the violation of a fairytale, and I found myself taking up just the task she prescribes. By imbricating Disney tropes with elements from my divorce experience, I wove a story both familiar and new, which sought to appease the need for category maintenance without accepting the ways in which I was positioned. As teachers and as parents, we can encourage students to creatively appropriate powerful elements of Disney tales in order to construct new horizons of legibility.

DISCUSSION QUESTIONS

1. This chapter focuses on the influence of three classic Disney films, *Snow White* (Cottrell et al., 1938), *Cinderella* (Geronimi, Jackson, & Luske, 1950), and *Sleeping Beauty* (Geronimi, 1959). More recent Disney fairytales have experimented with recasting and twisting these very storylines. In what ways have these new tales, for all their problems, made new identities imaginable?
2. How are these officially twisted Disney tales different from writing a twisted tale yourself, about your own life? What might it mean to write twisted tales collectively, as Davies did in *Shards of Glass*, or to collectively read tales we have written, as I did for this chapter?
3. Think of a time when you have felt written out of existence, or when your legitimacy within certain narratives has been challenged. What fairytale would you write to respond to these anxieties? In what ways does the genre allow you to make new possibilities legible?
4. How can the shared cultural "obviousnesses" of Disney tales be used as a tool for facilitating the development of new imagined possibilities for ourselves?

REFERENCES

Bell, E. (1995). Somatexts at the Disney shop: Constructing the pentimentos of women's animated bodies. In E. Bell, E. L. Haas, & L. Sells (Eds.), *From mouse to mermaid: The politics of film, gender, and culture* (pp. 107–124.) Bloomington: Indiana University Press.

Clements, R., & Musker, J. (Directors). (1989). *The little mermaid* (Motion Picture). United States: Walt Disney Pictures.

Cottrell, W., Hand, D., Jackson, W., Morey, L., Pearce, P., & Sharpsteen, B. (Directors). (1938). *Snow White and the Seven Dwarfs* (Motion Picture). United States: Walt Disney Pictures.

Davies, B. (2003). *Shards of glass: Children reading and writing beyond gendered identities.* rev. ed. Creskill, NJ: Hampton Press.

Do Rozario, R. A. C. (2004). The princess and the magic kingdom: Beyond nostalgia, the function of the Disney princess. *Women's Studies in Communication, 27*(1), 34–59.

Eigler, F. U., & Kord, S. (Eds.). (1997). *The feminist encyclopedia of German literature*. Santa Barbara, CA: Greenwood Publishing Group.

Geronimi, C. (Director). (1959). *Sleeping Beauty* [Motion Picture]. United States: Walt Disney Pictures.

Geronimi, C., Jackson, W., & Luske, H. (Directors). (1950). *Cinderella* [Motion Picture]. United States: Walt Disney Pictures.

Giroux, H. A., & Pollock, G. (2010). *The mouse that roared: Disney and the end of innocence*. Lanham, MD: Rowman & Littlefield Publishers.

Haug, F. (2008). *Memory-work as a method of social science research: Detailed rendering of memory-work method.* [PDF Document]. Retrieved from: http://www.inkrit.de/frigga/index.htm

Henke, J. B., Umble, D. Z., & Smith, N. J. (1996). Construction of the female self: Feminist readings of the Disney heroine. *Womens Studies in Communication, 19*, 229–250.

Hoerrner, K. (1996). Sex roles in Disney films: Analyzing behaviors from Snow White to Simba. *Womens Studies in Communication, 19*(2), 213–228.

Murphy, P. (1995). "The whole wide world was scrubbed clean": The androcentric animation of denatured Disney. In E. Bell, L. Haas, & L. Sells (Eds.), *From mouse to mermaid: The politics of film, gender, and culture* (pp. 125–136). Bloomington: Indiana University Press.

O'Brien, P. C. (1996). The happiest films on earth: A textual and contextual analysis of Walt Disney's *Cinderella* and *The little mermaid. Womens Studies in Communication, 19*(2), 155–184.

Stone, K. (1975). Things Walt Disney never told us. *The Journal of American Folklore, 88*(347), 42–50.

Wasko, J. (2001). *Understanding Disney: The manufacture of fantasy*. Cambridge: Polity Press.

Whelan, B. (2012). Power to the princess: Disney and the creation of the 20th century princess narrative. *Interdisciplinary Humanities, 29*(1), 21–34.

Zipes, J. (1995). Breaking the Disney spell. In E. Bell, L. Haas, & L. Sells (Eds.), *From mouse to mermaid: The politics of film, gender, and culture* (pp. 21–42). Bloomington: Indiana University Press.

CHAPTER THIRTEEN

Dis(ney)ability

Reconceptualizing Normalcy Through an Embodied Arts Research Curriculum

LAURA TRAFÍ-PRATS AND GINA POLENCHECK RUCHALSKI

This chapter examines how pre-service teachers negotiate their subjectivities in connection to the popular culture of their generation (Luke, 2010) through the development of an embodied arts research curriculum that is centered on bodies and on relationships between bodies in Disney fairy tale movies. An embodied arts research curriculum (hereafter, referred to as EARC) focuses on the criticality of subjectivity, understood as the intellectual curiosity, capacity of association, and risk-taking necessary to move from what is familiar into what is new through additive and associative processes that link known and unknown fragments of knowledge (Garoian, 2013). Our study was conducted with nineteen pre-service middle and early childhood teachers at the University of Wisconsin-Milwaukee in a summer intensive undergraduate compulsory course that focused on art and visual learning in elementary education. This course connects EARC with disability theory (Garland-Thomson, 1997; Siebers, 2008, 2010; Millett-Gallant, 2012) in order to reconceptualize corporeal difference in Disney fairy tale movies through creative engagements implicating images, human bodies, and material processes.

The group of pre-service teachers who participated in the study was diverse in terms of class, gender, race, and disability. Most of the students in the class had been engaged in the lifelong consumption of Disney products through films, toys, and theme parks. All but two students (who were older) had grown up during what some have called the "Disney Renaissance," which comprised the period of 1989–1999, and which signified the reengagement of Walt Disney Animation

Studios with traditional storytelling. Additionally, all of the participants declared to have seen one or more of the newer movies, *Princess and the Frog* (Clemens et al., 2010), *Tangled* (Greno et al., 2010), *Brave* (Andrews et al., 2012), and *Frozen* (Buck, Lee, & Del Vecho, 2014), which for some, signify a reengagement with the fantasy and escapist themes of the Renaissance period (Disney revival, n.d.). Several participants shared stories of watching Disney films in the company of children, in the role of parents, extended family members, or other caregivers.

Through our EARC, we considered this cross-temporal and intergenerational consumption of Disney fairy tale films as a pedagogical site where pre-service teachers shared and exchanged knowledge with members of their families, communities, and other consumers (Luke, 2010). We explored what happens when this knowledge overlaps with other forms of knowing typical of the field of teacher education, such as the development and practice of culturally relevant curriculum. We wondered, what knowledge relations would emerge? How would they be negotiated? What encounters, tensions, and contradictions would arise? What bodies would this encounter form, deform, and reform? In what follows, we begin with an overview of the theoretical foundations of the EARC, which are grounded in disability studies and in contemporary art theory. We then explore their applicability to an analysis of how bodies and relationships between bodies operate in Disney fairy tale movies.

DIS(NEY)ABILITY

We created the neologism "Dis(ney)ability" and use the concept to describe how Disney fairy tale movies construct narratives that privilege normalcy and that position extraordinary bodies as illegitimate. Normalcy refers to what a given society establishes as the ideal body and uses to differentiate between bodies that are valuable and bodies that are deemed to be unworthy of attainment because they deviate from the ideal. We bring together disability studies and contemporary arts research practices to explore how normalcy operates in Disney and how creative practices can shift its centrality. Here, we describe three ways in which disability studies contributes to an analysis of how individual subjectivities are developed in relation to Disney ideals, through (1) an aesthetic emphasis on ablebodiedness, (2) the rematerialization of bodies through creative self-representation, and (3) the challenging of totalizing narratives.

First, disability theory takes up an aesthetic of ablebodiedness as it interrogates the ideologies behind social norms, conventions, and modes of looking that structure what counts as normal (Siebers, 2008, 2010; Garland-Thomson, 1997; Millett-Gallant, 2012). In the case of Disney's protagonists, ablebodiedness is constructed as normal in the ways the characters embody contemporary standards of beauty in popular culture. Disney's state-of-the-art animation and highly elaborated production designs display the bodies of its protagonists within a myriad of artistic details and in harmony with the surrounding world. With their childish faces, big eyes, petite bodies, sexualized movements, and curious impulsive behaviors, their physical features contribute to the idea that aesthetic pleasure is tied to the viewing of a fully able body (Siebers, 2010). Corporally diverse bodies, that is, those that deviate from this norm—such as those of the ruffians in *Tangled*, the male members of the clans in *Brave*, or the trolls in *Frozen*—function to reaffirm the privileged norm by displaying its opposite (Garland-Thomson, 1997).

Second, disability studies challenges these idealistic perceptions of the body through rematerializing them via creative self-representation strategies that problematize how looking is a non-neutral process of knowledge-making, in which the stare and the gaze function with different implications. The stare is the response of the eye to something that takes the starer by surprise (Garland-Thomson, 2009). We see this in *Frozen* during the coronation party, when the crowd fearfully stares at Elsa after discovering that she projects ice in violent, uncontrolled ways. Elsa is horrified by these stares, as her feelings of being overexposed are amplified with the claims, insults, and accusations that emerge from the crowd. The result of this interaction is a stigmatization of Elsa's body, making it the source of all of the problems that will follow and provoking Elsa's flight from Arendelle.

While staring involves the interaction of at least two people, gazing operates in the separation of the viewer and the viewed, functioning as a space for voyeurism. From a disability studies point of view, the gaze distances the disabled, extraordinary body from other bodies, transforming it into a wondrous exotic spectacle that aligns with the traditions of the freakshow (Millett-Gallant, 2012). *Frozen* presents a powerful example in the central musical scene, where viewers gaze at Elsa as she builds her ice palace on the peak of a mountain. The scene consists of an ensemble of choreographed elements, such as a powerful music theme, an empowering ice construction, and the eroticizing touch of Elsa stripping off her clothes and revealing a tight gown, loose hair, dramatic make-up, and stiletto heels, producing an image that aligns more with contemporary celebrity culture than with the exposure of a body that has just been segregated from its community.

Disability theory scholars and artists consider that art research practices can subvert these objectifying workings of the stare and the gaze and produce a rematerialization of bodies. Millett-Gallant (2012) suggests that staring back and self-representing corporal diversity are strategies that contemporary artists use to confront the viewer, to solicit but at the same time reverse the gaze by shockingly exposing the fragmented body in affirmative ways that challenge the ideology of normalcy. We will discuss later how our EARC centered on a select number of artists whose work focuses on issues of self-representation and diversification of point of view.

Third and finally, disability studies challenges the frames of totalizing narratives through seeing social understandings of disability as a form of minority identity, not as a physical flaw (Siebers, 2008). Scholars within disability studies differentiate between a medical and a social model of disability. The medical model sees disability as an abnormality that needs to be cured, while the social model understands it as something socially and environmentally constructed (Siebers, 2008; Millett-Gallant, 2012). Some proponents of the social model defend an intersectional understanding of disability as "a cultural … identity" (Siebers, 2008, p. 4) with overlapping locations of gender, class, race, and disability, that "create figures of otherness" (Garland-Thomson, 1997, p. 6). Corporally diverse bodies function in bodily hierarchies and in distributions of privilege and power where there has been a "persistent intertwining of disability with femaleness" (Garland-Thomson, 1997, p. 20), and where women are presented as a physical variation "different, deviant, inferior, and insufficient" (p. 20) in relation to the normative type represented by the white male.

In the previously discussed examples from *Frozen*, we can see how extraordinary, deviant female bodies fill Disney fairy tale narratives. Rapunzel's body with hair power in *Tangled* constitutes another case. Both Elsa and Rapunzel are located in narratives in which social instability depends on, and is solved through, the female body—always via chance situations, which, instead of affirming the intentionality and social agency of these bodies, illustrate their exceptionality. Coincidentally, at the end of these movies, Elsa's and Rapunzel's tears resurrect Anna and Flint and, as a result, order is restored in their correspondent kingdoms. Corporal diversity is rendered as something transitory or illegitimate through a narrative that pursues closure and homogenization. In this totalizing narrative, normalcy is embodied through intersections of whiteness, privilege, youth, and femininity with the nuclear middle-class family, heterosexual marriage, and/or centralized-colonial-absolute power at its center. Millett-Gallant (2012) invokes the ontology of contemporary art research to transcend such totalizing interpretations. Disability theory thus connects with EARC as contemporary art debases interpretative frames and contests the exclusivity, unity, and fixity (Garoian, 2013) of Disney's images by amplifying the dynamics between viewers and bodies on display (Garland-Thomson, 2009). These ideas are developed in more detail in the following section.

MAPPING AND RECONSTRUCTING EARC

Our Dis(ney)ability EARC focused on intersectional constructions of disability and corporal diversity in contemporary art (Siebers, 2008). Its aim was to approach disability as something that happens to all bodies in different degrees, at different moments of life, and within different environmental situations, and therefore presents disability as a critical concept with which to question the pervasiveness of normalcy in Disney fairy tale movies. These ideas on normalcy, disability, and contemporary art research were presented and discussed in class through the exploration of the work of a large group of contemporary artists engaged in issues of corporeal diversity and/or critiques on the social normalization of the body. Participants then organized in smaller groups to develop further research on the artists in whom they were interested. Artists chosen for further exploration included Michael Ray Charles, whose paintings criticize and transcend culturally-manufactured stereotypes applied to Black bodies; Wendy Ewald, a documentary photographer who works with children through collaborative and ethnographic methods to create photographic narratives; and, Barbara Kruger, Poster Boy, Nicolas Lampert, and Banksy, who utilize montage to effect radical shifts both in images and in their public contexts of reception.

Additionally, the work of these artists inspired the teaching of specific contemporary art-making principles (Gude, 2004) that participants used to appropriate and transform Disney images. The principles included (1) *juxtaposition* of image and text as a way to create disjuncture between verbal and visual signs; (2) *hybridization* as the intermingling of various cultural references to both expose and to challenge stereotypes connected to race, gender, class, sexuality, and disability; (3) *recontextualization* as the appropriation and recombination of images to alter their meaning; and (4) *staring back*, or using the stare to confront the viewer and to self-represent a body in fragmented, problematic, and agented ways.

Finally, our curriculum was organized through two main art research projects that we called the *Disney oxymoron* and *Disney dis/ability*. In the *Disney oxymoron*, participants were asked to write collaborative Disney alphabets. Each member of a collaboration, for each letter of the alphabet, had to generate as many words as possible representing aspects of their own experiences with Disney. Once the alphabets were completed, participants had to choose two terms in their Disney alphabets that were contradictory, combine them, and juxtapose them with a Disney image that was representative of a significant childhood memory. We used image transfer on cloth and embroidery to play with a feminine and crafty mode of expression with the purpose of introducing further disjuncture in perceptions of Disney digitally-made images (see Figs. 1, 2, and 3).

The *Disney dis/ability* project focused on the art-making research that participants developed on the artists they chose and centered on the (re)appropriation of Disney bodies. Participants developed a body of work, provided an artist statement, and participated in a classroom critique. Additionally, participants used visual journals to document and to reflect on their learning processes, creating connections between text and visuals. In their visual journals, participants provided examples of intertextuality as they connected research on contemporary artists, documentation of art processes, self-reflections, artist statements, images and critiques of peers' artwork, sketches, material samples, finished artwork, and inspirational images. Below, we reconstruct the learning moments that structured our Dis(ney)ability EARC, which include a reflection on biographical connections to Disney narratives, engagements with notions of normalcy, and the study of contemporary artists who provided models for participants to reconceptualize Disney images with their own artwork. Using pseudonyms to refer to the participants, we describe selected examples of participant responses and art research work with the aim of showing the multidimensional aspects of their learning.

BIOGRAPHICAL CONNECTIONS

Our EARC began with a focus on participants' biographical connections with Disney. Participants narrated a significant childhood memory of Disney and analyzed it from a perspective of critical pedagogy inspired by the introductory chapter of *The Mouse That Roared: Disney and the End of Innocence* (Giroux & Pollock, 2010). This initial moment of our EARC also included the *Disney oxymoron* project. To represent this work, we have chosen the stories of Dani and Natalie because they reveal how participants negotiated different forms of knowing (e.g., family, popular culture, and critical pedagogy) and how these negotiations in multiple cases resulted in contradictory and complicated overlappings of dis/identification, critique, and differentiation (Luke, 2010).

We start with Dani's story. We have selected Dani because she often was loquacious, expressing views that differed from other students in the class, especially with those that, at the beginning of our project, defended Disney fairy tale films as innocent, non-political narratives. This is what Dani wrote:

> *When I was about four years old,* The Little Mermaid *was released. My mom took my twin sister and I to the theaters to watch it, which was a treat for us. At the end of the movie Ariel beats a spell and decides to remain a human and marry a prince that she fell in love with. As a child this really struck a chord in me. It was heartbreaking to me that Ariel decided to leave her beloved father and community to become human. My mother had to take my sister and I out of the theater because I was crying so hard. … Disney thrives on creating a homogeneous, regulated, and controlled environment through which its audience can experience wonder and joy. In the case of* The Little Mermaid, *Disney intended to tap into the audience's universal desire to witness an adventurous love story and live vicariously through Ariel's steamy romance. This, however, was lost on me. It seems that my values led me to root for Ariel's return to her family and community.*

In her story, Dani questioned both the powerful emotional themes and the romantic coupling as narrative devices that narrowed her experience and functioned in totalizing ways to oppress her. Dani's *Disney oxymoron* juxtaposed contradictory images of union and separation' Ariel hugging her father, Triton, and she and

Prince Erik waving goodbye. The term *conglomerate fantasy* refers to how the encounter of Disney fairy tale movies with people's lives results in an uneven and rough mixture. By playing with these disjunctions, Dani's piece transcends what she describes as homogeneous and controlled narratives to emphasize instead a non-romantic, located, and relational understanding of bodies-in-love connected to family and community (see Fig. 1).

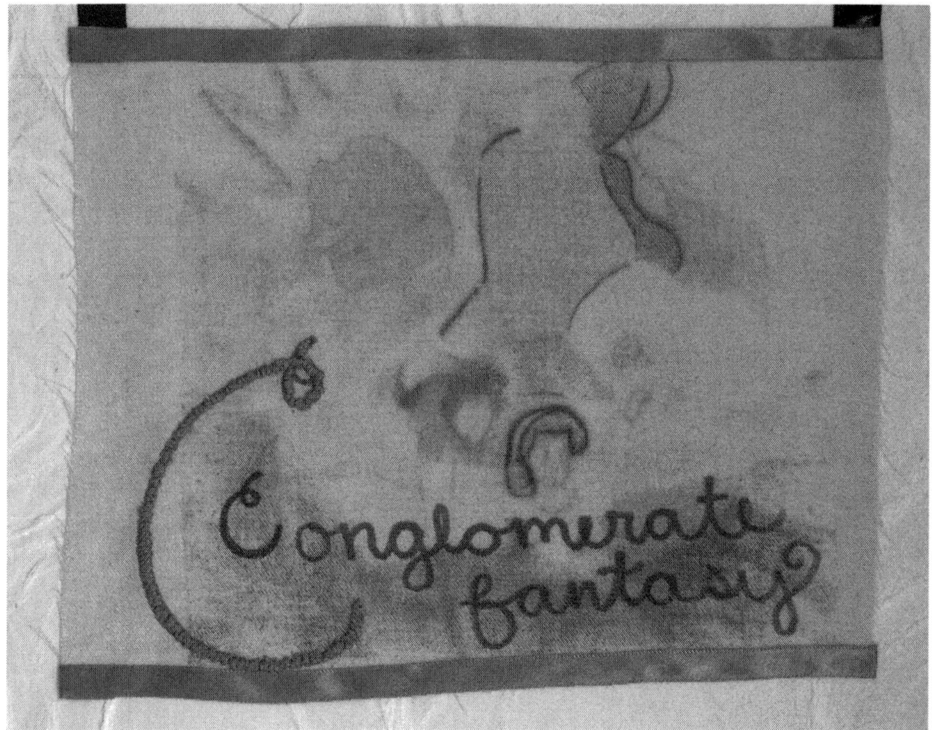

Fig 1. Dani, *Conglomerate Fantasy* (Disney oxymoron project).

Natalie was the only Hmong student in our class. Her Disney story engaged with issues of race and gender identity that connected with what Lynch (1999) describes as the struggles of Hmong youth in the United States for "reconciling older and emerging gender roles for women" (p. 59). Natalie wrote,

> *The dreams created by Disney are not innocent and must be questioned for the futures they envision, the values they support, and the firm identifications they offer. … Giroux and Pollock (2010) question the impact that Disney has in gender roles, culture, and childhood values. … I loved Disney movies since I was a kid. My dad would buy all of us the Disney movies that we liked and the toys that we wanted. Of course, I liked all of the Disney princess movies and owned some of the Barbies. But I wasn't obsessed with having the dresses and everything else, because I understood*

> *that we did not need everything and we could not afford it. … Mulan was my all time favorite because she was a little different from the other princesses. She was not about the fairy dust and the glittery dresses, she was a warrior. I related to her because of her race. She was Asian, just like me. As a young girl, I liked the girly stuff, but I had a tomboy side of me. I was active and liked action, so I looked up to Mulan.*

Natalie's narrative contained a desire for affirmative models of racial and gender difference, which Natalie tried to negotiate within the frames of Disney consumption and the family. In her *Disney oxymoron* titled, *False Truth*, Natalie chose an image that showed Mulan's face divided in two genders (see Fig. 2).

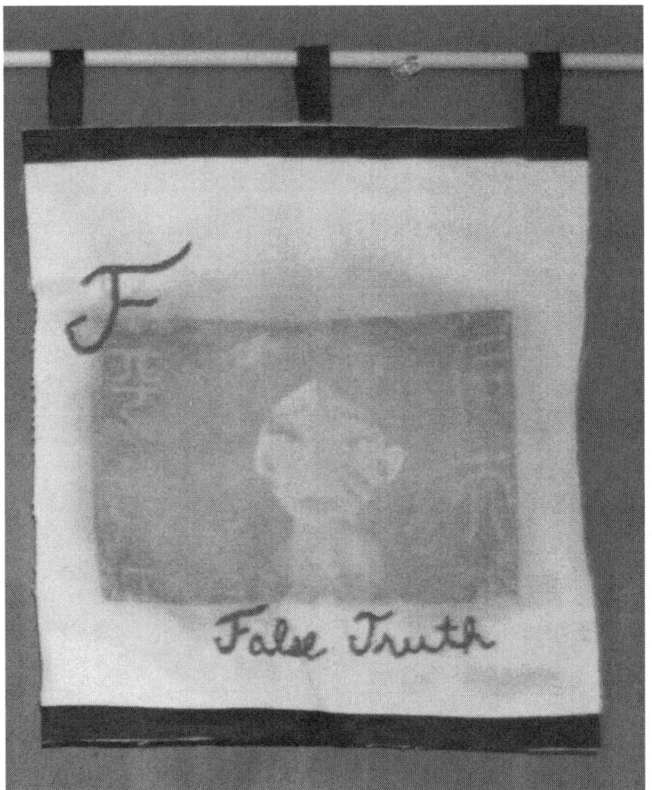

Fig 2. Natalie, *False truth* (Disney oxymoron project).

Natalie wrote about it in her visual journal: "[The image] represents her true self and the side her parents wanted her to be." The free, unrestrained, adventurous Mulan masqueraded-as-a-warrior, confirms that normalcy is male, but for Natalie became a model on which to build a fluid identity situated between what she described as girly and tomboy locations.

ENGAGEMENTS WITH NORMALCY

In this second moment of our EARC, we moved the focus away from biographical connections to center on representations of disability, corporeal diversity, and normalcy. Participants read Maudlin's (2008) "Life Goes On: Disability, Curriculum, and Popular Culture" and analyzed representations of disability and normalcy in relation to the movies that they used in their stories of childhood experiences with Disney. What was interesting about this moment is that for the first time participants used, and reflected on, the concept of normalcy, connecting it most often to issues of class, race, gender, and sexuality, because these were central to their own personal experiences. Delma's visual journal provides an example of how participants responded to the concept of normalcy in reference to their own lives:

> *There is a scene in* Toy Story *that has always stayed with me: the gas station at night. The whole movie made me feel safe and bounded, but this scene in particular made me think of how I always felt safe at night as a kid. ... But the more I continued thinking about it, I realized that that was not true. I grew up in the 1970s when crime was sky high and I never felt safe at night, and a lot of bad things happened to me too. This caused me to reflect that Disney has the power to cause me to remember—nostalgically—something that never was.* [It performs] *a kind of nostalgic truth. The Disney oxymoron is what is chosen and not chosen. Whose bodies are empowered, and whose bodies are different or normal?* (see fig. 3)

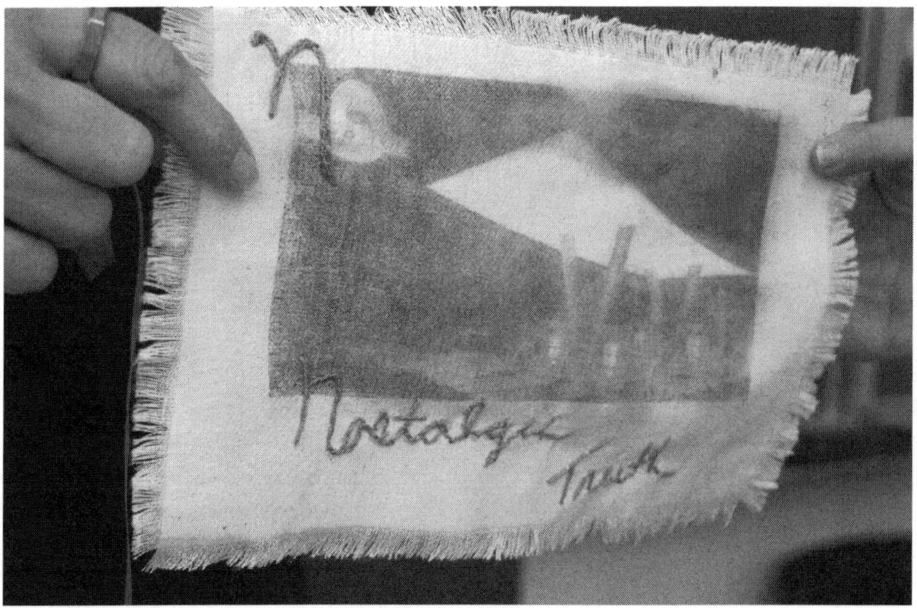

Fig 3. Delma, *Nostalgic truth* (Disney oxymoron project).

The concept of normalcy helped participants to both recognize and problematize their own bodies as grounds for the formation of knowledge and subjectivity. At the same time, the concepts of normalcy and disability also provoked resistance. Some participants opted not to discuss Disney through a disability studies perspective, and there were class discussions in which participants directly asked us why they had to analyze Disney through ideas that they could not really see in Disney movies.

RECONCEPTUALIZING IMAGES

In the third moment of our EARC, participants studied the group of contemporary artists they had chosen, analyzing how these artists appropriated and transformed popular culture and deployed diverse views of bodies and relationships between bodies. As a result of this research, participants created artwork centered on reconceptualizing Disney's images and bodies. However, many of our participants expressed concerns about their ability to understand contemporary art. They found it difficult to relate to some artworks, and felt lost when asked to use contemporary art research strategies to reinterpret Disney images. To move out from this blockage, we invited students to find connections between the art strategies used by their chosen artists and those utilized by Internet-based fan communities who appropriate and create alternative Disney imaginaries. To facilitate this process of understanding, we assigned the reading of Sandlin and Milam's (2010) "Culture Jamming as Critical Public Pedagogy" to help participants understand how popular culture could be appropriated and reused "to expose negative and oppressive, social, environmental, cultural or ethical consequences of the practices of multinational corporations" (p. 253). These two connections not only nurtured participants' interest in contemporary art but also made them see their consumption of Disney as something creative, where pleasure derived from the production of their own images, not just the viewing of images produced by others.

In the Disney dis/ability project, participants addressed Disney images through ideas and issues that their studied artists engaged with. Finding inspiration from Michael Ray Charles, one participant, McKenzie, questioned the absence of Black bodies in Disney movies. She created a number of sketches that led to the elaboration of a painting that appropriated *Brave*'s movie poster through the combination of different cultural references. McKenzie's painting presents the Black female body as a ground of identity where difference is claimed to be something exceptional, instead of something inferior (Garland-Thomson, 1997) (see fig. 4). McKenzie wrote:

> *I combined the image of Wonder Woman, an American icon of strong femininity, with the format of the "wanted" poster, Disney's* Brave *(Andrews, Chapman, Purcell, Sarafian & Lasseter, 2012) movie poster, and race … Merida's voluminous, kinky, curly, red hair struck me. I thought*

of the natural hair that many Black women work hard to tame as a way of subjecting to White standards of beauty. I wondered why, if Merida could be depicted with wild hair, Tiana, the only Black princess could not. … I also considered the Don Imus fiasco from several years ago when he referred to a tournament winning Rutgers female basketball team as a bunch of nappy-headed hos, a disqualifying comment that essentially devaluated their accomplishment and them as Black women. … I wanted to treat the subject of my piece with the utmost respect while not shying away from the topic. I knew it would be very easy to fall too far back on the myth of the strong Black woman or even the jezebel character. … I wanted the subject of my piece to show a Black hero/role model, who does not adhere to White beauty standards and embraces her Blackness, along with her intelligence, strength, vulnerability, and everything else. …

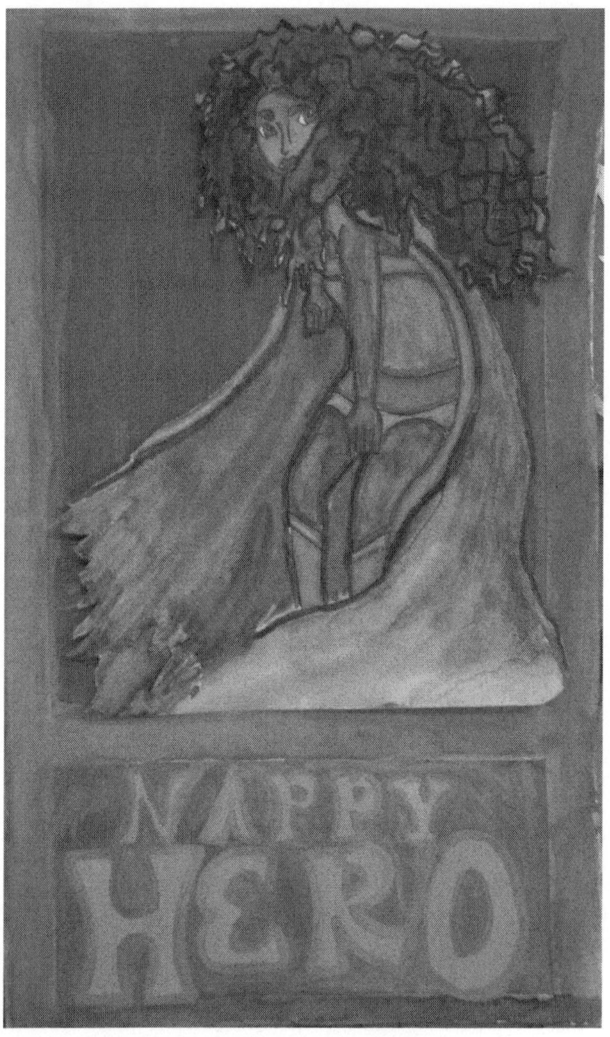

Fig 4. McKenzie, *Nappy Hero*, acrylic painting (Disney dis/ability project).

For her Disney dis/ability project, Cassandra was inspired by street artist Poster Boy's fast and crude appropriation and recombination of advertisements in the public spaces of New York streets and subways. She recontextualized Disney characters in ads of other products, using humor and language to reveal underlying issues concerning relations of gender, power, and privilege central to Disney narratives (see figs. 5 and 6). In her artist statement, Cassandra discussed how Poster Boy's aesthetics enhanced reflective processes and confronted viewers with Disney's involvement in the normalization of bodies and homogenization of cultural narratives:

> *For many, Disney is considered good children's entertainment. … Despite this, Disney creates a global influence that teaches children that there are set definitions of what happiness is and unrealistic expectations towards beauty. While it tries to appeal to the masses, it often isolates anyone living outside the Hollywood ideal. … I used the strategies of appropriation and juxtaposition of artist Poster Boy as a way to surprise the viewer, make her slow down, take a second to distance from Disney's spell, and perhaps question some of the unintended consequences. …*

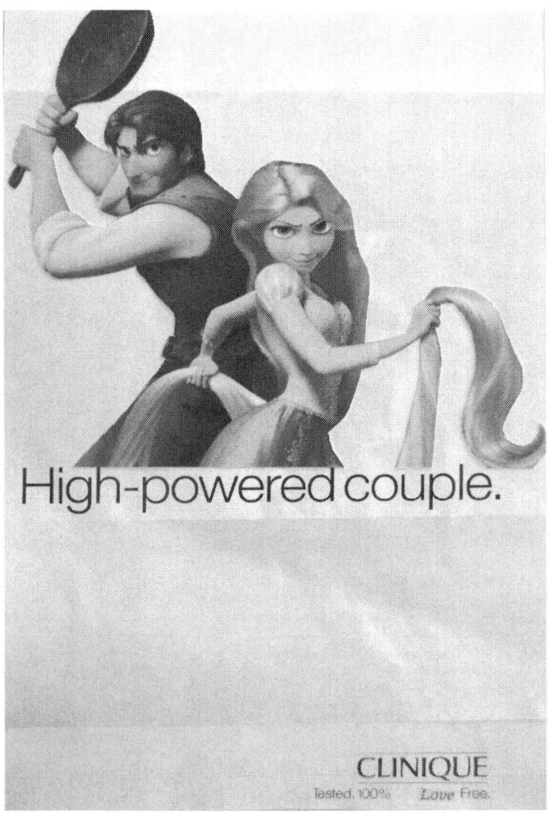

Fig 5. Cassandra, *High powered couple,* photomontage (Disney dis/ability project).

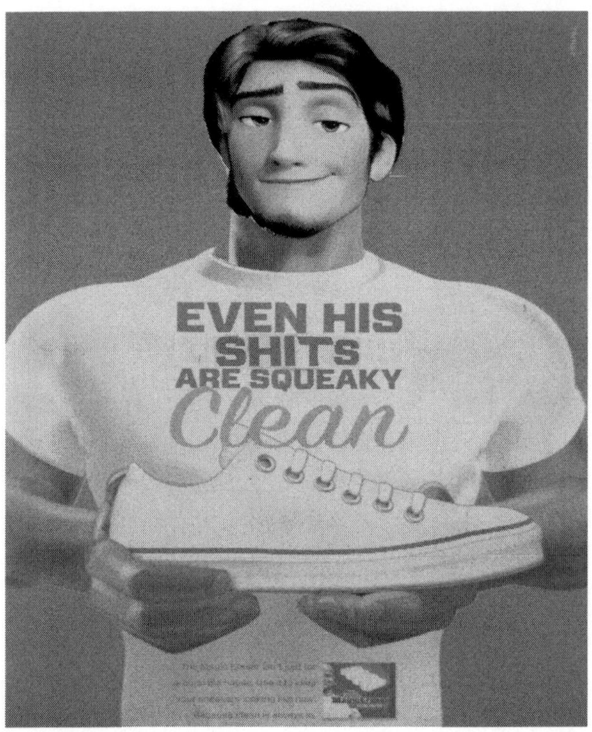

Fig 6. Cassandra, *Even his shits are squeaky clean,* photomontage (Disney dis/ability project).

In their *Disney dis/ability* project, Delma and Breeze utilized the artist Wendy Ewald's ethnographic collaborative strategies of photography to turn the camera on themselves and their classmates. They carried into their projects observations of, and conversations with, their class peers about the connections with Disney that they were articulating. They also asked their classmates to embody those connections in front of a camera for a portrait. Delma and Breeze associated words with each of their portraits, and created a second Disney Alphabet that added to the one we had already elaborated with the *Disney oxymoron* project. Breeze wrote this in her artist statement:

> *In our project, Disney is not a place of instant gratification but instead a place to re-evaluate the simplicity of Disney narratives. …* [The final] *installation is a transitional space … where the resulting images are free to be complex.* [They] *come together to highlight the many feelings that many adults have with Disney instead of coaxing viewers to think one way or another about this megacorporation.*

One of the more remarkable aspects of Delma and Breeze's project was that it taught participants about the affordances as well as the challenges of staring back, life performance, and self-representation. While participants like McKenzie had little problem performing ideas about subjugation and assimilation of beauty standards in *Dangerous* (see fig. 7), others like Dani or Lucía found it difficult to embody roles connected to their art projects. Dani's work was inspired in Barbara Kruger's photomontages, language games, and expressions of power. Delma and Breeze asked Dani if she would perform an image that combined the face of Merida with the phrase *Basic bitch* included in her Kruger-inspired body of work. Initially Dani denied performing such a role. However, in a second conversation she recognized that her decision contradicted Kruger's use of language as locational, interpretative, as something that can be appropriated and resignified in ways that challenge power and reverse the gaze (see fig. 8). In *Let It Grow,* an acrylic painting in the Disney dis/ability project, Lucía utilized the pose of Elsa in *Frozen*'s movie poster to create an image inspired in the complex uses of Black stereotypes in Michael Ray Charles' paintings (see fig. 9). Lucía wrote this in her statement:

> *I played with the power of the gaze by overexaggerating features of Blackness including a stereotypical African dress. My painting can create a negative emotional response, even provoke conflict. I use dissonance to expose and challenge racism.*

However, when asked to embody similar exaggerations, Lucía resisted the possibility of showing her naturally Afro-textured hair and recognized that she could not do without the products that she applied to tame her hair. Additionally, when Delma and Breeze asked her to pull her hair up as an alternative, she laughed and moved nervously, and performed the resulting image that we see in fig. 9.

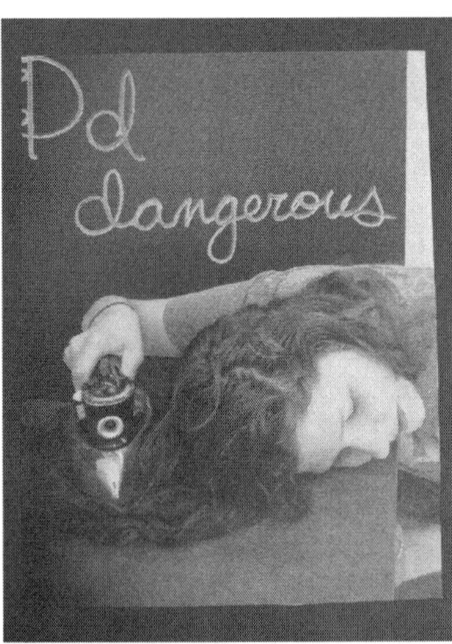

Fig 7. Collaboration between Breeze, Delma, and McKenzie, *Dangerous*, digital photographic print (Disney dis/ability project).

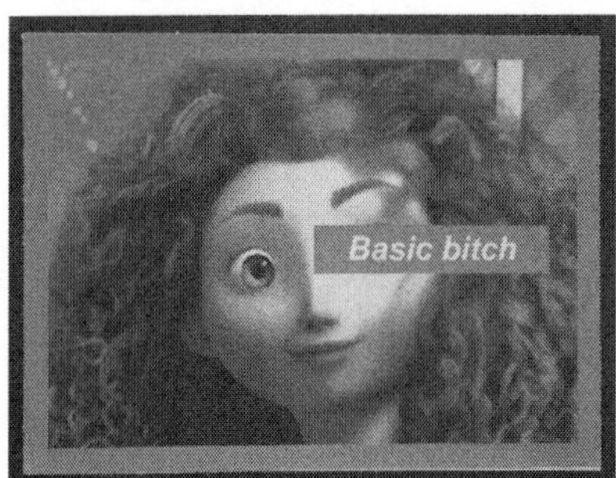

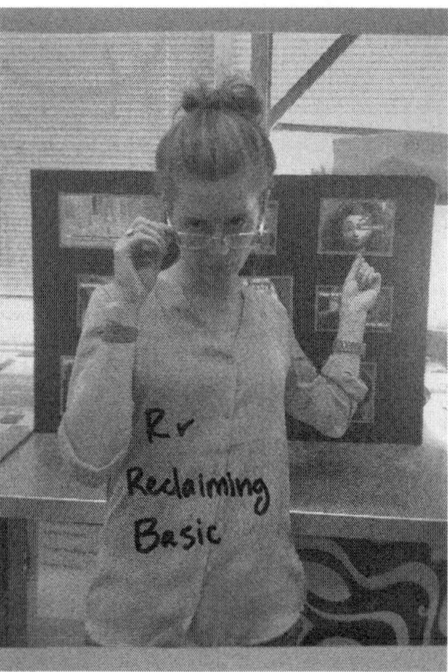

Fig 8. Dani *Basic bitch*, photomontage in digital print (Disney dis/ability project), and collaboration between Breeze, Delma, and Dani, *Reclaiming basic*, digital photographic print (Disney dis/ability project).

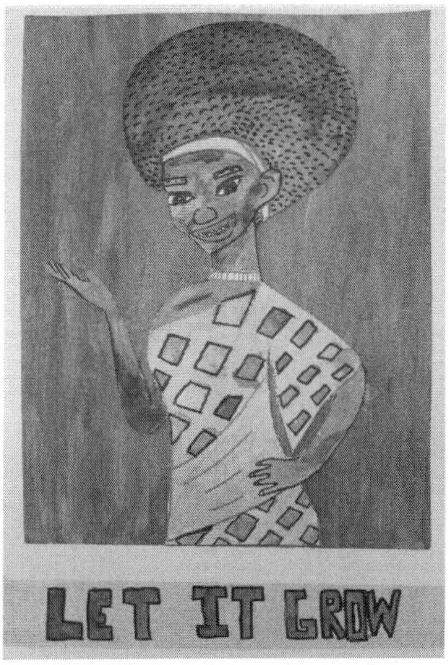

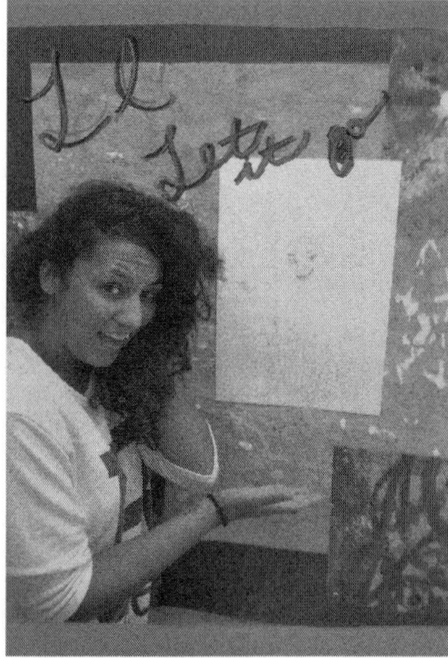

Fig 9. Lucía, *Let it grow*, acrylic painting (Disney dis/ability project), and collaboration between Breeze, Delma, and Lucía, *Let it go*, digital photographic print (Disney dis/ability project).

Dani and Lucía's resistance to perform their images facilitated an opportunity to teach how looking is not neutral but formative of notions about ourselves and others that affect how we want to be identified and how we relate (Millett-Gallant, 2012). Delma and Breeze's project confronted Dani and Lucía with the space that distanced their bodies from the bodies in their images and gave them an opportunity to continue reconceptualizing their own bodies, other bodies in display, and new understandings of art research.

CONCLUSIONS

Past and present Disney fairy tale movies have had a large impact on current generations of pre-service teachers, providing them with forms of knowing and senses of community that they share with present generations of children. In this shared culture, there are opportunities for strategic alliances between teacher education and embodied art research to open spaces for experimenting with models of curriculum and pedagogy centered on encounters between familiar and unfamiliar fragments of knowledge. To illustrate such an alliance, we have described here an encounter between pre-service teachers' knowledge of Disney's culture and the concept of disability as a minority identity. Initially a small number of our participants considered this as a partial and uninteresting knowledge connection. Nonetheless, we engaged in it because we believed in the importance of exposing pre-service teachers to ideas in the arts and the humanities that encourage reflection on issues defining contemporary experience, and possibly the lives of their future students. We explored how disability theory and embodied practices of art research can immerse pre-service teachers in practices of reconceptualization of Disney bodies beyond a cultural narrative centered in normalcy. One of the more important outcomes of this experiment was seeing pre-service teachers recognizing their own bodies as corporeally diverse and as grounds for knowledge and subjectivity. Our process was not linear or unproblematic. We encountered contradictions and resistances, but we also formed new knowledge, created new images, and maintained a sense of community and dialogue. We hope that the three themes we presented under the concept of Dis(ney)ability can be used and perhaps extended by other educators to engage in embodied arts research beyond the visual arts and organize curriculum and pedagogy on issues of normalcy, embodiment, and disability in connection to Disney.

DISCUSSION QUESTIONS

1. What are some examples of Disney films that privilege normalcy? What characters demonstrate contemporary standards of beauty that emphasize ablebodiedness as normal?

2. Our embodied arts research curriculum featured particular learning moments that engaged students in reflecting on biographical connections to Disney narratives, engaging with notions of normalcy, and studying the work of contemporary artists as inspiration for their own artwork that reconceptualized Disney images. How might you utilize these learning moments to enact your own exploration of Dis(ney)ability? How might these learning moments contribute to an examination of other socially constructed norms?

REFERENCES

Andrews, M., Chapman, B., & Purcell, S. (Directors), Sarafian, K., & Lasseter, S. (Producers) (2012). *Brave* [DVD]. Burbank, CA: Disney.

Buck, C., & Lee, J. (Directors), Del Vecho, P. (Producer) (2014). *Frozen* [DVD]. Burbank, CA: Disney.

Clemens, R., & Musker, J. (Directors), Del Vecho, P., & Lasseter, J. (Producers). (2010). *The Princess and the Frog* [DVD]. Burbank, CA: Disney.

Disney Revival. (n.d.) Retrieved from: *Disney.wikia*. Available at: http://disney.wikia.com/wiki/Disney_Revival.

Garland-Thomson, R. (1997). *Extraordinary bodies. Figuring physical disability in American culture and literature*. New York: Columbia University Press.

Garland-Thomson, R. (2009). *Staring: How we look*. Oxford, UK: Oxford University Press.

Garoian, C. (2013). *The prosthetic pedagogy of art*. Albany: State University of New York Press.

Giroux, H., & Pollock, G. (2010). *The mouse that roared: Disney and the end of innocence*. Lanham, MD and Plymouth, UK: Rowman & Littlefield Publishers.

Greno, N., & Howard, B (Directors), Conli, R. Lasseter, & J., Keane (Producers) (2010). *Tangled* [DVD]. Burbank, CA: Disney.

Gude, O. (2004). Postmodern principles: In search of a 21st century art education, *Art Education, 1*(57), 6–14.

Luke, C. (2010). Introduction: Feminisms and pedagogies of everyday life. In J. Sandlin, B. D. Schultz, & J. Burdick (Eds.), *Handbook of public pedagogy: Education and learning beyond schooling* (pp. 130–138). New York: Routledge.

Lynch, A. (1999). *Dress, gender, and cultural change. Asian American and African American rites of passage*. New York: Berg.

Maudlin, J. G. (2008). Life goes on: Disability, curriculum, and popular culture. In S. Springgay & D. Freedman (Eds.), *Curriculum and the cultural body* (pp. 113–130). New York: Peter Lang.

Millett-Gallant, A. (2012). *The disabled body in contemporary art*. New York: Palgrave Macmillan.

Sandlin, J. A., & Milam, J. L. (2010). Culture jamming as critical public pedagogy. In J. A. Sandlin, B. D. Schultz, & J. Burdick (Eds.), *Handbook of public pedagogy: Education and learning beyond schooling* (pp. 250–261). New York: Routledge.

Siebers, T. A. (2008). *Disability theory*. Ann Arbor: University of Michigan Press.

Siebers, T. A. (2010). *Disability aesthetics*. Ann Arbor: University of Michigan Press.

CHAPTER FOURTEEN

Online Fan Activism and the Disruption of Disney's Problematic Body Pedagogies

SARA LEO

In 2012, Disney-Pixar released *Brave* (Docter et al., 2012), a story about a headstrong and fearless Scottish princess named Merida, who rode horses, shot a bow and arrow, and rescued her family from a curse, all without the aid of a handsome prince. In May of 2013, Merida was slated for official induction as a Disney Princess. In preparation for her coronation ceremony, Disney released a redesigned image of Merida in various press releases and in web promotions. Fans immediately noted some major changes to the previously round-faced, wild-haired, tomboy-ish character. The redesigned Merida was thinner with a bigger bust and wore a more glamorous sparkly dress with a revealing neckline. Her face was narrower and covered in makeup. Her wild red curls were tamed and flowed luxuriously down her sides and back. And, perhaps most notably, the signature bow and arrows she carried had been replaced with a jaunty sash around her waist.

Immediately after the image was released, the social media backlash began. And it was fierce. Feminist bloggers and journalists took to the Internet to voice their outrage. Brenda Chapman, *Brave's* creator, even weighed in, calling the makeover atrocious and irresponsible. She argued:

> When little girls say they like it because it's more sparkly, that's all fine and good but, subconsciously, they are soaking in the sexy 'come hither' look and the skinny aspect of the new version. It's horrible! Merida was created to break that mold—to give young girls a better, stronger role model, a more attainable role model, something of substance, not just a pretty face that waits around for romance. (quoted in Liberatore, 2013, par. 6)

A Mighty Girl (2013), an organization dedicated to promoting positive, powerful, and healthy representations of young girls and women in the media, created a petition on Change.org to protest the Merida makeover and ask Disney to return Merida to her original state. The petition circulated widely on Twitter and by the time it closed, it had 262,196 supporters.

Disney's response to the Merida makeover social media backlash was swift. Fans celebrated when the made-over image was removed from The Disney Princess website and replaced with an image of Merida from the film. Disney's press releases at the time claimed they never intended to keep the redesigned Merida on the Disney Princess website and that she was only redesigned for the coronation (Brigante, 2013). However, a cursory glance at the rest of the Princess artwork on princess.disney.com suggests this may not have been the case. As Morrissey (2013) noted in *Jezebel*,

> And while it's good news that integrity of the Merida character has been saved, the same can't be said for the other 10 ladies in the Disney Princess lineup, who have all been victims of the same kind of redesign involving lots of makeup, hair extensions, plumped-up lips, breast implants, Restylane cheek injections, and an inordinate amount of glitter. (par. 9).

Indeed, in comparison to the rest of the revamped Princesses, Merida sticks out on the website like a sore thumb. It is hard to imagine that a company as meticulous in their design work as Disney intended for this to be the case all along. We may never know, of course, but it does appear that fan activism, in this instance, accomplished something significant in preserving the creator's original images of Merida on the Disney Princesses website.

In the aforementioned interview given in response to the Merida makeover, Brenda Chapman referred to the power that Disney images have to teach young girls how to be a woman (Liberatore, 2013). Education scholars call this type of out-of-school teaching and learning public pedagogy. They claim, "We are constantly being taught, constantly learn, and constantly unlearn. Education is an enveloping concept, a dimension of culture that maintains dominant practices while also offering spaces for their critique and reimagination" (Sandlin, Schultz, & Burdick, 2010, p. 1). Many of the spaces where this type of critique and reimagination happen today are on and through social media platforms. Thanks to social networking sites like Twitter, Facebook, and Tumblr, both formal and informal criticism of Disney pedagogies can be circulated more widely among mainstream audiences, allowing Disney consumers to 'buy in' and show support for critiques by retweeting, reblogging, and reposting. In the case of the Merida makeover, many people shared Chapman's anger over the issue and were motivated to act. But, this is not the only example of how online fan activism has actively challenged and disrupted Disney's public pedagogies.

In this chapter, I discuss how Disney fans and consumers use social media to resist and to disrupt some of Disney's problematic public pedagogies. To do this,

I will focus on a specific arena of Disney's public pedagogy—their pedagogies of the body. Though evidence on exactly how media images directly affect body image is mixed, research has revealed that girls as young as 3 years old are worrying about the size and shape of their bodies, and studies also show that young people who worry about the appearance of their body early in life are more likely to develop eating disorders when they are older (Hayes & Tantleff-Dunn, 2010). A lineup of Disney's Princesses confirms an overwhelming preference for light-skinned, slender-framed women with enormous doe-eyes and long, flowing hair. These images of femininity, as well as many other problematic, unrealistic, and potentially harmful body pedagogies that Disney has the power to promote, concern me as both a scholar and a parent.

BODY PEDAGOGIES AND PARTICIPATORY CULTURE

Through constant repetition of Princess and other images across their vast media landscape, Disney has the power to teach us how to have a body. However, as Foucault (1982) argued, where there is power, there is always also resistance. While Disney has the power to teach us how to have a body, we also have the power to resist those teachings. Right now, much of that resistance is happening on and through social media technologies and is participatory. As Jenkins et al. (2006) explained,

> a participatory culture is a culture with relatively low barriers to artistic expression and civic engagement, strong support for creating and sharing one's creations, and some type of informal mentorship whereby what is known by the most experienced is passed along to novices. A participatory culture is also one in which members believe their contributions matter, and feel some degree of social connection with one another (at the least they care what other people think about what they have create. (p. 3)

When fans encounter a Disney pedagogy they disagree with or find problematic, they can participate though social media to disrupt those pedagogies in a variety of ways. Fans can use social media for old-fashioned protest (as they did with Princess Merida), distributing critical information and demanding change among much wider audiences than previously accessible. But, they can also connect with each other via social media platforms and use digital media to reconceptualize and playfully contest Disney's problematic cultural products and messages in creative ways (Jenkins, Ford, & Green, 2013). In order to examine how Disney fans are taking advantage of this participatory online culture to resist Disney's harmful body pedagogies, I will focus on two of Disney's lesser-discussed pedagogies of the body—fat shaming and gender dimorphism—and examine the online fan activism surrounding them.

FAT SHAMING

The Disney-Pixar movie *WALL-E* (Collins et al., 2008) takes place over a thousand years into the future in which the earth, covered in garbage, is uninhabitable. Humans have long since abandoned the planet in favor of a large spaceship. These future space inhabitants have become 100% dependent on technology and consequently spend all of their time reclining in automated lounge chairs that provide everything they need from food to entertainment at the press of a button. As you can imagine, with limitless supplies of liquid junk food at their fingertips and no imperative to exercise, the humans of *WALL-E* are not exactly svelte. Farrell (2011) argued that Disney was able to rely on fatness as a shorthand for downward evolution because, "the 19th- and early 20th-century meanings of fat as designating an uncivilized body are alive and well today" (p. 117).

Prior to the time frame Farrell references, corpulence was viewed positively as evidence of success and wealth. According to Bordo (2003), in the late 19th and early 20th centuries, however, social power was "more connected to the ability to control and manage the labor and resources of others. At the same time, excess body weight came to be seen as reflecting moral or personal inadequacy, or lack of will" (p. 192). Both Bordo and Farrell posit that, though representations of overweight people may not be as severe or blatant as they were two hundred years ago, fatness is still used in popular media as a proxy for all kinds of devious or despicable behavior.

Fat shaming turns out to be one of Disney's most useful body pedagogies. Consider, for example, the character of Governor Ratcliffe as portrayed in *Pocahontas* (Bloodworth et al., 1995). His exaggerated double chin and oversized belly serve as symbols of his unchecked greed. Similarly, in *Robin Hood* (Reitherman, 1973), the Sheriff of Nottingham's huge midsection could be seen as an emblem of his corruption and buffoonery. But fat shame is not reserved only for villains in Disney films. Fatness is also used to reflect impotence or inadequacy such as the domestically helpless Seven Dwarfs in *Snow White and the Seven Dwarfs* (Disney et al., 1937) or Jasmine's bumbling incompetent father in *Aladdin* (Clements et al, 1992).

Bordo (2003) also explained how fat shame has been used to reinforce gender hierarchies by using soft, protruding body parts to "evoke helpless infancy and symbolize maternal femininity" (p. 208). Under this paradigm, the only non-shameful way to have a female body that is neither slim nor tight is to be either a mother or a child, neither of whom enjoys a particularly powerful social position. Disney Princesses manage to exemplify both of these body pedagogies, rendering them especially powerless. On one hand, of course, Disney Princesses are almost all portrayed as impossibly thin. Unlike the aforementioned villains, this lack of bulging flesh symbolizes restraint and virtuosity. However, they also have unusually curvy figures with relatively large breasts that jiggle when they move, which subtly reinforces the characters' maternal capabilities and cements their place in the gender hierarchy.

Farrell (2011) explicated how fat shaming was/is used to reinforce gender hierarchies by deflecting women's attention from "maintaining, let alone improving on, the political, cultural, and social rights they had gained in the previous decades" (p. 108). Ostensibly, women who are preoccupied with keeping their bodies slim and tight will not have extra time to devote to social improvement projects on behalf of their gender. In this case, it is no wonder that Disney Princesses always need a man to rescue them; they spend all their energy maintaining their implausibly small waistlines.

Finally, both Bordo (2003) and Farrell (2011) argue that negative images of fatness have historically been used to keep gender and other social hierarchies in place. For women, at different times throughout the past century and often simultaneously, it has been acceptable or desirable to be either extremely thin, or toned and muscular. Bordo (2003) noted that, while these two ideals are different in appearance, they have "a common enemy: the soft, the loose; unsolid, excess flesh" (p. 191). Bordo (2003) suggested that images of bulging flesh are often a metaphor for social anxiety about females' inability to control their impulses. The Queen of Hearts in *Alice in Wonderland* (Disney et al., 1951) comes to mind here as does perhaps the most well-known obese character in the Disney canon, *The Little Mermaid's* (Ashman et al., 1989) Ursula, who I turn to now.

In 2013, fat acceptance advocate and slam poet, Melissa May, came across a surprising image of Ursula in her search for a Halloween costume. The image was from a line of Disney Villain Designer Dolls, a set of limited-release figurines that reimagined each famous villain in a stylized and fashion-forward way. For this line, Disney's designers slimmed down Ursula to one-third of her original size, replaced her tentacles with a ruffled floor length gown, and erased her double chin in favor of a sharp protruding jawline and cheekbones. At first, May said, she laughed and passed it by. But the image stuck with her and eventually became her inspiration for a new performance poem, "Dear Ursula" (Jug Report, 2014). The poem begins with May's outrage over the slimming down of "the only Disney character who ever looked like me," and goes on to boast, "while you may not have had the waistline of a princess I'll be goddamned if you didn't have the swagger of a Queen." May calls Ursula sexy and admits she "made living in this body a little less like a curse." May goes on,

> Ursula, I don't want you cut down into bite-sized pieces.
>
> You weren't easy to swallow for a reason.
>
> I want you larger than life, flaming red lips, black flamenco dress—I want the thick of your tentacles, your conjurer's hands, the jiggle of your ample bust. I want you dressed to the nines on a runway, I want every little girl to see a heroine in a size 24. (Button Poetry, 2014)

The poem is powerful and inspiring (especially if you watch May perform it) and thousands of women clearly related to its message. Since performing the piece at the 2014 Women of the World Poetry Slam and subsequently putting the video on YouTube for public consumption, May's ode to Ursula has earned reblog after reblog and attracted attention all over social media on both formal and informal news sites.

According to Jenkins, Ford, and Green (2013), "the ready availability of old media texts [on the Internet] may inspire new acts of creation and performance—leading not simply to the making of new meanings but also to the creation of new texts and the emergence of new subcultural communities" (p. 100). These communities can form for a variety of purposes, from simple nostalgia to cultural critique to social transformation, all of which were at work in the creation and dissemination of May's Ursula poem and the fat acceptance community that embraced it. Under the control of these types of communities, what Disney created as a commodity (Ursula, the villain) can transform into a cultural resource (Ursula, the hero). Jenkins, Ford, and Green (2013) further argue that

> The fantasies of a commodity culture are those of transformation, while the fantasies animating nonmarket exchanges are based on shared experience. … When materials move from one sphere to the other, they frequently get reworked to reflect alternative values and fantasies. (p. 203)

Disney may be promulgating fat shaming through characters like Ursula for a variety of purposes, not the least of which is that making men and women feel bad about the size of their bodies is good for all sorts of business. But social media gives Disney consumers the power to modify Disney texts to reflect alternate meanings, as in the case of May's poem. While fan resistance to the body pedagogies of Ursula has not inspired any official response from Disney, there was another case of fan resistance to Disney's fat-shaming pedagogies that did result in concrete change, which I discuss next.

In January 2012, Disney's Epcot Center unveiled "Habit Heroes," a new ride it claimed was designed to tackle the increasing problem of childhood obesity. The visitor experience included various interactive rooms, each engaging children in a different virtual battle against the evils of a sedentary and unhealthy lifestyle (Jameson, 2012). This may seem ironic considering the ride is housed in a place where you can purchase a turkey leg the size of an average adult forearm, but the concept itself was not viewed as inherently problematic by critics. What stirred up controversy was how Disney chose to represent these supposed depraved lifestyles to children. A virtual cartoon villain embodied each bad habit, and children earned points for defeating and humiliating them. Among many others, the villains included Snacker, a plump middle-aged fairy in a skin-tight striped tutu with a tacky beehive hairdo waving donuts and cookies into the air with her magic wand, and Lead Bottom, a severely obese man with no neck wearing a wrestling costume and holding a remote, surrounded by empty bags of chips and other assorted garbage.

Dr. Yoni Freedhoff (2012), professor, author, and creator of the blog, *Weighty Matters*, accused the ride of reinforcing society's harmful negative obesity stereotyping and quipped, "What kid doesn't want to be made to feel like a personal failure while on a Disney family vacation?" (par. 10). Blogger and fat acceptance activist, Ragen Chastain (2012a), wrote that she "couldn't stop the tears" (par. 2) when she heard about the "Disney fat shame ride" (Chastain, 2012b, par. 1). She noted that fat kids are already subjected to shaming, humiliation, and bullying from society and that the Habit Heroes ride was akin to "[holding] fat kids down and [letting] park guests kick them" (2012a, par. 5). In addition to bloggers, various media outlets and public figures picked up the story, including nutritionist and author, Marion Nestle, who tweeted, "You can't make this up" (quoted in Williams, 2012, par. 3).

It was not long before Disney responded to the backlash and attempted to do damage control. Only three weeks after its launch, Disney took Habit Heroes.com "down for maintenance" and closed the Epcot exhibit indefinitely (Williams, 2012, par. 4). A visit to both the attraction and the website in 2015 reveals no trace of these original villains. Social media fan activism, in this case, was granted a clear victory. While cynics refer to social media activism as "slacktivism" and question the power that citizens can exert in online spaces, according to Portman-Daley (2013), social media has the power to encourage civic engagement, to educate citizens, and to democratize information, all of which can evoke meaningful change as it did in the case of Habit Heroes. In addition, Georgetown University's Center for Social Impact Communication and Ogilvy Public Relations Worldwide conducted a study that revealed that people who support causes through social media (e.g., blogging and posting icons on social profiles) are twice as likely to engage in supportive activities (both on and off the Internet) compared to their peers who don't support causes via social media (Georgetown University, 2011). Social media give Disney fans the power to disseminate their protest and critique among a global audience. They are using it to fight fat shaming and other problematic Disney body pedagogies such as gender dimorphism, which I will now examine.

GENDER DIMORPHISM

In the middle of *Beauty and the Beast* (Ashman et al., 1991), the pseudo-villain Gaston indulges in a self-titled musical brag fest to make himself feel better after Belle rejects his proposal of marriage. At one point in the song, in order to demonstrate his strength and prowess, Gaston proceeds to lift a wooden bench with three fully-grown women sitting on it above his head with one arm. He continues singing about his strength and attractiveness while the women's legs dangle above him like rag dolls as he tosses them about. Perhaps no other moment so typifies the stark contrast between the body pedagogies of men and women in Disney films.

Similar to notions of the body, much of what we know and believe about gender is socially constructed. According to Fine (2010), "the culture in which we develop and function enjoys a 'deep reach' into our minds. ... When the environment makes gender salient, there is a ripple effect on the mind" (p. xxvi). Culture teaches our minds to see differences in gender as prescribed and fixed. Then, as Fine explained, "When we categorize someone as male or female, as we inevitably do, gender associations are automatically activated and we perceive them through the filter of cultural beliefs and norms" (p. 66). One of the ways in which culture inscribes gender differences in our minds is through representations of body size. And these inscriptions can be powerful, even if they are so obviously unrealistic as in the case of Gaston.

Biologists use the term *sexual dimorphism* to describe the physical characteristics that distinguish males and females of the same species from each other. For example, the male cardinal is bright red while the female is mostly brown; a male lion has a large hairy mane around its head while the female does not. Sociologists have adopted this scientific term to observe the ways in which society understands and defines common differences in appearance between men and women. However, rather than thinking of these differences as biological in nature, they consider how they are socially constructed. They refer to this concept as gender dimorphism. A simple and obvious example of gender dimorphism in current Western society is how we dress baby boys primarily in blue and girls in pink. While one could observe a whole host of stereotypical physical differences between men and women in Disney films, one of the primary ways Disney represents men and women differently is through the size of their bodies.

Philip N. Cohen (2012, 2013, 2015), a sociologist at the University of Maryland, College Park, has a revealing series of posts on his blog, Family Inequality, about gender dimorphism and body size in Disney films. Though a picture is worth a thousand words on this topic (and I encourage you to read Cohen's blog posts, which contain images), I will mention a few of his examples here. Close-up shots from the movies *Hercules* (Clements et al., 1997) and *Tangled* (Conli et al., 2010) of their respective heroes and heroines holding hands reveal the heroine's wrists to be half the size of the hero's while the heroine's eyes appear more than twice the size of the hero's. A similar shot of Anna and Kristoff in *Frozen* (Del Vecho et al., 2013) reveals the same wrist and eye dimension comparisons, and Anna's eyeball has a larger circumference than her own wrist. Merida's parents from the movie *Brave* (Docter et al., 2012) are perhaps the most severe example. Standing next to each other, Merida's mother appears to be one-third of her father's total size and the his hand appears larger than her entire head and neck combined, while her hand appears roughly the size of one of his fingers.

Repeatedly, the most striking examples of Disney's gender dimorphism involve massive differences in male and female characters' eye, wrist, and hand sizes. A simple glance around at a group of humans will tell you that the eye size differences are obviously exaggerated, but to prove his point, Cohen (2013) looked at several studies measuring the actual diameters of male and female wrists to compare reality to Disney's portrayals. Among the studies, he found a range of diameter averages for women of 15.4 cm to 16.3 cm, and for men of 17.5 cm to 18.1 cm. So, while obviously extreme deviations could be reported, the difference between the smallest average woman's wrist and the largest average man's is unremarkable.

Not only are Disney's gender size portrayals false and misleading, but they have potentially harmful consequences, particularly for women who are consistently portrayed as weak and frail in comparison to men. According to Bordo (2003), "Female bodies have historically been significantly more vulnerable than male bodies to extremes in both forms [experienced and physical] of cultural manipulation of the body" (p. 143). Similarly, King (2004) posited,

> Woman's historical association with the body has resulted in her being judged by and valued for her appearance more than man, often above all else, and has also engendered the fear and dread of otherness. Even in this supposedly equal, liberated and progressive society femaleness is still disturbing enough to require supervision and containment by forms of discipline that men are not subjected to. (p. 36)

Though King's assessment is grim, she is quick to point out the possibilities for, and realities of, resistance. In fact, merely pointing out and challenging Disney's problematic body pedagogies in a public forum, as Cohen does on his blog, disrupts their power. And, Cohen's work has been cross-posted and distributed on various information platforms such as Time, Huffington Post, and Sociological Images, allowing more consumers to participate in the critique.

Disney fans are also using the affordances of digital technology and social media to re-create problematic examples of gender dimorphism in popular Disney characters and distribute them to a wide audience. Recently, Buzzfeed's Loryn Brantz (2014) digitally altered six Disney Princesses to show what they would look like if they had more realistic and proportional waistlines. The images struck a chord and were shared widely on various social media platforms. Many, women in particular, praised the aesthetic of the edited images; The Huffington Post also released an article titled, "Disney Princesses with Realistic Waistlines Look Utterly Fabulous" (Sieczkowski, 2014). Buzzfeed also published a similar story (Lewis, 2013) containing animated gifs of Disney's most popular Princesses that showed what they would look like if they had regular-size eyes. This type of resistance does not look like activism in the traditional sense. Disney fans who create these types of images are not necessarily demanding change; rather, they are subverting Disney's pedagogies by drawing attention to them and offering alternatives. According to Harrison and Barthel (2009), this type of active audience participation and production is a central feature of the social media paradigm. They explain, "The rhetoric of broad 'audience' participation can be viewed as one oriented to decentralized cooperative efforts rather than centralized single vision, and empathy rather than persuasion" (p. 172). Disney fans are using social media to talk back to Disney's pernicious body pedagogies in a public space where their interaction with the text transforms from a personal reader response to a form of broader resistance.

RESISTING PROBLEMATIC PEDAGOGIES

Examples of participatory fan activism on the Internet vary widely and defy formal categorization. And there are many more problematic Disney pedagogies related to issues of race, gender, class, and sexuality that have inspired creative and critical fan responses that have circulated through social media platforms. While there is certainly a wide array of valuable Disney criticism being published in traditionally formal spaces like books, journals, and documentaries, these criticisms are limited by time and space constraints of old media technology. The Internet provides spaces for fans to respond to lesser-known pedagogies like fat shaming and gender dimorphism both in real time as well as years after they occur. Disney wields an inordinate amount of cultural power and will continue to do so, but thanks to social media technology, fans are now able to participate in critique and resistance to Disney's problematic public pedagogies in ways they never have been before.

DISCUSSION QUESTIONS

1. Fat shaming seems to be an acceptable form of prejudice in American society because fatness is linked with an unhealthy lifestyle and is constructed as an issue of self-control. Why is that a problematic way to view fatness? Do you think it is a good idea to advocate for fatness? Why or why not?
2. Gender dimorphism is not a topic we tend to discuss very often in society. Can you think of other examples of gender dimorphism in popular culture?
3. Why might harmful body pedagogies be profitable for Disney to promote? What industries are bolstered by fat shaming and by gender dimorphism? Why?

4. Undoubtedly, since this book was published, many more instances of resistance to Disney's harmful body pedagogies have occurred through social media participation. Can you think of any? Do you think these types of resistance are making a difference? How? Why or why not?

REFERENCES

A Mighty Girl. (2013). Disney: Say no to the Merida makeover, keep our hero brave! *Change.org*. Available at: www.change.org/p/disney-say-no-to-the-merida-makeover-keep-our-hero-brave

Ashman, H., Donley, M, & Musker, J. (Producers), Clements, R., & Musker, J. (Directors). (1989). *The little mermaid*. [Motion Picture]. United States: Walt Disney Pictures.

Ashman, H., Hahn, D., Lasseter, J., & McArthur, S. (Producers), Trousdale, G., & Wise, K. (Directors). (1991). *Beauty and the beast* [Motion Picture]. United States: Walt Disney Pictures.

Bloodworth, B., & Pentecost, J. (Producers), Gabriel, M., & Goldberg, E. (Directors). (1995). *Pocahontas* [Motion Picture]. United States: Walt Disney Pictures.

Bordo, S. (2003). *Unbearable weight: Feminism, Western culture, and the body*. 10th ed. Berkeley: University of California Press.

Brantz, L. (2014, October 29). If Disney princesses had realistic waistlines. Buzzfeed. Available at: http://www.buzzfeed.com/lorynbrantz/if-disney-princesses-had-realistic-waistlines#.xtJ4mX32Y

Brigante, R. (2013, May 15). Exclusive: Disney bravely responds to Merida makeover outrage, says 2D look was for "limited" use only. Inside the Magic. Available at: http://www.insidethemagic.net/2013/05/exclusive-disney-bravely-responds-to-merida-makeover-outrage-says-2d-new-look-was-for-limited-use-only/

Button Poetry. (2014, March 28). Melissa May—"Dear Ursula" (WoWPS 2014). *YouTube*. Available at: www.youtube.com/watch?v=xLSnNSqs_CQ

Chastain, R. (2012a, February 24). Deeply disappointed in Disney. Dances with fat. Available at: danceswithfat.wordpress.com/2012/02/24/deeply-disappointed-in-disney/

Chastain, R. (2012b, February 27). When good intentions go bad. Dances with fat. Available at: https://danceswithfat.wordpress.com/2012/02/27/when-good-intentions-go-bad/

Clements, R., Ernst, D. W., Musker, & Pell, A. (Producers), Clements, R., & Musker, J. (Directors). (1992). *Aladdin* [Motion Picture]. United States: Walt Disney Pictures.

Clements, R., Dewey, A., Haaland, K., Musker, J., & Tobin, N. (Producers), Musker, J.,& Clements (Directors). (1997). *Hercules* [Motion Picture]. United States: Walt Disney Pictures.

Cohen, P. N. (2012, May 29). Tangled up in Disney's dimorphism. Family Inequality. Retrieved from: https://familyinequality.wordpress.com/2012/05/29/tangled-up-in-disneys-dimorphism/

Cohen, P. N. (2013, December 16). Disney's dimorphism, 'Help! My eyeball is bigger than my wrist!' edition. Family Inequality. Available at: https://familyinequality.wordpress.com/2013/12/16/disneys-dimorphism-help-my-eyeball-is-bigger-than-my-wrist-edition/

Cohen, P. N. (2015, January 4). Herculean dimorphism. Family Inequality. Available at: https://familyinequality.wordpress.com/2015/01/04/herculean-dimporphism/

Collins, L., Lasseter, J., Libbert, G., Morris, J., & Porter, T. (Producers), Stanton, A. (Director). (2008). *WALL-E* [Motion Picture]. United States: Walt Disney Pictures and Pixar Animation Studios.

Conli, R., Keane, G., Lasseter, J., & Scribner, A. (Producers), Greno, N., & Howard, B. (Directors). (2010). *Tangled* [Motion Picture]. United States: Walt Disney Pictures.

Del Vecho, P., Lasseter, J., & Scribner, A. (Producers), Buck, C., & Lee J. (Directors). (2013). *Frozen* [Motion Picture]. United States: Walt Disney Pictures.

Disney, W. (Producer), Cottrell, W., Hand, D., Jackson, W., Morey, L., Pearce, P., & Sharpsteen, B. (Directors). (1937). *Snow white and the seven dwarfs* [Motion Picture]. United States: Walt Disney Pictures.

Disney, W. (Producer), Geronimi, C., Jackson, W., & Luske, H. (Directors). (1951). *Alice in wonderland* [Motion Picture]. United States: Walt Disney Pictures.

Docter, P., Drumm, M. A., Lasseter, J., Sarafian, K., & Stanton, A. (Producers), Andrews, M., Chapman, B., & Purcell, S. (Directors). (2012). *Brave* [Motion Picture]. United States: Walt Disney Pictures and Pixar Animation Studios.

Farrell, A. E. (2011). *Fat shame: Stigma and the fat body in American culture.* New York: New York University Press.

Fine, C. (2010). *Delusions of gender: How our minds, society, and neurosexism create difference.* New York: W. W. Norton and Company.

Foucault, M. (1982). The subject and power. *Critical Inquiry, 8*(4), 777–795.

Freedhoff, Y. (2012, February 23). Disney's horrifying new interactive childhood obesity exhibit at Epcot. Weighty Matters. Available at: www.weightymatters.ca/2012/02/disneys-horrifying-new-interactive.html

Georgetown University. (2011, November 28). Slacktivism doing more than clicking in support of causes. Available at: csic.georgetown.edu/news/1308/slacktivists-doing-more-than-clicking-in-support-of-causes

Harrison, T. M., & Barthel, B. (2009). Wielding new media in web 2.0: Exploring the history of engagement with the collaborative construction of media products. *New Media Society, 11*: 155–178.

Hayes, S., & Tantleff-Dunn, S. (2010). Am I too fat to be a princess? Examining the effects of popular children's media on young girls' body image. *British Journal of Developmental Psychology, 28*: 413–426.

Jameson, M. (2012, February 21). Epcot exhibit joins fight against childhood obesity. *Orlando Sentinel.* Available at: articles.orlandosentinel.com/2012–02–21/health/os-epcot-health-exhibit-20120221_1_childhood-obesity-food-fight-bad-habits

Jenkins, H., Clinton, K., Purushotma, R., Robison, A., & Weigel, M. (2006). *Confronting the challenges of participatory culture: Media education for the 21st century.* Cambridge, MA: MIT Press.

Jenkins, H., Ford, S., & Green, J. (2013). *Spreadable media: Creating value and meaning in a networked culture.* New York: New York University Press.

Jug Report. (2014, May 26). Melissa May: 3 minutes to be remembered. Available at: jugreport.wordpress.com/2014/05/26/Melissa-may-3-minutes-to-be-remembered/

King, A. (2004). The prisoner of gender: Foucault and the disciplining of the female body. *Journal of International Women's Studies, 5*(2), 29–39.

Lewis, J. (2013, October 31). If Disney princesses had normal-sized eyes. Buzzfeed. Available at: http://www.buzzfeed.com/jenlewis/if-disney-princesses-had-normal-size-eyes#.xfRW19Rnw

Liberatore, P. (2013, May 11). 'Brave' creator blasts Disney for 'blatant sexism' in princess makeover. *Marin Independent Journal.* Available at: www.marinij.com/ci_23224741/brave-creator-blasts-disney-blatant-sexism-princess-makeover

Morrissey, T. E. (2013, May 15). Disney pulls sexy Merida makeover after public backlash. Buzzfeed. Available at: http://jezebel.com/disney-pulls-sexy-merida-makeover-after-public-backlash-494274022

Portman-Daley, J. (2013). Subtle democracy: Public pedagogy and social media. Currents in Electronic Literacy, 16. Available at: http://currents.cwrl.utexas.edu/2013/subtle-democracy-public-pedagogy-and-social-media

Reitherman, W. (Producer & Director). (1973). *Robin Hood* [Motion Picture]. United States: Walt Disney Pictures.

Sandlin, J. A., Schultz, B. D., & Burdick, J. (2010). Understanding, mapping, and exploring the terrain of public pedagogy. In J. A. Sandlin, B. D. Schultz, & J. Burdick (Eds.), *Handbook of public pedagogy: Education and learning beyond schooling* (pp. 1–6). New York: Routledge.

Sieczkowski, C. (2014, October 30). Disney princesses with realistic waistlines look utterly fabulous. Huffington Post. Available at: www.huffingtonpost.com/2014/10/30/disney-princess-real-waistline_n_6076634.html

Williams, M. E. (2012, February 28). Disney's fat-shaming fail: The mouse misfires with an ambitious, awful health campaign. Salon. Available at: www.salon.com/2012/02/28/disneys_fat_shaming_fail/

CHAPTER FIFTEEN

Learning to Live as a Disney Villain

JESSICA L. KIRKER

As a young girl, I found that Disney movies provided me with a salient image of the woman I wanted to be: a thin, big-busted beauty, brushing my flowing hair while blinking my wide, dreamy eyes, and donning a glittery gown as I waited for my prince charming to sweep me off to my beautiful palace wedding and happily ever after. Eventually I outgrew the fantasy of maintaining a princess image, but found myself wondering what my adulthood should look like as a wife, mother, art educator, and scholar. In Disney films, "older women are backgrounded as loving (preferably deceased) mothers (Haas, 1995) or, if powerful and independent, vilified as evil femme fatales or ugly hags" (Wohlwend, 2009, p. 59). My interests in media's effects on identity force me to replace my learned desire for a palace and prince charming with critical considerations of how mainstream media agents such as Disney project limited possibilities for satisfying identity roles. I am very critical of media's images of normalcy, and I find myself fighting against Disney's representations of young, White, docile, innocent beauties as an ideological persona. If I were depicted as a Disney character as I am now, I have no doubt that my critical, feminist, troublemaking self would squarely construct me as a villain.

While I can embrace this villainous subject position, it becomes problematic when my critical examinations of media conflict with dominant discourses of Disney, particularly those that occur in contexts that are regulated by social or professional customs, and vilify me to my co-participants in these contexts. This chapter is an autoethnographic recount of some of the struggles, challenges, and moments of success I've experienced as I've learned to navigate the discourses of Disney in a variety of (formal and informal) educational settings. I will highlight two vignettes that exemplify these crises in both my personal life (as a parent) and professional life (as an educator). It adds to the body of work surrounding Disney by discussing the challenges that scholars and critical pedagogues face as they balance their commitment to provocative pedagogy with their need to comfortably exist in society. Autoethnography is a way of understanding social realities in more meaningful ways by illuminating authors' experiences so that they and their readers may find new ways to confront their own personal dilemmas (Toyosaki, 2012). Autoethnographic stories can evoke chaos, disconnect, fragmentation, and incoherence rather than provide a settled story (Ellis & Bochner, 2000). Through telling these stories, I use my own life as a way of describing some possibilities theorists and pedagogues who have to make decisions about when to advance or to suppress their own feminist/critical race/social justice agendas.

IN/FORMING MY "VILLAINY"

Professionally speaking, I consider myself to be a postmodern feminist educator striving for social justice through art education. Postmodern feminists are concerned with identifying discourses that infuse gender with meaning, including visual forms (particularly media) as well as spoken/unspoken forms of communication (McCaughtry, 2004). Postmodern feminism also stretches beyond gender issues and explores the ways in which power, knowledge, and meanings are flexible and constructed. Embedded in feminist theory is the spirit of activism, and I choose to use it as a way to move towards social justice. Ballengee Morris, Daniel, and Stuhr (2010) state that social justice in art education is a *process* and a goal guided by democratic social values that seek to change the unequal distribution and access to resources that hamper equal participation of all social groups in society. As an art educator, I strive to teach adolescents and young adults to recognize and challenge dominant societal discourses and to respond to them in ways that promote equity, drawing on critical race theory to explore the social, political, and moral aspects of race as translated into my life and the lives of those I teach. For critical race theorists, racism is not an exceptional situation or act but deeply ingrained in the U.S. psyche (Ladson-Billings & Tate, 1995; Stovall, 2005). I also employ a Foucauldian consideration of the regulatory and normalizing nature of both discursive and non-discursive discourses. Social semiotics (Hodge & Kress, 1988) and mediated discourse theory (Scollon, 2001) help me understand the complexity of the web of social practices, sites of engagement, and positions of the participants of a discourse that is embedded within a larger social order that frames all of the various aspects of a particular exchange in my attempts to position the various facets of my own identity in relation to Disney when it is presented in both my personal and professional life.

The theories that construct my professional philosophies are guided by my personal experiences and beliefs; as a public school art teacher and parent, I often find myself struggling, living in tension, and negotiating as I engage, participate in, navigate, and manipulate popular discourses that revere Disney as innocent, even wholesome, entertainment. Becoming a parent has heightened my awareness of how language and images shape children's understandings of their own identity and the identity of others and I am increasingly conscious of the discourses that are presented to my children through family, playdates, school, and media. In the first vignette, I consider my position as a mother and discuss how I find myself silencing my beliefs for the sake of social acceptance for my children and myself. Conversely, in the world of academic discourse, it has been relatively easy to find audiences that support my feminist and critical race position and challenge limiting and normalizing societal influences such as Disney. These spaces inform my professional life as an art teacher. In the second vignette, where I speak as an art teacher in a public high school, I highlight how my desire for a provocative pedagogy is tempered by dominating discourses of normalcy that limit my ability to fulfill my goals as a feminist educator for social justice.

SILENCING THE CRITICALITY OF MY INNER VILLAIN FOR THE SAKE OF SOCIAL ACCEPTANCE

I knew this day was inevitable, but I secretly hoped it would not come. As I peered into my son's school cubby, I could see bright red and black cardstock shaped like that iconic silhouette reaching out for me; taunting me. I wanted to ignore it altogether, but I resolved to pick it up and try to minimize my natural tendencies for eye rolling at the sight of this variety of party invitation. Another mother was reaching for the same invitation a few cubbies down. In her other hand, she held her daughter's personalized Disney Princess-themed lunch bag. We simultaneously read the text and as she reached down to flatten the layers of her daughter's sparkly pink tutu, she said to me, "How cute are these invitations!? A Disney party—how fun! We love Disney princesses!"

I wanted to jump up and shout at her, "It is completely evident that you love Disney Princesses, but have you ever stopped to consider the expectations these characters set up for your daughter? Do you even realize what are you teaching her about what it is to be a woman in this society?"

But instead, I reached down for my son's coat and simply replied, "Yes, it sounds like a nice party. We'll definitely be there."

I felt so ashamed. What kind of feminist educator was I for passing up this opportunity to have a critical conversation about Disney and the construction of gender and sexuality for young girls? I felt like a traitor to my academic work as well as a negligent pedagogue. At the same time,

> *launching into a critical discussion of Disney's impact on identity construction and cultural norms amidst the frenzy of classroom dismissal would not give justice to the depth of discussion required and likely result in the loss of social capital as I become labeled as "the mother who hates Disney."*

I don't actually *hate* Disney, and I certainly won't make my son miss out on his friend's Disney-themed birthday party. But in the process of such acquiescence, I often find myself struggling with when to vocalize my critical interpretations of Disney's social influence and when to leave well enough alone. I find this particularly challenging when my professional self urges for conversations about children's media's influence on gender constructions in contexts where my audience might not be receptive to work of this nature. As many scholar-parents know, not every situation is an appropriate venue for challenging Disney's gendered discourses. Therefore, as a mother, I juggle raising my children with feminist sensitivities and producing social pariahs who won't be invited to any more play dates. In this case, I had to negotiate my criticality towards shallow versions of femininity fixated on princess fantasies with appeasing the popular discourses that regard the Disney brand as wholesome entertainment.

I'm speaking of discourse not merely in a dialogic sense, but with a Foucauldian lens that situates it as more than just linguistic speech, but rather as a sign system that relates to other social systems and symbols established through social constructions. From a Foucauldian (1975) perspective, discourses help to establish taken for granted assumptions that circulate within local and global societies; discourses serve as a way to govern ourselves and each other as they help enact power, discipline, and normalization. As a mother, I can't help but be concerned with issues of normalization as they relate to my own children. Research in social learning theory indicates that young children, even infants, learn identity primarily through observing and then imitating what they see in their environment, and then fine-tuning imitated behaviors through various feedback mechanisms (Carinci & Wong, 2009). Children situate themselves in the gender performances made available to them within prevailing discourses (Butler, 2004), so how can a mother's postmodern feminist ideals compete with the sort of narrow and limiting version of femininity that is displayed through the bombardment of sparkly pink tiaras and tutus?

Considering that postmodern feminist thinking challenges dominant patriarchal value systems that have been established in society through cultural interactions (Carinci & Wong, 2009), my first confrontation with a Disney discourse in my child's school context was a feminist pedagogue failure. I didn't take the opportunity to educate my audience about the socio-cultural impact on Disney's princess brand, despite its direct relevance to my audience and the educational setting of a pre-school classroom. Rather, social graces silenced me from reacting to the other mother's exuberant perspective that seemed more aligned to the dominant discourses of this *social* setting. Hodge and Kress's (1988) work on social semiotics helps me contextualize this exchange of discourses. They describe "logonomics" as rules that are policed by concrete social agents (e.g., parents and teachers) and are highly visible through politeness conventions and etiquette. They explain that "where structures of domination are unchallenged, a logonomic system serves the dominant by ensuring that acts of semiosis ultimately assure their dominance" (p. 4). In other words, logonomic systems rely on the participants to abide by the governing social rules of the discourses being exchanged. Hodge and Kress (1988) point out that every producer of a message relies on its recipient to react as the producer intended. In the context of the pre-school classroom, the little girl's mother never expected me to resist her exuberance for Disney, and I responded as she expected, despite my intuition to react differently. To resist or to challenge her speech would create an exchange that was unfamiliar to the logomonic system governing my son's school, and I wasn't prepared to completely dismantle this system. Therefore, my conformity to the logonomic rules bolstered the dominant discourse that *all parents* must love Disney Princesses.

Mediated discourse theory (Scollon, 2001) helps me analyze the materials, site, and social structure of this interaction in order to figure out why, despite everything I passionately believe about a feminist interpretation of Disney Princesses, I fell silent. Mediated discourse theory relies on the complexity of what Scollon (2001) refers to as the *nexus of practice*, the linkage of discursive and non-discursive social practices that have become well developed for the participants through engaging with/in various sites of practice over the course of their lives. Mediated discourse theory takes the position that it is the constellation of relevant and linked practices that make up the uniqueness of a particular site of engagement, not necessarily the specific practices and actions themselves (Scollon, 2001). In other words, the exchange between myself and the other mother did not define the discursive system of our children's classroom; it was revealed to us through our own experiences with conversations in that particular context. My son's classroom, like many preschool classrooms, is a site of teaching, learning, and modeling a particular way of behaving that emphasizes politeness through non-confrontational, supportive, and generally agreeable discursive actions. At that exact moment in that particular site of engagement, I was not prepared to dispute the dominant discourses that enraged my feminist self, despite the fact that my silence left me deeply dissatisfied.

As I further consider the conversation in my son's classroom, I also think about how dominant notions of femininity positioned each participant within this conversation. In terms of gender identity, style of dress, appearance, and behavior are strictly policed by social norms and are overt enough to be obligatory and ubiquitous, thus relegating verbal language to a secondary role whose meaning is given by the behavioral texts it invokes (Hodge & Kress, 1988). As she expressed her love of Disney Princesses, the other mother exhibited characteristics in line with dominant notions of proper femininity. She uttered her speech from bright, pink lips and beamed a wide smile with glowing, white teeth and eyes that shone under layers of perfectly applied make-up. Her long, tan body could literally look down upon mine from her three-inch high stiletto boots. I couldn't help but notice that my messy hair, tired and makeup-less face, and painting-spattered clothes, made me feel even more like the Disney dichotomy of the villainous, ugly hag in comparison to the bright-eyed, optimistic, sweet heroine.

Of course, I don't think the other mother perceived me as a villain during this pleasant exchange. The existence of this strong dichotomy is as fictional as a shallow fairytale plotlines. As I struggle to negotiate a balance along the continuum from pleasant chit-chat to an assault brought on through a drastic deconstruction of gender expectations, I consider past experiences when challenging prevailing normalizing discourses in social situations was met with disinterest or (more polarizing) disgust. Scollon (2001) notes that all social actions are based in tacit and (typically) non-conscious actions that comprise an historical body of an individual's accumulated experiences of social actions. As it turns out, I err on the side of the polite and passive heroine to save myself from being villainized by my social circles that are far removed from my comforting academic spaces that welcome critiques of normalization.

There is a tinge of anxiety when my personal and professional beliefs are challenged in spaces ruled by more strict social conventions. The parents at my son's preschool are polite acquaintances. We typically don't discuss things like politics, religion, money, or social beliefs. On the day that I picked up the party invitation, the other mother's style of dress and composure, the enthusiasm in her voice, the politeness encouraged in the space of the preschool classroom, the logistic urgency to get my son ready for dismissal, and the trend of cordial exchanges between parents of this school foreclosed upon a space or audience in which I felt comfortable challenging the prevailing discourse of Disney. Likewise, when we attended the birthday party, I complimented the hosting mother on her lovely decorations, never uttering a word about my disapproval of Disney's consumer culture. In doing this, the dominant Disney discourses defeated my feminist sensitivity, causing me to become a villain against my own professional/scholarly self.

THE SHENANIGANS OF THE TROUBLEMAKING TEACHER

Tonight is Back-to-School Night and I want to get my students' "Deconstructing Disney" projects hung in the hallway during my prep period. I smile as I hang up the projects, knowing that the students are proud of their work and their ability to create arresting images that will undoubtedly garner attention. Darnel was both excited and shocked that I was going to display his cartoon entitled, "How to Promote Racism in 5 Easy Steps, by: The Walt Disney Corporation." His cartoon was positioned towards the center of my display. Next to it, I hung Daija's (re)presentation of Disney princesses bearing average body sizes and more realistic hair and facial features. In the same row, I displayed Luis's re-creation of a Forbes *magazine cover that featured a castle constructed by bricks labeled with the names of Disney's holdings featuring the headline, "How to Build a Magic Kingdom Media Monopoly, One Corporate Takeover at a Time."*

By the time the first row was hung, another art teacher came out into the hallway. "You're not actually hanging those up again, are you? Have you forgotten about last year's response?"

*I certainly couldn't forget last year's response. Several colleagues complained to the administration about the content of last year's Disney display, prompting several administrators to express their concerns for displaying such controversial topics in the hallway. In light of last year's critiques, I hung even more contextual clues to give passers-by even more information about my lesson and students' work. As I finished up my display, a vice principal walked by and sighed, "not **again**, Kirker. ..."*

The above scenario provides a glimpse of separate nexuses of practice (Scollon, 2001) and logonomic systems (Hodge & Kress, 1988) as they are layered within my teaching environment. First, there is the discursive context of my practice as a White, female, middle-class, suburban-raised teacher in her mid-thirties teaching an ethnically diverse group of students in an urban environment where a majority of students qualify for free or reduced lunch. Second, there are strict logonomic rules to abide by in this school's context. In this particular case, it is not a space that is necessarily welcoming of a discourse that draws attention to topics relating to media corporations' influence on establishing racist and sexist norms in mainstream U.S. culture through the creation of arresting images. Each particular context has varied levels of regulatory restraints on the discourse I deliver, requiring me to manipulate both my speech and my visual messages.

The discourse I have found to be the least contentious consists of the exchanges within my own 11th and 12th grade Media and Visual Culture Studies class. In this particular general art class, my aim is to teach students to recognize and question images' overt and subconscious messages in shaping norms and values in their socio-cultural environment. The images produced through popular culture provide significant sites of learning for children and youth (Tavin & Anderson, 2003). Tavin and Anderson (2003) also note that the organizations that produce, distribute, and regulate most popular culture teach a sanitized perspective of culture while serving the interests of their own profit. In this particular lesson, we work to discover and deconstruct some of the sexist and racist messages in Disney media and consider how these messages get transmitted through seemingly innocent cartoons. The students then create artworks that render these messages visibly and explicitly challenged.

This lesson also allows me to introduce students to my own critical race pedagogy. Through a critique of White hegemonic discourse and power and the social disparities between races, critical race theory rejects notions of objectivity and neutrality (Donner, 2005). Critical race theory examines not only the inequities employed by White supremacy but also the mechanisms that internalize White supremacy in the public consciousness. It's no wonder that the students seem extremely interested in this topic; many are used to seeing childhood media and toys that reflect a White normativity. Disney normalizes Whiteness in the ways it represents exotic lands, voices, and cultures as dangerous and scary while the Western, White order provides safety and normalcy (Tavin & Anderson, 2003) and sells these heavily racialized messages to my students as mindless entertainment rather than as agents of socialization (Lugo-Lugo & Bloodsworth-Lugo, 2009). When other cultures or ethnicities are not explicitly demonized, they are rendered invisible or—perhaps worse—given anthropomorphized racialized characteristics.[1] The racialization of animal or other non-human Disney characters makes these characters and their stories powerful agents of socialization by providing audio-visual reinforcement of dominant White ideologies and maintenance of a racialized status quo (Lugo-Lugo & Bloodsworth-Lugo, 2009). Many of the anthropomorphized characters displaying ethnic characteristics also project subordination through their positions of servant or adversary to the hero, thus enhancing their sub-personhood.

Considering that the U.S. K-12 public school classroom has historically been a racialized (Delpit, 2006; Ladson-Billings & Tate, 1995; Vaught, 2011) and gendered (Bettie, 2003; McIntosh, 1983; Sadker, 2000) space, I am conscious of my position as a White woman as I teach about feminism and critical race theory. With this same consciousness, I brace myself for the backlash from colleagues and administrators who would prefer I decorate the hallway with still lifes of fruit rather than critiques of sexism and racism in Disney. My fluency in the language of standards and objectives allows me to follow the logonomic systems set forth by my administrators so that I can teach this lesson, but with a voice that is tempered by the regulatory nature of my position as a teacher within this context. Conversely, in the space of my classroom, my discourse feels open, free, and most congruent with my scholarly beliefs more so than most of my personal and professional experiences. One could argue that a high school teacher is typically in a position of power in her classroom, allowing her own pedagogical agendas to dominate, but the common practice of lively debates in my classroom indicates that the young adults I teach are willing to argue, challenge, and resist any authority figures, including myself or Disney as their teachers of culture. These diverse students seem to be genuinely receptive to my feminist, social justice-oriented teaching, providing me with a great deal of satisfaction and a space to speak and teach as I wish, even if it depicts me as a villainous troublemaker to colleagues.

Unfortunately, like my colleagues and administrators, the students in my arts methods courses for elementary pre-service teachers were also less receptive to the introduction of a discourse of criticality towards Disney. These classes, which took place in a large rural university, were comprised mostly of White, female, middle-class, suburban-raised women. Even though many students valued the exposure to this critical outlook of constructed childhood culture (Giroux & Pollock, 2010), several of my end-of-semester evaluations confirmed that the Disney discussion was the most unpopular material I covered. Some students were defensive of Disney, maintaining that it is not the only, or even the worst, perpetrator of racist and sexist images in childhood culture. Other students were downright hostile and exhibited a strong allegiance to Disney's traditional views of innocence, gender, and White supremacy. Throughout the teaching of this course, I experienced varying levels of success with confronting their own childhood nostalgia with sensitivity towards the influence of media images on the elementary children they sought to teach. In considering the contexts of discourses, Hodge and Kress (1988) note that the producers of messages have to rely on reception messages from their receivers which act as a kind of feedback which is, in turn, built into the producer's message. The message that is constructed with a knowledge of its intended feedback is framed to remain unchallenged, thus ultimately assuring its discursive dominance. In my attempts to gain students' receptivity towards my content, I constantly found myself navigating the cues of the classroom and adjusting my teaching so I could deliver my message without completely closing off the students. I had to validate the pleasurable and nostalgic side of Disney for the sake of my own critical agenda and, once again, to save myself from total villainy.

In both the cases of my pre-service teaching students and my colleagues at the high school, there are a significant few who embrace and support my efforts, but the discourses of objection towards these lessons seem to be the loudest. I feel confined by dominant discourses, and I fear they operate against my ability to provoke as intended. Though I don't perceive being a troublemaker to be a negative quality for a pedagogue, it can be professionally damning. In order to maintain workable relationships with my colleagues and ensure continued employment, I have to exercise some compliance and perhaps even politeness while simultaneously attending to my own pedagogical agenda of democratic dissonance and challenging the status quo. Polite speech is created by self-negotiation, self-suppression, and self-constraint (Hodge & Kress, 1988). It also caters to a context. It is not always simple and rational but full of conflict and lacking in clarity (Hodge & Kress, 1988). I feel extremely conflicted as well as calculating in how I address racism and sexism in Disney in professional spaces, but this is necessary to secure my employment. Though I don't mind being a villain, if my troublemaking ways close off my audience or remove me from the classroom altogether, then my tempered voice would become muted and thus completely ineffective.

CONCLUSION

It is valuable to try to understand social life and organize discursive research around the moments in which social actions take place (Scollon, 2001). This research acts as an exploration of experiences that led to a story of discovery (Rolling, 2008) to explore the factors that contribute to the suppression of my perspectives of Disney in acquiescence to dominant discourses and social conventions. These discourses create a decorum that regulates appropriateness and polite speech in line with what is expected from fairytale heroines and simultaneously positions Disney critics as villains. Throughout my social and professional life, I have to constantly renegotiate my roles as a parent, teacher, and scholar as they come in contact with my work about gendered and racialized identity construction.

This autoethnographic account of the challenges in being a Disney "villain" is not an apology for the critical compromises I have made to maintain a balance between my roles as a parent and a professional but rather an acknowledgment that all communication is positioned within multiple, overlapping, and conflicting discourses (Scollon, 2001). As educators of formal and informal learning environments go forth with a critical consideration of Disney, one of the world's most influential voices in shaping local, national, and global identities, we must be prepared for the complexity of navigating this discourse within the different contexts we encounter and the factors that regulate communication within these contexts. We must also come to terms with the fact that there might not necessarily be a concrete way to reconcile normative social relations with a consistent critical stance. As Hodge and Kress (1988) point out, politeness is riddled with conflict and self-negotiation, but silence is a signifier of exclusion from a relationship and lack of power. In that vein, I will continue to struggle, live in tension, and engage in the process of constant negotiation. I will not dismiss the value in the complexity of this discursive dance, as it allows me to reconsider my own theoretical positioning and how the articulations of perspectives position me in relation to the contexts around me. Learning how to compromise between my critical perspectives and social/professional relationships allows me to provoke my own self and to continuously learn from the process of doing so.

DISCUSSION QUESTIONS

1. Consider a time when dominant discourses operated against your own critical perspectives. How do you personally justify your decision(s) to speak up, to temper your speech, or to remain quiet?
2. Reflect on your past formal and informal educational contexts and think about how a critical analysis of Disney discourses would be received in these venues.

What are the dominating discourses of these spaces that make this type of critical work welcomed or discouraged? In what ways can critical pedagogues shape the dominating discourses of their professional contexts?

NOTE

1. A few examples include the childish and mischievous Pedro the Chihuahua from *Lady and the Tramp* (1955) who speaks with a Mexican accent; Sebastian the crab from *The Little Mermaid* (1989) who speaks with a Jamaican accent and acts as the lazy servant to Princess Ariel; and the threatening and villainous hyenas in *The Lion King* (1994) who speak with an urban African American vernacular.

REFERENCES

Ballengee Morris, C., Daniel, V., & Stuhr, P. (2010). Aligning our national visual arts standards with the social justice aim of art education. In T. Anderson, D. Gussak, K. Hallmark, & A. Paul (Eds.), *Art education for social justice* (pp. 22–31). Reston, VA: National Art Education Association.

Bettie, J. (2003). *Women without class: Girls, race, and identity.* Los Angeles: University of California Press.

Butler, J. (2004). *Undoing gender.* New York: Routledge.

Carinci, S., & Wong, P. (2009). Does gender matter? An exploratory study of perspectives across genders, age, and education. *International Review of Education, 55*(5/6), 523–540.

Delpit, L. (2006). *Other people's children.* New York: The New Press.

Donner, J. (2005) Toward the study of blackness: The development of a field of inquiry. In C. Brown & R. Land (Eds.), *The politics of curricular change: Race, hegemony, and power in education* (pp. 91–104). New York: Peter Lang Publishing.

Ellis, C., & Bochner, A. (2000). Autoethnography, personal narrative, reflexivity: Researcher as subject. In N. Denzin & Y. Lincoln (Eds.), *Handbook of qualitative research* (pp. 733–768). Thousand Oaks, CA: Sage Publications.

Foucault, M. (1975). *Discipline and punish: The birth of the prison.* New York: Vintage Books.

Giroux, H., & Pollock, G. (2010). *The mouse that roared: Disney and the end of innocence.* Lanham, MD: Rowman & Littlefield Publishers.

Haas, R. (1995). Disney goes Dutch: Billy Bathgate and the Disneyfication of the gangster genre. In E. Bell, E. L. Haas, & L. Sells (Eds.), *From mouse to mermaid: The politics of film, gender, and culture* (pp. 107–124). Bloomington: Indiana University Press.

Hodge, R., & Kress, G. (1988). *Social semiotics.* Ithaca, NY: Cornell University Press.

Ladson-Billings, G., & Tate, W. (1995). Towards a critical race theory of education. *Teachers College Record, 97*(1), 47–5.

Lugo-Lugo, C., & Bloodsworth-Lugo, M. (2009). "Look out new world, here we come"? Race, racialization, and sexuality in four children's animated films by Disney, Pixar, and DreamWorks. *Cultural Studies/Critical Methodologies, 9*(2), 166–178.

McCaughtry, N. (2004). Learning to read gender relations in schooling: Implications of personal history and teaching context on identifying disempowerment for girls. *Research Quarterly for Exercise and Sport, 75*(4), 400–412.

McIntosh, P. (1983). *Interactive phases of curricular re-vision: A feminist approach.* Wellesley, MA: Wellesley College Center for Research on Women.

Rolling, J. H. (2008). Contesting content, or how the emperor sheds his old clothes. *Qualitative Inquiry, 14*(6), 839–850.

Sadker, D. (2000). Gender equality: Still knocking at the classroom door. *Equity and Excellence in Education, 33*(1), 80–83.

Scollon, R. (2001). *Mediated discourse: The nexus of practice.* New York: Routledge.

Stovall, D. (2005). A sociological treatise on the racialized context of American education. In C. Brown & R. Land (Eds.), *The politics of curricular change: Race, hegemony, and power in education* (pp. 15–25). New York: Peter Lang Publishing.

Tavin, K., & Anderson, D. (2003). Teaching (popular) culture: Deconstructing Disney in the elementary art classroom. *Art Education, 56*(3), 21–24, 33–35.

Toyosaki, S. (2012). Praxis-oriented autoethnography: Performing critical selfhood. In N. Bardhan & M. Orbe (Eds.), *Identity research and communication* (pp. 239–251). New York: Lexington Books.

Vaught, S. (2011). *Racism, public schooling, and the entrenchment of white supremacy: A critical race ethnography.* New York: State University of New York Press.

Wohlwend, K. (2009). Damsels in discourse: Girls consuming and producing identity texts through Disney princess play. *Reading Research Quarterly, 44*(1), 57–83.

About the Contributors

Dennis Attick is an Associate Professor in the Department of Teacher Education at Clayton State University in Morrow, GA. His research interests include philosophy of education; critical pedagogy; and the confluence of popular culture, technology, and education.

Christina Berchini is an Assistant Professor in the Department of English at the University of Wisconsin Eau Claire. She earned her PhD from Michigan State University; her areas of interest and specialization are secondary English education/English teacher education, critical race studies, critical pedagogy, social justice, and issues in urban education.

Julie C. Garlen is an Associate Professor of Education in the Department of Teaching and Learning at Georgia Southern University, where she teaches courses in curriculum and instruction, early childhood education, and educational research.

Alphonso Walter Grant is a W. E. B. Du Bois Scholar and dual PhD candidate, Graduate Lecturer, and Instructor in Art Education and African American and Diaspora Studies at The Pennsylvania State University. He holds an MS in Art Education from Penn State and a BA in Political Science from Henderson State University's Honors College.

Marna Hauk catalyzes collaborative creativity for wisdom learning while innovating programs for The Institute for Earth Regenerative Studies and Prescott College. A Community Climate Change Fellow of the NAAEE and EPA, her research interests include climate resilience, sustainability education, biocultural biomimicry, and regenerative design. She has more than seventy refereed presentations and publications.

Joyce Olewski Inman is an Assistant Professor of English and Director of Composition at the University of Southern Mississippi. Her research interests include social and cognitive linguistics, basic writing programming, and the ways space and locale—including Disneyfied spaces—influence students' perceptions of writing.

Jessica Baker Kee is a PhD candidate in Art Education at Penn State University. She completed her BA in Art History at Duke University and her MAEd in Art Education at East Carolina University. She has worked as a public and private school teacher, a federal disaster relief agent, and an educational research consultant; she currently conducts arts-based participatory ethnographic research with students and with teachers in New Orleans.

Jessica L. Kirker has been teaching for over fifteen years. She has taught art to every level from preschool to collegiate, with the majority of her career spent teaching high school students. Her primary research focuses on racial and gender inequality in public schools and art education for social justice.

Sara Leo is a PhD candidate in the Curriculum, Instruction, and Teacher Education program at Michigan State University. Her areas of study include media education; public pedagogy; and critical issues of race, gender, and sexuality, particularly as they relate to young children, parents, and the intersection of schooling and society.

Alejandra Martinez is a full researcher at the National Council for Research in Science and Technology, Argentina. She conducts research in the field of communications, media studies, and gender and has completed her postdoctoral research in Film Studies at the University of Illinois at Urbana-Champaign.

Stacie K. Pettit is a Professor of Teacher Education at Augusta University. In her research, she takes a critical look at current issues in education, particularly related to English language learners and the use of social media in education.

Shannon Puechner is a PhD candidate in the Department of Curriculum and Instruction with a specialization in Critical Literacy at the University of Minnesota. Her scholarly interests include Foucault and queer theory in education; critical discourse analysis; critical literacy; sexuality education; and antiracism and anti-bullying curriculum, pedagogy, and policy.

Cole Reilly is an award-winning educator who earned dual-PhDs in Curriculum and Instruction and Women's Studies at Penn State. He is an Associate

Professor at Towson University, where he focuses on teacher preparation, identity/philosophy formation, and development, particularly with regard to social studies, socially just curricula, and culturally responsive and/or feminist pedagogies.

William M. Reynolds teaches in the Department of Curriculum, Foundations, and Reading at Georgia Southern University. He has authored, coauthored and coedited numerous books including, *Expanding Curriculum Theory: Dis/positions and Lines of Flight* (2004), *The Civic Gospel: A Political Cartography of Christianity* (2009), *A Curriculum of Place: Understandings Emerging Through the Southern Mist* (2013), *Critical Studies of Southern Place: A Reader* (2014), and *Expanding Curriculum Theory: Dis/positions and Lines of Flight,* 2nd ed. (2016).

Gina Polencheck Ruchalski is an art educator at Bay Lane Middle School and an MS in Art Education candidate at the University of Wisconsin-Milwaukee. She is currently finishing her thesis on how disability aesthetics and quality arts curriculum support pre-service educators in negotiating disability in K-12 contexts.

Laura Rychly is an Assistant Professor of Teacher Education at Augusta University. Her research interests include the role of language in classrooms and identity development.

Jennifer A. Sandlin is an Associate Professor in the Education, Culture, and Society program in the School of Social Transformation at Arizona State University, where she teaches courses focused on consumption and education, public pedagogy, and curriculum theory.

Kelli M. Sellers is an Instructor of English at the University of Southern Mississippi. Her research interests include narrative theory, folklore, and the ways in which stories shape our understanding of language and identity.

Manisha Sharma is an Assistant Professor of Art at the University of Arizona. She has taught art education in K-12, community and higher education settings. Her research interests include border pedagogies and the pedagogical development of South Asian visual culture with a focus on social justice.

Laura Trafí-Prats is an Associate Professor of Art Education at the University of Wisconsin-Milwaukee. Her research focuses on adult-children cooperative inquiry, creative interactions, multidimensional forms of visual thinking, and art-based research. Her studies pursue the resingularization of children's experience and experiment with emancipatory processes inspired in contemporary art practice.

Index

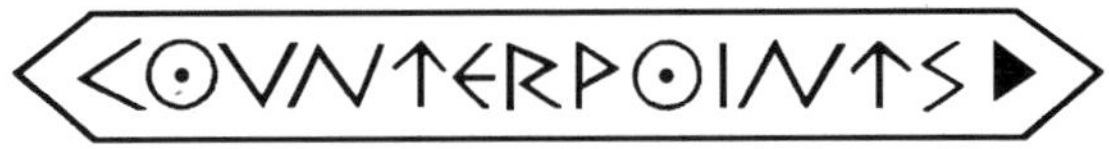

Studies in the Postmodern Theory of Education

General Editor
Shirley R. Steinberg

Counterpoints publishes the most compelling and imaginative books being written in education today. Grounded on the theoretical advances in criticalism, feminism, and postmodernism in the last two decades of the twentieth century, Counterpoints engages the meaning of these innovations in various forms of educational expression. Committed to the proposition that theoretical literature should be accessible to a variety of audiences, the series insists that its authors avoid esoteric and jargonistic languages that transform educational scholarship into an elite discourse for the initiated. Scholarly work matters only to the degree it affects consciousness and practice at multiple sites. Counterpoints' editorial policy is based on these principles and the ability of scholars to break new ground, to open new conversations, to go where educators have never gone before.

For additional information about this series or for the submission of manuscripts, please contact:

Shirley R. Steinberg
c/o Peter Lang Publishing, Inc.
29 Broadway, 18th floor
New York, New York 10006

To order other books in this series, please contact our Customer Service Department:

(800) 770-LANG (within the U.S.)
(212) 647-7706 (outside the U.S.)
(212) 647-7707 FAX

Or browse online by series:

www.peterlang.com